I—*Frontis.*　　　　THE POSTMAN.

"Literature is likely to be an important means of elevating and purifying the native. All Africans, from the lad that writes his Grammar exercise to the postman that conveys a written message in a split wand, have a liking for *kalata* (letters)."—Vol. II., p. 261.

THE
COLONIAL HISTORY
SERIES

General Editor
D. H. Simpson
Librarian of the Royal Commonwealth Society

AFRICANA

AFRICANA

OR

THE HEART OF HEATHEN AFRICA

BY THE

REV. DUFF MACDONALD, M.A., B.D.

with a new introduction

by

George Shepperson

In two volumes

VOL. 1. NATIVE CUSTOMS AND BELIEFS

"The proper study of mankind is man"

1969
DAWSONS OF PALL MALL
London

First published 1882
Reprinted with new introduction 1969

Dawsons of Pall Mall
16 Pall Mall, London, S.W.1.

SBN 7129 0347 X

Introduction © Wm. Dawson & Sons Ltd. 1969

PRINTED BY Unwin Brothers Limited
THE GRESHAM PRESS OLD WOKING SURREY ENGLAND

Produced by offset lithography

A Member of the Staples Printing Group   (HCO 3391)

INTRODUCTION

ON the sixth of July, 1964, another part of the British Empire in
Africa, Nyasaland, the country around the great Central African
Lake, became an independent State under the old African name
of "Malawi". Almost eighty-six years before (on the twelfth of
July, 1878, to be precise), the first ordained missionary of the
Established Church of Scotland went out to the southern part of
the Lake Malawi region to minister to the little group of Scottish
artisans and a doctor which his Church had dispatched, two years
previously, as the nucleus of what came to be called the Blantyre
Mission after the birthplace in Lanarkshire of David Livingstone.
Like the celebrated explorer, who had stirred the conscience of
the Western world with his description of a once peaceful and
industrious African society at the foot of Lake Malawi which was
being savagely torn apart by the Arab slave traders and their
Yao intermediaries, he was every inch a Scot and bore the
indisputedly Scottish name of Duff Macdonald. And, like
Livingstone again, he went home from these disturbed Central
African regions, after three years of difficult and devoted service,
with his reputation damaged. But Duff Macdonald, unlike
Livingstone, never returned to Africa. His book, however,
Africana; or the Heart of Heathen Africa, which was published a
year after he went back to Scotland, shows the profound impression that Africa had made upon him and it contains much of
the evidence by which his services to its indigenous inhabitants
are to be judged.

Duff Macdonald was born on the fifth of October, 1850, at
Keith in Scotland. While he was still young, his parents had

moved to Aberdeen. He was educated at its Grammer School and, like Dr. Robert Laws, the famous missionary whose name will always be associated with the other Scottish Mission in Malawi, Livingstonia, Duff Macdonald went on to the University of Aberdeen where he graduated in both Arts and Divinity, completing his Bachelor of Divinity degree in 1875, the year in which Laws was establishing his Mission on the shores of the Lake. After Macdonald graduated in Divinity, he became assistant minister in the parish of Lybster, Caithness, and was then ordained and inducted to the charge of Pulteney Town, Wick, in March, 1877.

In that year, Macdonald was approached personally by friends of Dr. MacRae, the Convenor of the Foreign Missions Committee of the Church of Scotland, and asked if he would go out to the Blantyre Mission as clerical head. In spite of all the efforts of the Committee, the Mission had not been successful in attracting an ordained minister to join its staff which remained entirely lay and possessed no member with any theological or linguistic training. At first, Macdonald hesitated about accepting this invitation. In view of his ultimate removal from the Blantyre Mission, the reasons for his hesitation are worth noting: he felt that the Missionary Regulations under which he would be required to serve permitted the Committee to dismiss him summarily, without any regular legal process such as was the right of a parish minister in Scotland. But Dr. MacRae's missionary enthusiasm prevailed over his doubts; and Macdonald gave up his Scottish charge and went out, with his newly married wife, to the Shire Highlands of Malawi—where David Livingstone had been forced, for the first time in his life to use a gun against hostile Africans.

This incident in the life of an experienced, single-minded missionary deserves to be remembered not only as part of the background to Duff Macdonald's African career but also as a standard by which his removal from Blantyre' by the Foreign Missions Committee of the Church of Scotland may be judged. Livingstone's hand had been forced by the anarchy and war that the slave trade had brought to the area. These were also part of Duff Macdonald's inheritance in Malawi. By the time he reached the Shire Highlands, there was the additional problem of disciplining the escaped and freed slaves and other Africans who were crowding into the Blantyre Mission, with its security, prestige and opportunities for learning something of the strange but exciting new life which the white men were bringing to Malawi. The lay workers at Blantyre—from a country whose symbol was almost as much the tawse as the thistle—had introduced flogging as a disciplinary measure. For Macdonald, there was the further complication of the abuse of power by some of the white artisan members of the Mission who were setting themselves up as landlords and employers of labour in their own right. Livingstone, too, had had his troubles with the European artisans on his Zambezi expedition of 1858–1864; and it is a common occurrence in colonial history that the worst exploiters of the underprivileged are often those who have once been underprivileged themselves. Duff Macdonald's "poor whites" were as much of a problem as the predatory slave traders and the undisciplined African wards of the Mission. The depth and ramifications of this "poor white" problem are illustrated by the fate of George Fenwick who was originally an artisan member of the Blantyre Mission, eventually became a trader, killed an African chief when they were both in liquor, and had his head cut off in revenge by the chief's followers. It was difficult for such a young and inexperienced man as Duff Macdonald to exert his authority over people like Fenwick, far away from home in a land where the traditional restraints on the behaviour of both Europeans and Africans were under attack constantly by the slave trade and the "New Imperialism" from Europe.

Macdonald was thus placed in an almost impossible position; and he could not fall back for help on the power of the British State because Great Britain did not assume formal control of the regions around Lake Malawi until a decade later. Something was almost certain to go wrong. An African thief was flogged too severely and he died; the whole wretched business was vented in the British press; and the Foreign Missions Committee of the

Church of Scotland summarily recalled Macdonald. He left Blantyre in August, 1881. Although he was subsequently exonerated from much of the blame for the disgraceful situation at the Mission, he had been made the scapegoat, and his subsequent career in the Church was undistinguished, although six years before his death in 1929 his old University belatedly recognised his worth by awarding him the Doctorate of Divinity.

Macdonald's defence of his three years in Africa is to be found in *Africana*, particularly in the second volume. The reader of it will be able to judge for himself how valid is the assertion by a historian that, although Macdonald was "scholarly and well-intentioned", he "lacked the intense moral conviction and force of character required to control the situation".*

There can be little doubt, however, about Macdonald's scholarly interests and abilities: they are clearly displayed in *Africana*, especially in the first volume which is devoted to a study of African customs and beliefs in the Blantyre area, particularly amongst the Yao. If Macdonald had not felt obliged to use part of *Africana* for his defence, and if he had been able to spend more than three years in Africa, it is possible that he might have produced a more substantial study—although it could be asserted that his book gained from his being forced to get his observations and opinions into print quickly, for they have a freshness which too much emotion recollected in tranquillity at a later date might have destroyed. As it is, Macdonald's study of Central African customs and languages is substantial enough for its period.

Its period, indeed, must not be forgotten, otherwise some of Macdonald's language and attitudes may be misunderstood by the modern reader and give offence, particularly to those of African origin. "Heathen" is a word which has joined "native", "savage" and other of Duff Macdonald's expressions in the present-day African's list of solecisms which he has drawn up in reaction to colonialism with its often arrogant or amused attitudes towards the indigenous cultures. Macdonald never displays these

---

* A. J. Hanna, *The Story of the Rhodesias and Nyasaland* (London, 1965), p. 59.

attitudes; but he sometimes reveals a paternalism towards Africans and the confidence of Victorian Christianity which accord ill with the legitimate pride and aspirations of modern African nationalism. (Perhaps the worst that could be charged against Macdonald here is the concluding comment of the sixth chapter on childhood and youth in his first volume in which, in discussing the initiation ceremonies—which he calls "Mysteries"—into adulthood, he declares, "Few things better shew the degradation of the African heathen than the fact that the instruction at the Mysteries is the only kind of formal teaching to be found in his country.") Macdonald had not, however, absolute confidence in the transmission of his own culture to Africa. "What," he wrote in the second chapter of his first volume, "has all our boasted civilisation done? Are we any happier than these natives? . . . As the missionary is surrounded by the heathen, he feels that his message to them has not so much to do with civilisation. They are not disposed to trouble about mechanical improvements in their unsettled land." It was an attitude towards Africa which anticipated, to some extent, that of Albert Schweitzer; and it may too easily provoke the African's response that the white man has tried to delay the economic development of his country—although this would certainly not have been Macdonald's intention.

Within the limitations of his times, this Scottish clergyman-scholar, the heir of a long tradition of careful, systematic scholarship in manse, school and university, and of the sociologically-orientated Scottish thought of the age of Adam Smith· and Adam Ferguson, was genuinely interested in the African societies which he encountered; and he made a serious attempt to appreciate them and to interpret them within their own terms of reference. He indicated his method at the start of his book when he criticized some white observers of the African: "One cause of error is that we mix up what the African tells us with our own ideas, which are European. As a consequence of this, we put questions to him that he cannot understand." Macdonald tried, as David Livingstone had done before him, to analyse African customs and beliefs according to their function in their particular societies. In this, in a primitive manner, he anticipated the approach of the "functionalist" school of later social anthropologists. By his evident skill in observation and his sympathy with much, if not all of the African viewpoint, he produced an invaluable account of African society, particularly Yao society, in the Shire Highlands when it was still relatively untouched by the white man's way of life. Macdonald made, moreover, an attempt to systematize his observations and not simply to produce a random collection of notes, which justifies calling at least the first volume of his *Africana*, proto-social anthropology.

The Scots have always been great linguists. Macdonald reveals this national characteristic in his serious attempt to analyse the Yao language, the first of its kind. Furthermore, his attention to what he calls African 'traditional literature' and the collection of folk tales with which both volumes conclude illustrate that he came from the country of Sir Walter Scott, with its love for the "tales of an antiquary", as so much of its own old way of life was uprooted and destroyed by alien cultures. Macdonald was not only determined to preserve as many of the old African tales as he could; he was also anxious to bring to the Africans of his area in Malawi translations in their own languages of what he deemed best in the foreign literatures. Before he left Africa, Macdonald had translated into the Yao language part of *The Pilgrim's Progress*, many of Aesop's fables, the Gospels of Matthew and Mark, and some historical parts of the Old Testament. Here again he worked within the Scottish tradition of translation, from the days of the King James Version of the Bible.

Duff Macdonald's *Africana* has always attracted the attention of some students of Africa and of race relations. But until their numbers increased to their present-day levels—reflecting the full-scale entry of Africa into the modern world and the emergence of race as a threat to international as well as national peace and harmony—there has been no demand for *Africana* to be reprinted; and many readers have, consequently, missed the riches that, in spite of all its limitations, it has to offer. For students of the history of the method of the social sciences, its conceptualization and its proto-social anthropological approach have much of interest. For historians of the British and other empires, it illustrates the problems of transition from unofficial to official government. At a time of an increasing interest in Scottish history and nationalism, it supplies material for the appreciation of the difficulties of Presbyterianism in its expansion into the foreign mission field; and it reveals that even the most confessedly democratic of eccleciastical organizations has it bureaucratic and oligarchic problems. Above all, *Africana* should make its greatest appeal to students of Africa, particularly if they are of African descent and come from Central Africa. It is an unrivalled source-book for the study of many aspects of the indigenous cultures of Malawi, especially of the Yao, in their early contacts with the Europe of the period of the Scramble for Africa.

"Every race", wrote Duff Macdonald, "considers itself perfection, and points to a mote in the eye of a brother race." This, perhaps, explains, although it cannot excuse, some of the shortcomings in his book. But that Duff Macdonald was able to make such a statement is an indication of the source from which it drew much of its strength. And the strength in *Africana* more than compensates for its weakness.

GEORGE SHEPPERSON

AFRICANA;

OR,

THE HEART OF HEATHEN AFRICA.

BY THE

Rev. DUFF MACDONALD, M.A., B.D.,

LATE OF THE CHURCH OF SCOTLAND MISSION, BLANTYRE, EAST CENTRAL AFRICA.

VOL. I.—NATIVE CUSTOMS AND BELIEFS.

"The proper study of mankind is man."

LONDON: SIMPKIN MARSHALL & CO.
EDINBURGH: JOHN MENZIES & CO.
ABERDEEN: A. BROWN & CO.

1882.

TO

ħ. ħ. m.

THIS WORK IS INSCRIBED

IN REMEMBRANCE OF

THE GREATEST TRIALS PATIENTLY ENDURED

FOR THE GOOD OF AFRICA.

PREFACE.

Heathen Africa is a wide word, but not so wide as might at first sight appear. A large part of the continent has been reached by Mahommedanism, and Christian Missions are everywhere making bold inroads, so that the portion of Africa left entirely to the light of nature is less than is often supposed.

My main object is to contribute to a better understanding of the African heathen, and the reader acquainted with books on the "dark continent" will perceive that the greater part of the information given in these pages is entirely new. My knowledge was gained while I worked in the African Mission field. Unfortunately I arrived at the scene of my labours to find that the Directors of the Mission had set up a peculiar Civil Administration which, as might have been expected, soon gave rise to great difficulties. Hence, although I was labouring with increasing success, and daily gaining the confidence of the natives,

I was suddenly recalled by the Directors.* Although no longer privileged to labour in Africa, I have still the deepest sympathy with its people, and am led to publish these volumes in the hope of stimulating Christians to more hearty endeavours in behalf of this dark land.

A knowledge of these Africans is interesting for its own sake. Besides, we cannot believe that God has maintained such multitudes of human beings for so many generations without our being able to learn lessons from them.

It is only when one has had an opportunity of understanding these races for himself, that he knows how much they require the help of Christendom. While from that dark land Christians hear the words, "Come over and help us," seldom do they realize how urgent is the call. That call is associated with the shrieks of the helpless slave who is sacrificed at the tomb of his oppressor, with the last cries of a fond mother poisoned by a superstitious son, and with the sighing of a wife torn from the home of her affection and compelled to drag out a miserable captivity among men whose hands are red with the blood of her kindred. When labouring in Africa, often have I been asked to explain why I

* Since then the Church altered their decision, and practically found that it was groundless.

was "so long in coming" when I knew that its people were living in darkness, and such a question every Pioneer Missionary may expect to face. I cannot express the feelings of many a heathen African more touchingly and at the same time more truly than by quoting the following which comes from Mr. Gill, a Missionary in the South Sea Islands :—

"At one of the fellowship meetings which the native Christians of the South Sea Islands had among themselves, an old man rose and said, 'I stand among you to-day a solitary and lonely man. Once I had a wife : dear she was to my heart; she is no more. Once I had five noble sons; they are all gone. O that terrible night, when my wife went out to the brushwood, never to return, when my boys left my home to be slain by our deadly enemies!' He paused, and there was a deep silence; the tears rolled down his cheeks. 'These things do not occur now,' he again said; 'Christianity has put an end to these bloody wars. But there is one thing I want to ask, Can it be that the Christian people in England have had this Gospel of peace for many long years, and never sent it to us until now? O that they had sent it sooner! Had they sent it sooner, I should not be to-day solitary, sad-hearted, mourning my murdered wife and children. O that they had sent it *sooner!*'"

As Missions to solitary stations among aboriginal tribes require to be conducted in a careful and well-defined manner, I have pointed out many difficulties by which the success of such enterprises is liable to be impaired.

With reference to the assumption of Civil Jurisdiction, which brought one or two East African Missions under public notice, I have said little except where any incident illustrated Mission difficulties or African customs, and on this subject I must refer the reader to Missionary Magazines—in particular the *Missionary Review* for 1882. But lest I should appear indifferent on the matter, I may, without obtruding the subject, introduce one or two remarks calculated to benefit the youthful Missionary. Such a man is generally full of zeal and enthusiasm, and the last thing in the world that he fears is the danger of being confronted with misrepresentation or doubtful diplomacy. But such a danger is possible—it is one thing to go to the heathe as the servant of the Lord, and quite a different thing to go as the agent of a Committee. While Mission Directors incur some risk by setting up a Civil Jurisdiction, the real danger falls upon the agents they employ. If any of these agents say, " I am here commanded to act as a judge or a chief, I am perfectly aware this is a difficult task, but I am bound to do my best to obey," he soon finds he is greatly blamed : and, on the other hand, when a man reasons, "My superiors have set up a strange organisation here. But these men are the great Leaders of the Church. They have been studying Missionary methods before I was born. I have no doubt they understand their plan. But I cannot understand it : I must leave it entirely alone and devote all my attention to Spiritual work,"—condemnation as certainly follows.

Again, when an ordained Minister becomes a Missionary, he is held to lay aside his ministerial *status* and become the agent of a committee, while a Licentiate who is set apart for work among the heathen is "ordained" in the same sense as a beadle may be said to be ordained—he may talk of "magnifying his office," but he holds it only during the pleasure of a committee who, after he has performed his duties most diligently, may with the greatest complacency, turn him forth to starve !

Such are some of the difficulties that are thoughtlessly thrown in the way of Mission work.

There is, however, a more pleasant side to contemplate. I desire to say with emphasis :—"Savage tribes are *not* difficult to get on with, Heathendom is *not* an unpromising field," and such is the experience, I think, of all Missionaries as they go forward, believing that

"He shall have the heathen for His heritage, and the uttermost parts of the earth for His possession!"

I have pleasure in acknowledging that for several of the illustrations I am indebted to the courtesy of the Rev. H. Rowley, the talented author of the Story of the Universities' Mission to Central Africa.

CONTENTS OF VOL. I.

N.B.—The figures and letters in brackets refer to the sections (and not to the pages).

INTRODUCTORY.

CHAPTER I.—First Impressions.

CHAPTER II.—Arts and Literature.

CHAPTER XVI.—ETHNOLOGY.

CHAPTER XVII.—AFRICAN PHILOLOGY.

CHAPTER XVIII.—AFRICAN PHILOLOGY—*Continued.*

CHAPTER XIX.—ESTIMATE OF NATIVE CHARACTER.

LIST OF ILLUSTRATIONS.

VOL. I.

INTRODUCTORY.

INTRODUCTORY.

THERE are no books, so far as we are aware, that aim at giving a systematic account of the beliefs and customs of any of the tribes in Eastern Central Africa. Indeed, it is not long since these tribes have been known at all. Those beliefs and customs are to a great extent *Arcana Africana,* and form the main subject of this work.

Those that know how long it takes to become thoroughly acquainted with new races of people will object to a work like this appearing so soon. To this objection we would reply that, after a Christian Mission has been established for a few years in a district, the views of the people around may become so modified, especially on religion, that it is difficult to distinguish how much is native and how much is imported. This is specially true of these Africans. They rapidly throw aside everything that is native, and grasp after the views and customs introduced by the foreigner. Even as it was, we often got answers that seemed to be an echo of our teaching, but we made a point of rejecting every statement of this kind. The reader may rest assured that we have here put before him no religious belief that was suggested or modified by Christian teaching.

Again, there are some that think it is not possible to give an account of native beliefs and customs, because they differ so much in different districts. The same objection might be raised with reference to English beliefs and customs. A man that wished to give an account of the Religious beliefs of the people of England, would find that he had undertaken a difficult task, but such an account, so far from being impossible, might be made not only perfectly accurate, but also highly interesting and profitable.

So in the case of Native Law. We have seen the natives settle their disputes in methods so many and so different, that we might have said "There is no such thing as Native Law" Might not the very same opinion be expressed with reference to English Law?

As we tried to reduce Native beliefs to an intelligible form, we were often discouraged by finding that one man would make a statement that his nearest neighbour would contradict. But as years passed on, I discovered that this accident was not so much the fault of the African, or of his belief, as of the European that questioned him. In many respects there is a greater fixity of belief in Central Africa than in England, although it may be freely admitted that these African customs are subject to many modifications due to local ingenuity and caprice. On the subject of Native Law the reader is ever at liberty to read between the lines that *our statements may be often modified* by a maxim which is but ill concealed in Native Jurisprudence *by the maxim, " that might is right "*.

DIFFICULTIES

There are enormous difficulties to overcome before we can be sure that our statements are correct. We once knew a man of good abilities try to get information on a small section of native customs, and the result was in wonderful disagreement with facts. We were so tickled at the production that we went to our friend's informer and read over the expressions one by one, half inclined to ask regarding each " Would you be surprised to learn ?" In most cases he was very much surprised indeed ! The causes of error are so numerous and subtle as to deserve extended notice.

IMPORTING EUROPEAN IDEAS.

One cause of error is that we mix up what the African tells us with our own ideas, which are European. As a consequence of this, we put questions to him that he cannot understand. Many of our questions strike the African exactly as a question like the following would strike a European, " If seventy miles of the sea were burned, who would be the losers, the Insurance Companies ? or the Harbour Commissioners ? or —— ?" If an African put this question to a European the European would laugh at him ; but if the European put it to an African, the latter would be more polite, and would think that the European was very ingenious in finding out a supposition that would have never occurred to himself ; and although the African knows that the difficulty could never arise in his own country, yet he feels bound to believe that the poor European is perplexed by it, and states what he thinks *would happen* in Africa on such an extraordinary occurrence: thus *he gives an answer*, which the ingenious European carefully lays past.

For instance, a person that had never been out of England would see nothing amiss in asking a Makua or a Machinga, " If a dog were to tear your trousers and your housemaid were to mend them, how much would you give her in addition to her ordinary wages?" Now the native will not say " We wear no trousers," " Women in our country never sew," " No one receives wages in our country for domestic service," " Special services are not defined, and if they were, the duties of a housemaid would not be anything like what they are in England". Instead of making statements of this kind, which would all be interesting to his questioner, the African will take up the question as it stands, he will consider that it is quite worthy of the genius of a European, and will probably answer that the housemaid would get " two fowls, one hoe, and a string of beads !" And he may reply without the least hesitation ; for if he be a professional oracle-man, remember he has been trained all his lifetime to answer hypothetical questions. He would reason that if a man possessed trousers, and servants, yea, a female that obtained wages and had been taught to sew, he ought to give her some handsome present for what she did beyond her ordinary duties, and then our oracle would state what was his idea of a handsome present. His answer is utterly misleading, but he deserves credit for his polite attempt to humour the

European, who forthwith translates the answer into
pounds, shillings, and pence !

Another cause of error is found in

NATIVE POLITENESS,

One evening I questioned a professional judge on a
point of native law ; he replied by stating what was entirely untrue ; when I pointed this out he merely laughed
at the circumstance ; he thought he had invented something that would appear better to a foreigner. He
reminded me of a Scotch guide who kept telling what
was false, because the Southerns all liked to hear that
some " old king was killed beside the great big stane ".
Bishop Steere says—" In Africa they never say *no*, they
always say *yes, certainly ;* but possibly you are no
nearer your object ". One must be careful never to
suggest an answer to a native ; if the native and his
questioner are strangers to each other the former will
make it a point of etiquette to find out what answer the
stranger would like, and may by and by take occasion
to compliment him on his cleverness and the accuracy of his knowledge ! Statements made in answer
to direct questions are not to be relied on unless the
questioner has had years of experience in conversation
with natives, and knows the subject he converses about.
What is arrived at in an indirect manner is almost
always more valuable. I lay down these principles as
to native evidence with some confidence, as I have
tried them in hundreds of cases, especially in endeavours to fix the exact meaning of native words. One

statement where the word occurred spontaneously was worth ten statements contrived for the purpose of eliminating the meaning.

In my first efforts to learn African languages I found that a great deal of what was said to me, especially by interpreters, was quite useless, simply because the poor fellows were trying to adapt their language to a European capacity !

NATIVE IDIOMS.

When one attempts to obtain information through interpreters, without knowing anything of their peculiar idioms, he is liable to the strangest blunders Those that try to speak with him carry their African idioms into English. Natives have great difficulty in knowing the difference between *before* and *after*. Boys that have been writing English essays for more than a year, think nothing of writing deliberately about what men did on the earth *before* they were created. There is another idiom still more fitted to produce confusion, and when an Englishman writes down in a multitude of instances what is the reverse of the truth we are often able to point out the cause. He puts to a native the question, " He did not go, did he ? " The native replies " *Yes*," where an Englishman would say " No ". Consequently every question put in this form will be answered in a manner that cannot fail to mislead. In the same way natives confound the active and the passive voice in verbs.

DISTRACTING CIRCUMSTANCES.

Even after one has become familiar with some of their

idioms he cannot trust to all the information that he supposes himself to acquire. I had begun to hold conversations with the natives, in their own tongue, about six weeks' after my arrival, and I well remember that I often got information exactly similar to what Mr Pickwick got from his cabman When a native sees a person noting down anything, he makes up his mind to say something worth noting ! So much did I feel this that at one time I endeavoured to keep my book out of sight. While they were unaccustomed to it, it introduced into the conversation an element that was very unnatural. One plan I took was to have a pencil in my hand which I pretended to be playing with. I thus got down some new words upon my thumb-nail, and was beginning to congratulate myself on the success of my stratagem. After I sat for about ten minutes another man approached our group, when my friends hailed him in these words, " Come here and talk with the white man. He is writing on his fingers. He has written three new things already !" After this I saw that such a trick was quite useless. Not only had they seen it all, but they could tell how many words I had written. Great was the laughter that followed, and the new comer examined the guilty thumb-nail !

ROMANTIC INFORMATION.

I sometimes got romantic information that I was sorry at a later date to have to put my pen through. Thus with reference to the High Priest of a new government (98), I gathered from one man that the first person *seen*

by the chief after his installation became the High Priest
of his government.   I had carefully noted down that a
little *boy* playing in the village found his way to the house
of one important chief on the morning after his installation, and was the first to see His Royal Highness ; for
whom, as a matter of fact, he now officiates as sacrificer,
&c.   Then, *having taken up* this meaning of the incident,
I was farther informed that the chief made a note of the
first *five* people that he saw in case of the death of any ;
and my informer was eager to know who was the first
man that I saw after coming to Blantyre.   Subsequent
information threw discredit on the beautiful story   But
the peculiar thing was that I found long afterwards
another native make the very same statements.   This
referred me back to my old notes.   All I could say about
it was that the word I had translated *see* meant also *find*,
that a *boy* might be over 50 years for anything that the
native word indicated, and that it was not clear from my
text whether the chief was *seen* by the boy or the boy
by the chief.

Much of what we have written was not made the
subject of special investigation, except where we found
any doubt arise or any verification necessary.   Our
special object was to obtain such an accurate knowledge of the language as would enable us to give a
good translation of the Bible.   Most of the knowledge
gradually grew upon us as we mingled with the natives,
and for the purpose of translation attended closely to
every word that we heard.

Other parts, especially those that refer to religion,
were the subject of special inquiry.   It is walking in the

dark for a missionary to endeavour to appeal either to the feelings or to the reason of a people whose prejudices and beliefs are unknown to him, and how he is to convince them without appeals to their feelings or their reason I cannot tell. I would have given much to have had an account of those beliefs put into my own hands when I left for Africa.

I have tried to make all my statements as accurate as possible, but it would be too much to expect that in such a difficult investigation 1 should have escaped the influence of these many and subtle sources of error.

THE VALUE OF STUDYING NATIVE CUSTOMS AND BELIEFS.

WHAT is the use of minute investigations among the ignorant heathen of Central Africa ? We reply that such investigations throw light on many points that men of science consider to be of great importance. To take a few instances :—

I. IN THE SCIENCE OF THE HUMAN MIND.

(A) THE SENSES.

Some speak as if men were made at first with the power of perceiving only a few colours, for instance, black and white, and that by and by they trained themselves to perceive brown. One argument advanced in favour of this view is that many native languages have words for black and white, but no word for brown. Now I knew several languages where the natives called brown and black by the same word ; but they knew that there was a great difference between brown and black. I found that they could discriminate every shade of colour that I could discriminate myself.

(B) THE INTELLECT.

Many facts that I shall lay before the reader will seem so strange that he may doubt whether these savages have the same minds as Europeans, whether they reason or think in the same way at all. It is true, however, that after one places himself in their circumstances, and tries to see and feel as they do, he will understand all their strangeness ; he will even see that it would have been still more strange if their reasonings and conclusions had been different.

(C) THE FEELINGS AND EMOTIONS.

Have we in Europe so developed ourselves as to become possessors of emotions that are entirely wanting in savage Africa ?

We have what is called gratitude : have these heathen ? Without any hesitation I answer that they have, and that even though we define gratitude as being much more than " an acute sense of favours to come ".

Again we have pity. A stranger might think that they were destitute of this. I have said to a boy, " Don't carry that fowl so, you give it pain ". At this he would laugh. It would become the standing joke for a day or two. Everyone would be told that the Englishman said that " the fowl would be sore ". A whole village would collect at the strange report and receive the news with loud laughter. Yet all would admit that it was a cruel thing to pain the fowl; but they did not reflect that their method of carrying the fowl gave it pain. They were used to their own way, and thought no more of the matter than a butcher does of killing an ox. At the same time they have fables in their language, which show a desire to enter minutely into the feelings of the lower animals. For instance, they represent fowls as reasoning on their hard fate in being killed for their master's supper.

(D) MORAL PHILOSOPHY.

It has long been disputed whether men have a "Conscience" that distinguishes between right and wrong; or whether they merely look at certain actions that please or profit them, and call these actions good and the opposite actions bad.

Savages have been referred to on this subject. We have found that they distinguish the good from the evil in the same way as Europeans do, and usually agree with our conclusions. They know the difference between an injury of accident and one of intention. As to the moral judgment, "A man *ought* to do such a thing," "It is his *duty*," we find this lesson is brought home to slaves or inferiors by positive law. In others there are aspirations more akin to the exuberant activities and bright dreams of youth. They would rather ask, "How can we do best ?" as did the Ancients who talked of a *summum bonum*. As the spirit of the world became older and sadder this view gave place, and the idea of "duty" was more emphasised by moralists. Spirited Africans savour more of the Golden Age of Moral Science.

It is to be remembered that appeals to savage nations form only a part of scientific investigations like the above.

II. IN ETHNOLOGY.

On looking at the many different races that inhabit the earth, some say that they did not all spring from the same stock, others that they did. If we say that they are all of one family we should try to show how some broke away from the rest, and at what time. Now let us make a supposition to show how the *customs* of races might come in here.

In LIGHTING A FIRE some tribes rub a stick along a groove ; other tribes have an improvement on this, they produce fire by making a little notch or hole in one

SOUTH AFRICAN MAKING FIRE.

stick, and whirling the other round very rapidly with the point of it in the notch. Now we may hold that before mankind discovered the second method, many nations, like the South Sea Islanders, who knew only the first, had broken up communication with the rest of their kindred ; but that the Africans who use the improved method had likely been with the main body of mankind till the time of this great improvement.

Again, take the case of COOKING. Some tribes have no pots. They boil water by throwing hot stones into a skin. They must have separated very early from their more cultivated brethren. Others waited till some one fell on the plan of boiling water in a hollow stone. Others waited on till it was discovered that clay could be shaped into a kind of pot, and then carried this important discovery to the land of their adoption. Boiling with hot stones was the only way known to certain American, Australian, and Polynesian tribes ; some tribes in Africa also used this method. The Esquimaux had pot-stones. It seems to have been the daubing of these with clay that first suggested pottery.

I have taken down traditions from African natives that point to some recollection of the hollow stone, used either by themselves or some other race ; but the tribes here treated of know the value of clay pots. Of course they are far behind the Indians, who have metal pots.

With regard to THE CAUSE OF DISEASE there existed a widespread belief (held by many tribes in America and Australia, as also by these Africans) that disease came from bones, horns, balls of hair or something of this kind. The ancient Egyptians at a very early date considered that disease was to a great extent caused by excess of eating. The inference is that these tribes had not staid long enough to benefit by this wisdom of the Egyptians.

Other peculiar customs are spread over many tribes,

and might be used in a similar manner.   Many of these
are observances in FAMILY LIFE.   Among the Kaffirs a
son-in-law must not see the face of his mother-in-law.
This custom is found among South American tribes.
Sometimes a father has to fast after the birth of his
child, or take some such method of showing that he recognises that he as well as the mother should take care
of the young stranger.

When races are found knowing nothing of the art of
writing, and making no attempt to use stone or bricks
for building, we feel that a wide gulf separates them
from the most ancient races of history.   Of course it is
to be remembered that they might have once been aware
of such arts.   Many Africans, as a matter of fact, have
seen Portuguese architecture for centuries without
adopting it.

III. IN THE SCIENCE OF RELIGION.

A position has often been maintained that there is no
tribe without some knowledge of God.   This bears on
investigations in the science of mind and on primitive
traditions and ethnology.   We do not now dwell on
native religion, as it will claim special attention in
subsequent chapters.

Besides throwing light on many subjects like the
above, a knowledge of tribal beliefs and customs is of
vital importance to the missionary and also to the
trader.   Indeed, any attempt to deal with people
without knowing their customs and beliefs is a mere
groping in the dark.

LIBERATED SLAVE-WOMAN, BLANTYRE.
(Photographed in ordinary Costume.)

LIBERATED SLAVE-GIRL, BLANTYRE.
(Trained to Household Work.)

Chapter I.

FIRST IMPRESSIONS.

A.—DRESS, TATOOS, ORNAMENTS, &c.

The *dress* of the native is very scanty : sometimes we see full-grown men and women whose wardrobe does not consist of a square foot of cloth. We have even seen the primitive fig-leaves not sewn together, but simply taken down for use, along with the tip of the branches on which they grew. One tribe, called the Mangoni, is fond of wearing skins. Other tribes towards the north of Lake Nyassa are still more primitive in their dress, or rather want of dress. The usual costume in the Blantyre district is a piece of calico about two yards broad, and rather longer, which is put round the middle of the body : the dress of a man does not differ from that of a woman, except that the latter may occasionally cover her breasts. The breasts and arms are usually left quite bare. There is no hat on the head, nor shoes on the feet. When we tried to translate the words, " If any man sue thee at the law and take away thy coat, let him have thy cloak also," we found a difficulty, for if a native were stripped of *one* garment, he would generally be left in a very helpless condition.

The chiefs, or principal men, dress as the rest of the people, only they may have a few more folds of calico about their loins.   In certain families, as in the Abanda family of the Wayao tribe, the chief of the district, or. of a village, wears a band of cloth round his temples as a kind of crown.   Before the arrival of the missionaries, shirts, although very rare, were not entirely unknown, and there existed a belief that while men might wear them, they were not the proper thing for women. Bark cloth (H.) is extensively made and worn.

The *tatoos* (nembo) are sometimes dreadful inflictions, and when the larger marks are made the children roar as if they were distracted.   The Angulu have marks like "flies," the Wayao tribal mark is above the nose, the Anyasa make very large rude tatoos, which might be described in those words that Henry Salt, the Abyssinian traveller (1814), uses with reference to the Makua, a tribe not far distant, and much spoken of by the Wayao, under the name of Makuani.   "The Makua practise tatooing so rudely that they raise the marks one-eighth of an inch above the surface."   He writes also :—"They file their teeth to a point, so that the whole set has the appearance of a coarse saw".   The natives here are fond of knocking out a front tooth in order to produce a beauty mark.

Ornaments are worn chiefly by the women in Africa as elsewhere.   Beads and bangles are in great request. Many have armlets and anklets of brass or iron.   The most striking female ornament is the lip ring.   Little girls have first a small hole (lupelele) bored in the upper lip, in this they place a stalk of grass, which prevents the hole from filling up, next they insert a thicker stalk of grass, then by means of bits of twigs, &c., the hole is made larger and larger, till it can receive

NATIVE WOMAN WITH BEADS, TATOOS AND LIP-RING.

this ring. Hardly any female is without it. They say it makes them look "pretty"; the bigger the ring, the more they value themselves! At Zomba, a small hole is bored on the side of the nose, and a tack (exactly similar to those large headed tacks or "tackets" used in the sole of a boot), is put in. This tack, *chipini*, is made of lead; some of the ladies used to express much surprise when I showed them that it would write on my book.

Occasionally, a woman will wear an enormous wig made of beads. The beads are so manipulated as to present the appearance of having been " threaded " on the hair of the head. Some females do actually thread beads on the separate hairs of their head, but the usual way is to put them on a cluster of strings, and then wear like a wig. Sometimes they allow their hair to grow till it is very long—it may be sticking up about 8 inches above the head—and then it looks exactly like the fleece of a black sheep. But this is unusual, as the natives are obliged, for the sake of cleanliness, to shave their heads often. The men have scarcely any beard or whiskers. On the shaving of the head for a death (40), not even the eyebrows are allowed to escape. There is no end of capricious shaving, for instance, they shave one side only, or the whole head except a patch in the middle.

CHARMS *(mbiji)* are very often worn round the neck by both sexes. These are little pieces of wood like what fill the gourds of the Sorcerers (I.). They are worn on a small string in the same way as beads.

We may mention here that great quantities of beads are worn round the loins in strings as thick as cart ropes. When a person is from home and wishes to buy anything, he falls back upon this portion of his property which is really his " purse ". Besides this, a native carries a bag (msaku), which may contain a box with lime (swakala), which he uses in chewing tobacco : a snuff box is also common. Ladies partake of these " regales " to a less extent.

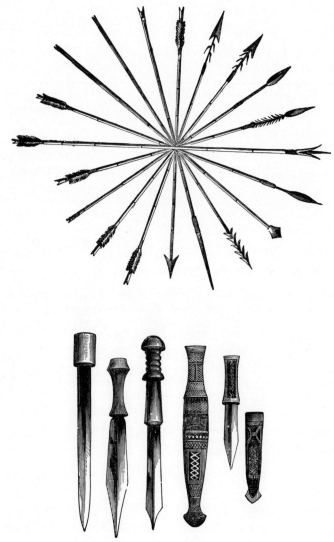

I—19   NATIVE KNIVES AND ARROWS.

B.—WEAPONS.

The men go armed generally with guns. (The country is full of flint muskets marked the "Tower," and introduced by the slave trade.) Often they carry their *bows* with half-a-dozen arrows. They never go unarmed. One chief used to be fond of carrying a large *spear*, which served as a kind of staff. Most of them carry knives as well. These weapons are necessary for protection against beasts of prey and other enemies, and may be used where game is seen. The Mangoni carry a shield like the Zulus.

On coming down from the Lake region to the Portuguese settlements at Quilimane, one of the first things that strikes us is, that natives under the Portuguese Government go about without carrying any deadly weapon. On the hills round Blantyre, a man scarcely sits down to sew his wives' calico in his own village without having his bow and arrows by his side.

They do not seem to be expert marksmen; but they were able to send their arrows very much farther than I could do, let me try never so hard. They were fond of asking us to competitions of this nature. One time Kumpama of Cherasulo challenged us to a shooting match—his arrows against our guns! They allowed us, however, to stand too far back, and the arrows of his bowmen fell short of the target. Little boys are to be seen using their arrows from their earliest years, and they shoot small birds very cleverly.

They use the assagai, but more for thrusting than for throwing. Apart from war, chances for its use occur

when they steal upon a buck before he awakes. A large
broad spear is used in killing fish.

Some carry knob-sticks, or staves of a similar nature.
They are useful for shaking the dew or rain off the long
grass, as well as for defensive purposes. Little axes of
various kinds are carried in the hand; they may be
borne as credentials where a chief has to send by an
unknown messenger. The usual African axes are said
to resemble those used in Britain in the Roman period.

C.—HOUSES.

The houses, or huts (nyumba) in which they dwell,
are all round. It is misleading to say that they
dwell in them, as they scarcely enter them, except to
sleep, or when driven by bad weather. Sometimes the
women boil a pot inside the house, but often the
cooking is done outside; all the meals are eaten outside.
When the head of a house has any sewing to do, he
does it on a mat before his door, or in the village forum.
His wife does not sew, and most of her occupations (57)
are necessarily outdoor. "A house," says the native,
" is made to sleep in."

The walls form a circle—say about twelve feet in
diameter—and are made of strong posts, sometimes
close to each other, but generally with spaces between,
where bamboos and grass are brought into requisition.
The framework of the roof is placed upon the top of
the circle, and some thatch is thrown on. The floor
and walls are plastered with clay.

Two doors (mlango) are marked out before they
plaster, but one of these is generally shut up, and may

even be dispensed with. There are no windows. The wall is not above 3 feet high, the roof projects so as to form a small verandah in which a person may sit. Sometimes there are apertures in the wall calculated to let through the muzzle of a gun.

The houses being occupied chiefly during the night, part of the floor is often raised for a bedstead. The bed, which is merely a mat made of bamboos or reeds, and is not nearly so soft as an ordinary door-mat or hearth-rug, is laid on this mound. By the side of the " bedstead " are placed a few logs of wood which form a fire during the night. The head of the house lies nearest to this fire, while his partner is placed on his other side, as he remarks, *away from the fire.* Blankets are unknown. The cloth that covers the man during the day may be drawn over him at night. Quite as often he lets it remain round his loins. Occasionally it seems as if a little flour had been spilt on the ground beside his head. He will not speak of this to a stranger, but you are on holy ground, and let me tell you in a whisper that it is an *offering to his gods.*

Candles are not used, the logs that smoulder in the fire give a little light. They burn beeswax occasionally, and when light is required, a little dry grass may be readily obtained. The native retires to rest soon after dark, and is astir at the first streaks of dawn.

The fire is in the middle of the floor, and there are no holes in the roof as in the old Highlands of Scotland. The houses are without any chimney whatsoever, and the smoke goes curling about in the roof and may ultimately escape through the thatch or at the doors,

The roof is beautifully black and glossy inside, but outside it has an ugly brown appearance.

A European finds it a most inconvenient thing at
first to enter a native hut, the smoke so fills his nose,
mouth, and eyes, but when he sits down to talk to an
invalid, the inconvenience is of course less than when
he stands upright; at best the atmosphere resembles a
London fog. In native huts it is sometimes difficult
for a man of ordinary stature to stand upright. The
doors of the houses are never over 3 feet high. What
pigmies the natives must be! We have heard a learned
professor arguing that the height of the doors in certain
very ancient houses proved that the human race was
not degenerating in stature, but this argument, true in
many cases, would not do here. If the native wants to
stand upright, he never thinks of trying to do so in his
doorway.

The roof of his house is generally made a store; he goes
up from the outside, removes part of the thatch, and puts
in his corn. Bags of beans are hung up round and round
on the pillars inside. Sometimes there are one or two
pots filled with beans, and hermetically sealed with clay
on the top to preserve such vegetables. There are no
fenders or fire-irons to be seen. Tables are unknown,
and chairs are hardly used at all, although men clever
at wood-work make very small chairs of various forms.
Implements of agriculture are stowed away in the house,
so are the cooking utensils, the man's bow and arrows,
the sleeping mat already mentioned, and—our inventory
is complete! Some part of the house may be occupied
by live stock. The fowls are sometimes put up stairs

in the store, and sometimes in a corner so as not to disturb the other members of the family ! But laying-hens (mkolo) and fowls with chickens have very special privileges, and are not always confined to their corner !

Another item of importance to the inmates of a native house is the rats. They swarm in all corners after dark. They nibble at the maize that is stored in the roof, and also at the feet of their lord and master below. As we sit in conversation with a number of natives we cannot help observing their feet. Very generally they are all nibbled round the sides, and, thick though the natives' skin may be, we can see that many bites have reached the quick flesh. When a person dies in a house at night, if the death be unobserved, the body may be terribly eaten by the rats before morning. What is the meaning of tolerating these vermin ? Leave that to the natives themselves. A great feast day will come. These rats will be caught in hundreds, and either eaten on the spot or laid up as stored pro-visions. Some natives set traps in the house even during the close season, but this is not nearly so profitable ; for if one or two rats are caught during the night, the others will eat them, and the fondest ex-pectation of " butcher meat " will be blasted.

After calling attention to the fowls and the rats, we have done with the live stock. There are indeed " smaller cattle," but they are too numerous to be specified. They are not a burden to the house itself, but are generally borne by the other inmates. We have often seen a native sit patiently while two or three others kept searching among his hair. A favourite remedy is to shave the head quite bare, and smear the head and the whole body with certain vegetable oils.

D.—CLIMATE AND PRODUCTIONS.

The climate strikes us at first as being much too hot, but after a while we feel it more comfortable. Then we can nearly always anticipate the weather. It is quite amusing to hear an arrival from England saying "This is another fine day!" When we meet a man at home, and have nothing to say, we nearly always call his attention to the state of the weather. When two natives meet each other the usual salutation is— " Where are you going ? " the weather being so uniform that it may be taken for granted. The temperature in the shade at the hill settlements was hardly ever over 105° or under 42°, 70° being about the average. On the plains the heat was excessive.

The rainy season begins about October. We have nearly six weeks of very hot weather about January without much rain. By and by the sun returns over-head again, and we have the latter rains. About April the dry season sets in.

On the productions of the country we may remark that there are fruits in almost endless variety in the bush, but they are generally very small, and few of them are so good that we care to taste them twice. The *masuku* and *mbembu* are used very much by the natives. Sugar cane, tobacco, india-rubber are all to be found growing throughout the country. The natives chew the stalks of the sugar cane, chew and smoke tobacco, and relish the apple-like fruit found on the india-rubber vine.

Thrifty housewives make various vegetable dishes (maponda) of leaves and grasses that a European would be inclined to despise. In the hot season that precedes the rains sometimes food is very scarce, and then roots and herbs still less savoury are called into use. Moreover, there are certain edibles of this kind, which are used only in years of famine. Before the arrival of the missionaries such famines were exceedingly common, but they were not all caused by the climate, many were caused by war.

Nature is here so bountiful that, in ordinary circumstances, food is no object. The only season associated with hunger is a month or two immediately before the rains. If the rains do not come early, the old food may be quite finished. As soon as the rains begin, vegetable life flourishes with such luxuriance that the season of want is immediately forgotten. Once or twice in travelling during the season when everything is dried up, we have found a little boy sitting weeping on account of "hunger," and the expression "hunger is painful" (sala kupoteka) reminds us that most natives know the fact by experience. Much of this is due to the tediousness of their cooking. If a party arrive half starving at a village, it may be several hours before anything can be cooked. The people do not keep flour on hand, but mill it as it is required for each meal; and as their meals are at 11 at noon and 6 at night, parties arriving in the interval must tighten their belts. Native travellers could casily sympathise with Esau when he sold his birth-right.

E.—FOOD AND COOKING.

The cooking is done by the women; but every native is a born cook. When a buck is shot out in the bush, even little boys will cook it at once. The staple food at Blantyre is maize ; among the Anyasa millet; and at the mouth of the Shire, rice. Maize and millet are ground into a fine flour (utandi, ufa), which is made into a kind of porridge (ugali, nsima). This is eaten without salt, but ought to be accompanied by some relish, as beans or meat. This porridge takes the place of bread in their meals, as the natives make no bread. Another way of using maize or millet is in the native beer (ukana, mowa), the only beverage in common use except water, which they drink out of the running streams. They drink stagnant water also. Their method of drinking is peculiar, as they literally throw the water into the mouth with their hands.

The natives have regularly only two meals a-day, but they may eat maize stalks or sugar cane or other vege-tables from morning till night. There are often feasts, as on the occasion of hoeing-matches (65), wakes, and marriage settlements. Beer is used greatly in those cases, and beer drinkings may be got up also without any special occasion. Sometimes they last for several days, the last day (lia kusasula) is specially distinguished for cooking porridge and fowls. Such solid food is not ex-pected on the other days. There is also singing, dancing, and drumming. The exercises generally continue the whole night. The parties that do most to keep up the interest in such dances are paid.

There are no live stock except the small species of fowls and the rats that we have already mentioned. Some natives keep ducks—Muscovy ducks, which do not require a pond. Richer people, as village chiefs, possess goats. The Magololo chiefs have sheep and a few cows.

The Wayao have a superstition against cow's milk, goat's milk, and dairy produce of every kind. (In the same way young people will not eat eggs; it would make them barren.) They eat hippopotami, elephants, monkeys, moles, beetles, and even caterpillars. They take kindly to meat that has begun to putrify. Yet they make a distinction between what animals are to be eaten and what are not. Any creature that will eat the flesh of a deceased human being is unclean. It is msawi (106). For instance, while some eat the raven or kite (likungulu), others protest that it feeds about the graves.

A person could travel far and wide and trust to native hospitality. If we arrive at a village at the time that the native is taking his meals we are invited to partake. A great drawback is that a person not brought up on native food will be unwilling to risk his health by partaking of their fare. It cannot be expected that the traveller will fare better than his host. They soon begin to know people that do not eat freely of native food, and from motives of politeness they are slow in offering it. If we pass through a village its inhabitants quietly ask some of our native retinue whether there is any chance of our tasting the native beer,* and if it be found that the beer will not be refus(d, the poor creatures go and search for a cup (if they have one in the whole village). They judged that, as we were more familiar with cups than with calibashes, the cup would be the more acceptable. The natives that accompanied us on any journey were presented with loads of the various fruits of the season. If one wish to stay all night he will get a house to sleep in. Natives receive hospitality quite freely, and are prepared when their host comes to their home to treat him in the same way When a party from one chief goes to visit another chief, one of their credentials is a present.

It is a breach of etiquette to eat alone if any one be present. When a native is at food he shares it with those around him, indeed he goes on dividing till he has only a mouthful left for himself. Etiquette does not bind us to partake of their food, but it is a sign of friendship to do so as far as possible. The natives have no spoons, and Englishmen would burn their fingers severely in eating porridge in the fashionable manner.

F.—WORK.

The natives go to work at sunrise, and continue until the sun is overhead. After this their day's work is finished, and they partake of their first meal. One reason why the morning meal is so late is that it would be

---

* Livingstone says this is the most wholesome form in which they use their corn owing to their rude cookery.

difficult to have it ready before the people go out to work. In the afternoon the men sit down and converse. Some do light work, as sewing, but a great many remain quite idle. The women will be found pounding maize. They are nearly as strong and tall as the men, perhaps owing to the heavy work they do. By sunset the second meal is ready.

They have little notion of the division of labour. Natives have not arrived at such a pitch of education that one of them would spend his days in making the sixth part of a pin. The little girls from their earliest years are initiated into all parts of the mysteries of hoeing, reaping, milling, and cooking. The men are equally ignorant of the advantages and disadvantages of division of labour. Each man builds his own house, and makes his own furniture. The only trade that can maintain a special existence is working in iron—a trade embracing mining, smelting, and forging. Even in this case most natives know the secrets of the trade; but to be specially successful they need to obtain a charm.

Agricultural work is the great means of a livelihood. It yields a great return, for every seed the natives sow they expect to reap hundreds. A little before the rains they begin to hoe their ground. They first clear all the trees and wood, which they collect in heaps and burn on the spot. They use no other manure. When they do work for the English they say they hoe very slowly, because they are told to hoe deep; but when they hoe their own land they hoe fast, as a scratch on the surface is considered sufficient. When the rains come they plant. After the maize grows they set up the soil round the stems as farmers do with potatoes.

Each house has generally what we might call a garden ; but the natives have no fancy for flowers. The wild flowers in the wood they recognise as being very pretty ; but they laugh at any one that plucks them. They fancy that a lover of flowers culls them for some charms. The natives have no word for a garden as distinct from a cultivated field or farm, but they have often round their houses little beds of tobacco, great quantities of manioc, and several other useful plants. Indian hemp is also much cultivated, and is nearly as bad as opium. Near Mazaro opium is cultivated by a Portuguese Company.

F². —RACES AND CHIEFS.

As we pass out of Portuguese territory we find ourselves in the country of a chief called Matekenya, on the Lower Shire (Chiri). His people are the Achikunda. When we reach the Ruwo or Ruo we are perhaps about two days from Blantyre by land. Here we come to what are called the Magololo, whose paramount chief is Makukani, although many of the others, as Katunga and Chiputula, seem to view themselves as independent of him. Still they say that if he commands they must all follow him to war. These men though aliens, have established themselves as rulers over the Anyasa. There is no Magololo tribe here. Passing through these Anyasa we ascend to Blantyre, where we find ourselves with a chief called Kapeni, who rules another tribe called the Wayao (Yao), with whom we are best acquainted.

Then about Zomba, which is other two days farther on, we encounter the Machinga, who speak practically the same language as the Wayao, and this language carries us far beyond. Several great chiefs on the east side of Lake Nyassa are Machinga. Again, when we stand on the south side of Mount Zomba and look over Lake Chirwa* (Shirwa) towards the rising sun we see mountains that are peopled by the Angulu (or Walolo).

The tradition is that the Anyasa first inhabited the land everywhere about Zomba; but that the Angulu, who lived at one time on the other side of the river Lujenda, began to fight the Machinga. The Machinga then went and encountered the Wayao, who, in turn, pressed on and drove from their home at Zomba the Anyasa tribe, many of whom now live under the Magololo on the Lower Shire* (Chiri), *i.e.*, the Shire below the cataracts.

The Anyasa are also called Anyanja, both words in different languages of the district mean river- or lake-people. The word Wayao (or Achawa) suggests a derivation from the personal pronoun. Yao regularly means "their" *(ipanje yao* means their property). So the Awa of Achawa is identical with the personal pronoun. I am inclined to interpret the name as "The people that hold their own!"' until I find something more satisfactory. The Machinga are

---

* Ch is the proper spelling, but sh has gained acceptance. The Arabs cannot pronounce the ch; while the natives cannot pronounce the sh.

really the same tribe, and are called the "fighting branch of the Yao". The derivation of their name is in harmony with this view.

It is instructive to note the descriptions that these tribes give of other tribes that live at a distance, and are barely known to them. I had heard such strange particulars about the Makua that I thought they must be a peculiar people; now so they are, but only just as the Wayao are peculiar. It was the old story; every race considers itself perfection, and points to a mote in the eye of a brother race. The language of the Makua is quite similar to Machinga. I travelled to London with a Makua with whom I had little difficulty in conversing.

There are two great Wayao chiefs in the district of Blantyre, who are called Kapeni and Kumpama, and whose head quarters are at Mounts Sochi and Cherasulo respectively. These are the two large territorial chiefs. Mkanda of Cherasulo, was at first a headman of Kumpama's, but rebelled, and lives on the southern side of that mountain; an easy day's march from Blantyre. Kumpama's territory begins about six miles from Blantyre at a stream called the Luunsu, and extends to the Namasi, on which is the old site of the Magomero Mission. The next great centre of population as we march to the north-east is Zomba, one side of which is owned by Chemlumbe, a Yao chief. The other side belongs to Malemya, a more powerful man, who is a Machinga. A little way beyond there is Mount Chikala, where a still more powerful chief called Kawinga resides; he is also a Machinga. If we look towards the south from Zomba we see a great mountain, Mlanje, this marks the domain of Matapwiri. When we wish in Quilimane to ask for a man who speaks Chiyao or Machinga, we ask for a person from Matapwiri's country. There a Matapwiri is used for a simpleton—one that has not seen the world. It is with this chief that the Yao of the coast are most associated, as the slave gangs for Quilimane used to set out from his village.

G.—TRAVELLING AND SALUTATIONS.

Native Roads.

The native roads are never straight ; at best they glide along by an easy succession of curves. Sometimes the amount of curvature is very annoying. The path is little more than a foot broad. Each side is covered with tall grass, which reaches over the traveller's head. You can only see four or five paces in front, and you can never predict what course the path will take after that. The causes of curvature are numerous. Here a tree fell down long ago and lay across the path. While it still lay every traveller went round the end of it, and the original path was abandoned, and replaced by grass that no traveller will care to interfere with. At another place the path turned aside to go through a little village ; but the village has passed away years ago. At another spot some one had hoed a field, and made the road go round its border. There are cases too where the path may have deviated to avoid marshes and difficult crossings. On many roads we lose one mile in every five. After the grass is burned, or in bad soil where very little grass grows, one may have the pleasure of going in a straight line; but where the grass is at all represented no one can pass through it without the greatest exertion. If a person leave a native path with the idea of taking a short cut, he may get into a tangle of long grass and bushes, where his progress will be not more than one mile in four hours.

Grass Fires.

One of the best sights in Africa is a large grass fire. No fireworks in Britain can for a moment compare with this. Broad plains will keep burning for weeks. At the mission on the side of Mount Zomba, which overlooked a plain of several days' journey, the sight of these fires was very impressive. The trees in the country suffer much.

Salutations.

The natives in saluting each other say " moni "—a corruption of the English "morning". So general did this word become that we have heard people inclined to fancy that there must really be a native word " moni !" The native salutation is " mugonile ?" " Have you slept well ?" Sometimes friends will ask each other " Are you well ?" " Is all well at your home ?"

A party arriving at a village observes the greatest formality. After getting an introduction to the chief of the village he begins to explain the object of his visit. The explanation is generally most tedious—it seems to go from the creation downwards—every step being carefully traced, whether in action or in motive, till the moment of the arrival !

The natives have the greatest respect for the older people. The title of father is given to such. If we ask anything of a younger man about 30 years of age he will say " I am only a child ; ask the old men of gray hairs" All the English are saluted as father ; even a white child of a few months is saluted in the words, " moni, moni, atati !" (morning, morning, father).

The Inferior Position of Women.

The women hold an inferior position. They are viewed as beasts of burden, which do all the harder work. When a woman meets any men on the path the etiquette is for her to go off the path, to kneel (tindiwala), and clap her hands to the "lords of creation" as they pass. Even if a female possess male slaves of her own she observes this custom when she meets them on the public highway. A woman always kneels when she has occasion to talk to a man. The custom very rapidly disappeared in the region of the missionaries. When we saw a woman go out of her way, carrying perhaps half a hundred-weight on her head, with the intention of kneeling down, and reflecting, as she must, that with her load she might have difficulty in getting up, we have often playfully shouted out, " You are losing your way ; this is the path," and she took it for granted that she might dispense with the clumsy ceremony.

CHAPTER II.

NATIVE ARTS AND LITERATURE.

H.—TRADES AND MANUFACTURES.

The chief method of obtaining a livelihood is by cultivating the soil. Near a lake abounding with fishes, the cultivation of the soil, though not abandoned, may take a secondary place. In districts abounding with game, the men as a rule hand over all agricultural work to their wives and slaves. Fishing and hunting are looked on as being more dignified occupations than hoeing.

Work in Iron.

Skilled labour is exemplified chiefly in their blacksmiths. Still the smith does not live so exclusively by his trade that he can neglect his farm, and in his operations he has sometimes so many assistants that his peculiar position is compromised.

Iron is found in many places. It is dug up and brought to a furnace or small kiln (ng'aso) made of clay. A charcoal fire is kept blazing by means of clay pipes or hollow bamboos, which communicate with the bottom of the kiln, and are used as the pipes of a bellows. For a bellows they use a goat's skin. Of iron they make hoes, spears, arrow-heads, knives, &c. Their hoes have no iron ring for fixing a handle. A hole is bored by means of a heated iron (there are no drills) in the handle, and the end of the hoe is inserted.

When a man wants a pocket handkerchief, it is to the blacksmith that he must go. The pocket handkerchief is made of iron and shaped somewhat like a spoon. The point of it is turned up so as to enter the nostril, and as the native has no pockets, it is hung round the neck.

Wood-work and Basket-work.

The worker-in-wood has hardly a distinct trade. Nearly every man does his own wood-work. They make mortars by hollowing out part of the trunk of a tree with a bent axe. The work takes about four days. Drums are made in the same way—their ends are covered with python skins. Certain drums are beaten on the breast ; the larger are not lifted from the ground. We have heard the sound of some of those at five miles' distance. Chairs in imitation of animals are cut out of the trunk of a tree ; but the legs are easily broken, as they run at right angles to the cleavage of the timber. Similarly they make large birds, wooden pillows, and plates.

Many things are made of bamboos (milasi) and reeds (matete). The tribes on the hills thus make beds and baskets in endless variety. The beds are not clumsy. One can easily " take them up and walk ". They are mats made of thin slips of bamboo, which are sewn together by a bamboo needle. They remind us of a Venetian blind, only the slips lie side by side without overlapping. They can be folded up in the form of a cylinder and carried conveniently under the arm (but the native carries his loads on his head). The borders of their baskets are thin broad pieces of wood, which are bent into a circular form, and sometimes curiously carved. A similar ornamental device, simpler in pattern, is seen on their clay pots. Good hats are made of the mlasa.

Bark Cloth, &c.

They go and strip a tree of its bark, which they soften in water, and beat with an ebony hammer till it forms a cloth. This was the ordinary clothing of the people before the missions. Now it is worn above other clothes on a rainy day. It very soon tears. The work is very tedious, much beating being required. One hears the sound of the hammer long before he comes to the spot. The piece of bark is laid on a large log ; after being well hammered, it becomes quite thin. The cloth thus formed is much wider than the original piece of bark had been.

Cotton grows plentifully. All the natives can make thread of it. One of their most tedious occupations is to make cloth. They do this in a very rude manner, and only make small strips at a time. Each thread has to be put separately in its place by the hand. Very few natives have courage for this tedious manipulation ; but the cloth when made is strong and highly esteemed ; it resembles bath towels.

They dye the English calico that it may last longer, but they preserve gaudy dresses without dyeing. A root is used for soap where the European article cannot be got.

Their pots are all made of clay by the women. Some of their clay vessels are a beautiful red. In their cooking they use no metals; English pots and pans speak to them of arts that are far beyond them. Their food is boiled in a clay pot, which is propped up on three stones. Another pot is turned down to serve for a lid.

Men of considerable skill are called alupa or apalu, and are believed to have strong medicine or charms.

If any one were to describe our English industries, he could not dispose of the subject in a short paragraph. But in Africa these industries do not strike us so much. They are not such a large item in human life. We see none of the working at high pressure that meets us everywhere at home. There are no crowds of pale-faced men and girls rushing along almost mechanically in response to some factory bell. There are no poor clerks cooped up in dingy counting-houses—no students with aching heads, trying to dispense with sleep. There are no careworn parents whose hard toil barely supports their children. The African has about him an air of stillness and repose that is in beautiful harmony with the scenery around. His life is not a struggle for existence. He does not care to work against time. Ambition does not drag him behind its chariot wheels. If we were to rank the Africans in classes, we should put down most of them as "gentlemen in easy circumstances". Their circumstances are easy not because their gratifications are many, but because their wants are few.

The way in which their industries come before our

notice is like this.   We take a walk in the country.   By
the side of some brook we find a man or two digging for
iron ore.   They are surrounded by companions with whom
they keep up a cheerful conversation.   Some are ready
to assist in carrying the ore to the furnace.   They
carry clay also, which is to be plastered on their kiln.
How are these loads to be transported ?   There are no
carts, no wheelbarrows, and no roads suitable for either.
Neither have they any boxes or baskets.   What are they
to do ?   One lad darts into the bush and cuts a bundle
of wands ; he then takes his knife and splits each wand
(if he be not content to use it whole), and there, he says,
is his basket.   The white man replies, " Yes ; these
wands might make a basket if you had anything to tie
them together".   Immediately the youth tears off strips
of bark, and exclaims, " Here's the black man's rope,"
and soon the load is tied up in the middle of his
basket.

As we pass along the stream we find indications
of agricultural work also, but on these we do not dwell,
as it is the more special trades we wish to illustrate.
Already we see women washing their grain at the stream
for we are advancing on little hamlets.   Now we hear
the peculiar tap, tap, tap of the hammer on the bark-
cloth, as it mingles with the notes of the birds.   Under
the trees we can descry a group of men splitting up
bamboos and smoothing the slips to form a bed.   In a
shaded verandah we find an old woman or two moulding
some soft clay.   It looks a shapeless mass, but it is " in
the hands of the potter ".   Each worker has found some
ochre, for she is fond of ornamental tints.   A potsherd

I—40 NATIVE PIPES AND POTTERY.

is by her, and she has calculated the precise form she will give her vessel.

Soon we reach the village green. Here we find a number of men sitting doing nothing. It may be that one is sewing a cloth, while the others loll upon mats and dreamily watch his hands. An ardent youth may approach the group and astonish us by taking from under his loin cloth a reel and some cotton, which he proceeds to make into thread. There are in that dark group all the elements of human nature that we find in busier lands. But in African life there is nothing of the bustle and hurry and scramble, nothing of the care and worry, the headache and heartache, that are found in England.

We cannot leave the group without asking ourselves, " What has all our boasted civilisation done ? " Are we any happier than these rude natives ? We shall see by and by that they are not exempt from hardship and injury. Their valleys and mountains witness many a sorrowful scene. But after we have placed a police-man in every corner, hardship and injury are still in our midst. Does it not seem as if there were some bank-ruptcy about human nature ? For a hundred genera-tions we have tried all manner of experiments with Governments and Institutions. We have moved them backwards and forwards like pieces on a draught board. In all this have we not been proving our bankruptcy ? We have been diligently trying the most improved methods of book-keeping, but the result has only been to chase the deficit out of one column into another. The deficit is still there !

Yes. But above the clouds and storms we have the blue vault of heaven. The pale factory girl, the over wrought mechanic, the anxious student may all have a peace that passeth understanding. As the missionary is surrounded by the heathen, he feels that his message to them has not so much to do with civilisation. They are not disposed to trouble about mechanical improvements in their unsettled land; but in their unsettled land they are arrested by an expression like " Fear not them that kill the body, and after that have nothing that they can do". Startling words to those that pass their days in fear of them that kill the body ! These are surely whispers from some other world ! Those dark figures have often gazed upon " the heavens above and the earth beneath" without making much of the vast mystery. They are likely to make more of the Scripture message. One of the oldest will turn on his mat and quietly remark, "Father, if you are speaking the truth, we are all living in darkness".

I.—THE LEARNED PROFESSIONS.

What corresponds among the Africans to the clergymen, doctors, and lawyers of modern England ? It will be found that in Africa these professions are not distinct, just as in Mediæval England the monks did all the teaching, healing, and advising. With reference to worship we shall find that the chief of the country and the chief of a village take prominent places.

The Physician.

The healing art is practised most purely by the

Msing'anga. Some of the methods are these :—*Cupping* by means of a horn, whose end is stopped by bees wax. The blood that fills the horn is thrown to the ground, and the disease falls with it. *Counter-irritation.*— Sometimes the physician will be content by making a number of incisions chiefly along the legs ; on other occasions he will rub in vegetable ashes. *Administration of medicine*, which consists chiefly of plants and their roots ; the Yao word for medicine means also a tree. The natives extract arrows by cutting all round the wound. They never amputate in order to heal, but they are able to cut off limbs very neatly, and are fond of practising the art on criminals and enemies.

But a great part of the treatment is by charms. Even where the native knows a good cure he looks on it as a charm, and his use of it is accompanied by much senseless mummery. This will be understood when we remember that diseases are supposed to be caused by witchcraft.

The Sorcerer.

This brings us to speak of a more terrible member of the learned professions, viz., the sorcerer, diviner, or witch-doctor (mchisango). The " cup wherewith he divineth " is called chisango.

He is appealed to after the physician or herbalist has failed. He is asked to tell what witch causes the disease. He may find one, and the person that he accuses of witchcraft goes with a present to the sick person, who recovers immediately.

The diviner may be consulted on any matter. He is

the great adviser of the people in all their difficulties. A person goes to him, and puts as many questions as he likes, and receives answers. These conversations are very interesting ; but all that I have heard are so very intricate that it is impossible to do justice to them in an abridgment. " My female slave has gone away, what am I to do ? " The diviner tells what he is to do if she have gone to Cherasulo, and what he is to do if she have gone to another place. He mentions what will happen if he goes to ask for her according to the individual that he may ask, &c., &c. Part of the advice may have reference to the spot where he will obtain a medicine helpful in his negotiations.

While these diviners give their response they shake a small gourd* filled with pebbles, and inspect pieces of sticks, bones, claws, pottery, &c., which are in another gourd. They often give sound advice, and they pretend to get it by this inspection, as it might otherwise give offence to their client.

Some of the diviners are the most intelligent men in the country. They claim high fees. One time we told a diviner very candidly our opinion of his art, insisting that his advice was sound, and deserved to be paid for, but that he knew as well as I that it did not come from the withered-looking contents of the gourd, but from his own judgment. The man took no offence, and though he lived at some distance he made a point of coming thereafter to our Sabbath meetings.

These men are the great agents in detecting and

---

* Stanley calls the sorcerer " the gourd-and-pebble man ".

trying witchcraft. In one respect they, and not the chiefs, form the judicial tribunals of the land, although they play into the hands of the chiefs or any rich man that pays handsomely. After they have detected a criminal he must be tried. The trial takes place by the drinking of the poisoned cup—mwai. Consequently the diviner had better be on good terms with the professional "pounder of poison" (mpondela mwai), whose duty it is to administer this poisoned draught to the accused. This, in case of guilt, at once convicts and punishes, the poison causes death. In case of innocence the poison is vomited, and the accused is acquitted.

The witch-detective is at the head of the divining profession, and is referred to in almost every case of death, and sometimes in smaller cases, as where life was in danger (107).

K.—MEDICINES AND CHARMS.

A great many trees are supposed to have virtues. Each native knows this, and becomes to some extent his own doctor. Pain in the stomach is treated by the bark of the mbawa ; headache by rubbing externally with ashes of the msolo, as also by certain charms put round the temples. The first thing a native does in headache is to tie a string tightly round his brow. The symptom of cold and shivering is treated by bathing in " water of the mkako ". For ulcers they use the mlonde. Ulcerated legs is one of the commonest maladies that attack children. For a time English treatment of these was brought into discredit, as the children would carelessly tear off the dressings and bandages.

One native treatment was to tie on a broad leaf by strips of bark (which serves as their thread), and leave it till the sore had improved.

A common war medicine is to eat the heart of an enemy.

Medicine to keep the hunter from danger and to render him successful is much prized. Elephant medicine they buy from each other at the highest prices they can afford. They have many miscellaneous charms—some tied about their bodies, others on their guns. They have a very effectual arrow poison.

One time a leopard was killed by strychnia. A chief and his Prime Minister came to Zomba Mission very secretly to beg for this "medicine"; it was to be sprinkled into the mortars where the flour of their enemies was pounded. The experiment was trusted to by its promoters as likely to be very successful, a point which was not at all doubtful. Great was the disappointment when the poison was refused.

The goats belonging to the Mission seemed to get on very well, and Mr. Buchanan was beset with many entreaties for a medicine to increase the goats of the neighbouring chiefs.

When a fowl hatches, the egg shells that have been forsaken by the young brood are carefully collected and hung up in the house of their owner to preserve the chickens from hawks and other dangers.

After they have planted their crops, the field is often protected against theft by charms which they buy. Pieces of string, either twisted from native cotton or made of the bark of a tree, are thus used.

On one occasion Dr. Macklin was called to prescribe for a woman. He asked to see her tongue. His quick observation detected at the same time signs of excitement and temper about her, and he advised her to try to be agreeable with her husband and friends. It appears the woman was a great scold ; and the natives were astonished to find that the Doctor could discover this by looking at her tongue ! That he had a great " charm " was beyond all doubt.

L.—TRADITIONAL LITERATURE.

These people have, of course, no writing. We met with many that had never seen a book before. The sight of pictures impressed them so much that their first impulse was to run away supposing that the little painted lion or leopard was dangerous. By and by some one in the crowd discovers that this lion is quite thin ! He has looked at the back of the paper and found that the body of the lion is not there ! Some of the boldest, after we assure them of safety, will even put their hands upon him. The attitude of old and young is one of utter, speechless amazement.

But these people are rich in a traditional literature. It meets us in at least four distinct forms. 1. Ndawi or conundrums. Some of them are quite short, as " the house without a door," for an egg. An incredible number of these is in common circulation, and known to most boys and girls. I noted down over 150 of them.

There are other conundrums in the form of a little story.

2. Ndano, or tales. These are also called ndawi, because many of them resemble the conundrums in having a double meaning. Some of these, we might almost say most of these, when complete have songs in them, which are repeated every now and then at each crisis in the tale. They are often recited in this form on public occasions.

I got one old man that was as enthusiastic in his recitals as the old Homerids are said to have been. When I was writing to his dictation my private study became a small theatre. In vain I reminded him that the nursery was near ! His voice was audible in the outside, scores of yards from the house. School children stopped their games, and came giggling about, and demure old natives would turn off the public highway and advance in amazement. Yet even so my old man was not satisfied—his enthusiasm, he thought, fell short of the occasion, and he introduced two young women to sing responses to the chants. The natives do not speak of "telling a tale," but of "singing a tale" (kwimba ndawi).

3. Nyimbo or Songs. These may be extemporised—music, responses and all, on the shortest notice. But there is a great collection of old songs, many of which can be identified as being the songs of several tales (L. 2), even where they are used independently. Indeed the singers could seldom point to the corresponding tale ; it was only when we happened to know the tale before that we could claim the song for it. Still many songs we believe to be quite independent. The music is a simple chant. Those that are not reciting join in

responses. The language of the songs is more difficult than that of the tales, and still more difficult is the language of the catch-word literature (L. 4).

Many of their songs aim at being an echo of tuneful nature around them. One beautiful chant imitates a little brook as it goes murmuring down its stony channel. The singers intentionally render this song in a subdued voice. I could not find any corresponding tale. It calls up to my mind the idea of a mother sitting with a few children on the bank (chiko) of a small stream as she has finished her hoeing, and rests for a minute before going home. She warns the children against the Likwanya or prickly bush that grows by the stream. This strain sung so softly has a soothing effect, and might well make the children sit down on the bank, engrossed with the sound of the rippling stream imitated in the music.

Sung in a company of little girls it is rendered thus—

1st Voice. Likwanya likunyanya ku chiko.
Response.   *Anyanyale.*

1st Voice. {   singing   } Likwanya likunyanya ku chiko.
2nd Voice. { simultaneously. } Anya-nya-nya-le e.

1st Voice. { simultaneous. } Anya-nya-nya-le e.
2nd Voice. {   } Likunyanya ku chiko.

1st Voice. { simultaneous. } Likunyanya ku chiko.
2nd Voice. {   } Anya-nya-nya-le e.

Response.   *Anyanyale.*

After this the girls that have sung the parts marked 1st voice and 2nd voice fall back on the response; and a 3rd and 4th voice take these parts. All the voices that are not reciting join in the response.

Another song has reference to a large bird, the

ndututu.   One voice designedly imitates its notes as it
converses with a few women ; while another voice imitates as distinctly the pounding of corn in which these
women are engaged.

4. The fourth form of their literature is in certain
catch-word compositions (chitagu), which have double
meanings.   The following is a specimen when there are
two speakers or reciters :—

The First Says.	The Second Says.
Nda.	Nda kuluma.
Kuluma.	Kuluma mbale.
Mbale.	Mbale katete.
Katete.	Katete ngupe.
Ngupe.	Ngupe akane.
Kane.	Kane akongwe.
Kongwe.	Akongole chimanga.
Chimanga	Chimanje macholo.
Macholo.	Gachole wandu.

Long tales are carried on in this way.   One effect
sought after is to bring together words similar in form,
but differing in meaning, as if we were to catch up the
last word of our sentences thus :—

Come forward, shew thys*elf* !
Elf dost thou call me, vile pretender ?

In this form of literature we meet with plays upon
words—an unusual phenomenon in unwritten languages.
In the conundrums proper (L. 1) we met with only one
case of a play on words.   We are asked, " What is the
girl that decks herself ?"   The word for " deck " happens
also to mean " shine," and the answer is " the moon ".

Having now spoken of the forms in which this literature has been handed down we shall say something of its matter or contents.

A great part of it consists of fables regarding the lower animals where the characteristics of these animals are brought out. The rabbit is the clever hero of all the tales, much as the fox is in European tales. The hyena (litunu) is celebrated for its greediness. The litunu is a large carrion eater, which stands, we think, rather higher than the lion. In one tale the hyena is always begging food from the lion. The lion makes a buck climb a tree, so that its shadow is reflected in the water ; this reflection is pointed out to the hyena, who at once casts himself into the river.

The following may stand for an example of their tales :—There was once a hyena and a leopard. They went a journey, and the hyena picked up a tortoise, and told the leopard, saying, " See, I have picked up my* tortoise ". The leopard said, " Give it me that I may see it ". He gave it him, then the leopard threw the tortoise away. One day they heard that the tortoise was a doctor. Then the hyena and the leopard arranged to go to the tortoise, and beg medicine for hunting. They went, they found the tortoise, and said, " We have come for medicine for hunting ". The tortoise gave the leopard beautiful spots, and the hyena ugly spots, because the hyena had wished to eat the tortoise ; then he gave them horns of medicine, and said to them, " If you find meat that died of itself you must not eat it ". Then the hyena and the leopard

* Native idiom.

went to hunt.   On the path they found an animal that had died of itself. The hyena said, "Leopard, my friend, behold an animal that has died of itself". But the leopard said, "Come, let us go away". The hyena said, "Pshaw ! we must not eat meat that died of itself ?" Then the leopard said to the hyena, "That doctor said to us, should you find meat that died of itself, you must not eat it". The hyena said " Pshaw ! not quite !" The leopard went to the bush, but the hyena returned to the doctor, and said, "Tortoise, I have found meat that died of itself.   Is it a transgression to look at it ?" The tortoise said, "No, it is not a transgression".

The hyena went to his meat and gazed on it.   Then he went back again to the doctor and said, "I have looked at it".   Then he said again, "Is it a transgression to lick it ?"   The tortoise said "No".   The hyena then went to his meat and licked it.   Then he returned again to the tortoise and said, "Is it a transgression to remove it from the path ?"   The tortoise said "No". The hyena then went to his meat and removed it off the path, and threw it far away.   He returned again to the tortoise and said to him, "I have removed it".   And the tortoise said, "Very well".   The hyena asked again saying, "Is eating it a transgression ?"   The tortoise said, "You will not swallow it ?"   The hyena said "No". Then he went back to his meat and ate it, and came back to the tortoise and said, "I have eaten that meat". But the tortoise said, "You have transgressed, hyena, you will not be a hunter, but the leopard will be a good hunter, I gave him a horn of medicine".   So the leopard caught much meat, but the hyena did not know how to catch meat. The tortoise had said, "Hyena, O chief, your name is hyena".

We may here note that the naming of the animals is a subject on which they have many legends. The names, too, in most of their legends about persons, are significant, and accord with the moral of the story.

It must not be forgotten that all the natives' names have a meaning It is common for men and women to bear the names of animals ; thus we may have a Mr. Cock, Mr. Lion, and so on. We almost think that their children when hearing these stories for the first time would think of " hyena," "leopard," &c., as being people who bore these names.

Several stories relate to fowls and birds. Fowls are stated to have been at first wild, and after a while to have been domesticated. One fowl was visited by a guinea-fowl. The latter was greatly astonished that the housewife threw out food for them—that a comfortable house was provided—and every kindness shewn ; but just as all these things were favourably impressing the guinea-fowl the hungry husband returned and said, " Kill that fowl as a relish for my porridge".

Many such tales evince a wonderful sympathy for animals. The natives are greatly distressed by the visits of a large crow to their crops. Yet they have a tale which makes them excuse the depredations. " Once on a time a chief was puzzled over some case, and could get no advice till a crow came and put matters quite right. This crow was handsomely rewarded by a gift of beans and other seeds. It proceeded to carry these home, but dropped many on the way ; now when the

crow rifles the native's fields it is looking for some of
those lost seeds and their fruit."

They have a great many tales embodying theories on
the creation of the world, to which we shall allude below
(13). The introduction of arts and manufactures is also
an important theme. We are told of a woman that found
people with plenty of corn, but no porridge. They
simply chewed their grain. This lady produced a
mortar and procured flour. Hollow stones they say
gave place to pots, in the same way as caves were
abandoned for houses. They speak of a time when they
hoed with wood. It was after they could use iron
knives that they dug down, and could put in their posts
as they do in their modern houses. The first clothing
was bark. Death was introduced by a woman who
taught two men to sleep ; she held one's nostrils, and he
never awoke. "Death and sleep," the legend remarks,
" are one word."

Monkeys were at one time human beings who quar-
relled with their friends, and went to stay in the bush.
Though the natives admit that the monkeys are their
cousins, they are not slow in pointing out where they
differ from men. We said to one woman who was
severely censuring the monkeys for eating her crop,
that she should give them some corn to see whether they
would not raise a crop for themselves. She replied
that monkeys would not leave their seed in the ground—
they would pick it up and eat it. It is not everyone
that would have fixed so promptly on such a characteristic difference between men and monkeys. They
give many tales of experiments tried to make human

beings out of monkeys, specially in the case of women that were barren and wanted a child ; but, after the most careful training, these " children " always rejoined their own " kind ".

Relation to Tales of Other Lands.

There are also many wonderful tales regarding people that crossed lakes or rivers ; but at the time we did not note these so carefully, as we considered that it was possible that our narrator might modify it in accordance with teaching that he had heard from the Scriptures.

Since we arrived in England, however, we find that Bishop Callaway has written down stories exactly similar, and indeed hardly so circumstantial, which he received from the Amazulu. On looking over his collection we find several that correspond, chiefly as regards the most striking feature of the story, with some of ours. This shows what we had been convinced of long before, that some of these traditions had been recited at a period when the ancestors of the Amazulu and of these Nyasa tribes were one people.

The following is an instance of the kind of resemblance :—In one of the tales of Bishop Callaway a young man tries to destroy the cubs of a leopard. He kills them one by one ; and the point by which the deception was carried out was to hand the cubs to their mother one by one. When only one cub was left he handed this cub several times according to the number of children. The leopard thought that the same cub handed to her three times was three cubs. In a collection of ours that was sent home in 1880, and since printed, a "rabbit" or fox cheats a lioness by the same peculiar strategy.

In the stories themselves there is little to give us any note of time or antiquity. They are liable to modification too in important particulars. Thus one man will tell a wonderful story of what a hero effected by his gun. He judges that a European would despise the hero if he were armed only with a bow and arrows. But another narrator of the same story may remark on his variation that guns did not come till long after.

After we have had a tale written, we have, in order to obtain explanations, asked the same man to repeat it, and where he had given any expression that seemed to vary from the more usual form of language, we have observed that he kept as faithfully to such expressions as if he had been reading from a book. We had little doubt that, as he confessed, he had before him some recital that had produced an impression in his early years.

As to the amount of this species of literature it is difficult to be certain. The number of conundrums (1) we think does not much exceed 250. I find that I have written out more than 100 tales (2), and I have listened to at least 150 others which I did not write out. I merely noted new words and points in grammar. The traditional songs (3) may be as numerous as the tales. Of the catch-word compositions (4), at least the longer ones, I should not expect to find more than 50.

Before I left I had difficulty in finding new specimens

of 1, 2, and 4. Mr. Buchanan, in his study of the language, was collecting specimens of native literature at the same time, and we had begun to think that we had nearly exhausted the field so far as the more pointed tales were concerned. New reciters generally wished to give us what we had already. Our contributors represented a wide district. My list included Wayao, Machinga, Anyasa, Angulu, Achipeta, Achikunda, and Awisa. But the tales seemed to be common to all these tribes. A Machinga was generally familiar even with the tales of a native of Quilimane. Where this was not so we considered the tale as merely local and of no antiquity.

We have given translations of several tales in the appendices.

ETHOLOGY.

Chapter III.

BELIEFS ABOUT GOD.

ARTICLES 1—107.

The following statements on the Ethology or the customs of these races are taken from the very words of the natives themselves. Natives are generally quite agreed as to what their customs are. Where they gave different views I have noted both, after finding that both had real authority. I do not think I have admitted any point of importance without having heard at least four natives on the subject. The statements are translations, as far as possible, from the *ipsissima verba* of the negroes.

1.—THE NATURE OF MAN.

An ancient philosopher was asked by his friends when he was dying what they should do with him after his death. "All very well," was the reply, "if you can catch me." The Materialist tells us that there is nothing to catch, that there is nothing that runs away from the body at death, but the Spiritualist says, " You have only the remains of the man there—only the instrument that he used to work with ".

What is the position of these African tribes with regard to this question ? They are unanimous in saying that there is something beyond the body which they call spirit (lisoka) or pure spirit (lisokape). Every human body at death is forsaken by this spirit ; but the spirit of a child that dies about four or five days' of age gets nothing of the usual attention (45).

2.—IMMORTALITY.

" Do these spirits ever die ?" Some I have heard affirm that it is possible for a troublesome spirit to be killed (5, 4). Others give this a direct denial. Many like Kumpama of Cherasulo say, " You ask me whether a man's spirit ever dies. I cannot tell. I have never been in the spirit world, but this I am certain of, that spirits live for a very long time." This is a good specimen of cautious answers that the natives often give, and it expresses the belief that they act on with reference to departed spirits.

3.—WHO THE GODS ARE.

In all our translations of Scripture where we found the word GOD we used *Mulungu*, but this word is chiefly used by the natives as a general name for spirit. The spirit of a deceased man is called his Mulungu, and all the prayers and offerings of the living are presented to such spirits of the dead. It is here that we find the great centre of the native religion. The spirits of the dead are the gods of the living.

Besides lisoka (1) and mulungu there is another word for spirit, viz., *msimu*, which is much used in reference to offerings.

4.—WHERE THEY ARE FOUND.

Where are these gods found ?　At the grave ?　No. The villagers shrink from yonder gloomy place that lies far beyond their fields on the bleak mountain side.　It is only when they have to lay another sleeper beside his forefathers that they will go there.　Their god is not the body in the grave, but the spirit, and they seek this spirit at the place where their departed kinsman last lived among them.　It is the great tree at the verandah *(kwipenu)* of the dead man's house that is their temple, and if no tree grow here they erect a little shade, and there perform their simple rites.　If this spot become too public the offerings may be defiled (40), and the sanctuary will be removed to a carefully-selected spot under some beautiful tree.　Very frequently a man presents an offering at the top of his own bed beside his head.　He wishes his god to come to him and whisper in his ear as he sleeps.

These gods are not confined to one place.　In answer to prayer they can protect a man during a long journey, and return with him in peace.　When all the villagers are driven from their homes by war these spirits have power to go with them to a new village.　The spirit of an old chief may have a whole mountain for his residence, but he dwells chiefly on the cloudy summit.　There he sits to receive the worship of his votaries, and to send down the refreshing showers in answer to their prayers.

5.—HOW THE GODS GIVE EVIDENCE OF THEIR EXISTENCE.

How do the natives know that these gods attend to them ? How do they judge that their deceased ancestors can see them through the darkness of the grave ?

(1) They judge from the way in which prayers have been answered.   If they pray for a successful hunting expedition and return laden with venison or ivory, they know that it is their old relative that has done it, and they give him a thank offering.   If the hunting party get nothing, they may say " the spirit has been sulky with us " *(akwete lupuso)*, and refuse the thank-offering.

(2) Besides this, their god appears to them in dreams. They may see him as they knew him in days gone by. When they dream of the living there is nothing wonderful in that ; but when they dream of the dead it is the departed spirit come to visit them.   Such a dream impresses them very much.   That being is altogether different since he entered the spirit world.   Now he is a god with power to watch over them, and help them, and control their destiny.

(3) The appearance of the gods in dreams is still too hazy.   Their craving for clearer manifestations of the deity is satisfied through the prophetess *(juakuweweta)*. She may be the principal wife of the chief ; in some cases a woman without a husband will be set apart for the god.

The god comes to her with his commands at night. She delivers the message in a kind of ecstacy.   She speaks (as her name implies) with the utterance of a person raving with excitement. During the night of the communication her ravings are heard sounding all over the village in a high key.

The whole hamlet is wrapt in slumber, when all at once the midnight stillness is broken by those mad shrieks. The startled inhabitants think it is war—slavers have come—their first impulse is to run away. Their fear soon subsides. It is the prophetess. They are anxious to hear what she has to say, and return to bed again. Or there may be a great meeting in the morning, when the prophetess appears—her head encircled with bhang or Indian hemp, and her arms cut as if for new tatoos.

Various gods reveal themselves thus in various places, either local deities (11), like Mbona of Cholo, or more ordinary gods (25-28).

(4) The gods may appear in animal forms. Some spirits may appear for mischief. If a dead man wants to frighten his wife he may persist in coming as a serpent. The only remedy for this is to kill the serpent, when some go so far as to say that this troublesome spirit is dead, but others say that though the trouble is ended the god is only reduced to a pure spirit (lisokape).

6.—DISTINCTIONS AFFECTING THE GODS.

It is usual to distinguish between the spirit and the form it takes. A spirit often appears as a serpent. When a man kills a serpent thus belonging to a spirit,

he goes and makes an apology to the offended god, saying,
" Please, please, I did not know that it was your serpent".
The departed may assume the form of other animals.
A great hunter generally takes the form of a lion or
a leopard ; and all witches *(asawi)* seem to like the form
of a hyena.

There is also a distinction between the spirit and
the spirit's messenger. The spirit, it is said, will
not take the form of a bird, but will send a bird with
its message. We have this well illustrated in the legend
about Che Mlóngolo, which became so popular amongst
us at Blantyre. A little boy was allowed by his father
to accompany a caravan to the coast ; he picked up
some curiosities, for which an Arab gave him exceedingly
beautiful cloth. His uncle coveted the cloth, abused
the boy very much, and ultimately killed him. A little
bird flew to his home at the village, and sang on
the trees to the women as they pounded their corn,
" Ti, ti, ti, diridya ; Ti, ti, ti, diridya, they have slain
Che Mlongolo because of his cloth ".

7.—THE PRIESTS.

A certain amount of etiquette is observed in approaching the gods. In no case can a little boy or girl
approach these deities, neither can any one that has not
been at the mysteries (52). The common qualification
is that a person has attained a certain age, about 12 or
14 years, and has a house of his own. Slaves seldom
pray, except when they have had a dream. Children
that have had a dream tell their mother, who approaches

the deity on their behalf. (A present for the god is necessary, and the slave or child may not have it.)

Apart from the case of dreams and a few such private matters, it is not usual for anyone to approach the gods except the chief of the village. He is the recognised high priest who presents prayers and offerings on behalf of all that live in his village. If the chief is from home his wife will act, and if both are absent, his younger brother (mpwao). The natives worship not so much individually as in villages or communities. Their religion is more a public than a private matter.

When we went to Blantyre we were accompanied by two small boys that had lived in Quilimane. One night after we were in bed we were startled by a terrible screaming. This was heard by a friend who lived in another house at a short distance from ours, and he came to us judging that we had among us at least a leopard. But the screams were found to have a different cause. The younger boy wished to carry into practice our exhortations about prayer, and for this purpose knelt down on his little mat or bed. The older was more cumbered with much serving, like Martha. He wanted to make his bed tidy, and without ceremony threw the little worshipper off the mat, telling him that it was not proper for him to pray, as he was not a white man (msungu). The rudeness gave rise to fighting and screaming. We mention the incident to show that the bigger boy would hold that he belonged to the village of the white man, and that the white man ought to approach the gods on his behalf.

The chief of a village has another title to the priest-

hood. It is his relatives that are the village gods.
Everyone that lives in the village recognises these gods ;
but if anyone remove to another village he changes his
gods. He recognises now the gods of his new chief.
One wishing to pray to the god (or gods) of any village
naturally desires to have his prayers presented through
the village chief, because the latter is nearly related to
the village god, and may be expected to be better
listened to than a stranger.

8.—VILLAGE GODS.

On the subject of the village gods opinions differ.
Some say that every one in the village, whether a relative of the chief or not, must worship the forefathers of
the chief. Others say that a person not related to the
chief must worship his own forefathers, otherwise their
spirits will bring trouble upon him. To reconcile these
authorities we may mention that nearly every one in the
village is related to its chief, or if not related is, in
courtesy, considered so. Any person not related to
the village chief would be polite enough on all public
occasions to recognise the village god : on occasions
of private prayer (which are not so numerous as in
Christendom) he would approach the spirits of his own
forefathers.

Besides, there might be a god of the land. The chief
Kapeni prays to his own relatives, and also to the old
gods of the place. His own relatives he approaches
himself, the other deities he may also approach himself,

but he often finds people more closely related, and consequently more acceptable (7) to the old gods of the land.

9.—MONOTHEISM, POLYTHEISM, OR PANTHEISM?

After we have settled that there is an object of worship, there are still a great many different positions to hold.   We might be Pantheists, Polytheists, or Monotheists.

The position of Pantheism is seldom indicated by natives when describing their religion.   We once thought that the class of nouns (in the native language) that *Mulungu* belongs to was an argument in favour of their Pantheism.   One class of native nouns is nearly co-extensive with human beings, and Mulungu is not in this class.   But the argument at best is weak.

While Mulungu means a spirit, it may also be used as a proper name.   There are two classes of expressions where it is used as a proper name.   The first class points to a kind of Pantheism.   Mulungu is said to be " the great spirit (msimu) of all men, a spirit formed by adding all the departed spirits together".   These and various other expressions of the same kind indicate a grasping after a being who is the totality of all individual existence, and are not unworthy of notice. If they fell from the lips of civilised men instead of savages they would be regarded as philosophy.   Expressions of this kind among the natives are partly traditional, and partly dictated by the big thoughts of the moment. The second class of expressions where we have Mulungu

used as a proper name certainly points to a personal
being. By the Wayao he is sometimes said to be
the same as Mtanga (12). At other times he is a
Being that possesses many powerful servants ; but is
himself kept a good deal beyond the scene of earthly
affairs, like the gods of Epicurus. In the native hypo-
theses about creation "the people of Mulungu" (wa ku
Mulungu) play a very important part. This Mulungu
in the spiritual world—the world beyond the grave—
is represented as assigning to spirits their various places.
He arranges them in rows or tiers.

After making an induction of all that we have heard
about Mulungu (carefully excluding, of course, every
statement that seemed to be in the least modified by
Christian teaching), we should say that their religion
in its worship was practically Polytheism. At the same
time the spirts are often asked to act as mediators with
some higher being. Beyond their Polytheism their
language contains a few expressions that remind us of
Pantheism, and a great many that speak to us of
Monotheism.

The derivation of the word Mulungu throws some
light on the subject. Henry Salt (1814) says that
among the Makuas it means "the sky". We have heard
Yao expressions that would prepare us to accept this
interpretation ; and the Yao word may be sometimes
used for rainbow (which is either Mulungu or ukunje wa
Mulungu) : it is singular too that Chilungu means
earthquake. We think a more correct view lies in the
derivation stated by Bleek, which makes it originally
mean " great ancestor ".

10.—NUMBER OF THE NATIVES' GODS.

We saw that every human being has a Mulungu
or spirit (2). This position every native will uphold,
except perhaps in the case of a young child who has not
reached six days of age, and has not been formally
introduced into the world or "taken out of the house"
(kopoka m' nyumba) (44). If a child of six days has
been introduced into the world though only a day before
its death, its spirit is entitled to offerings, and receives
these offerings at least from its parents. When the
little child meets the parents beyond the grave it will
say, "You remembered me; I saw what you were
doing".

The spirit of every deceased man and woman, with
the solitary exception of wizards and witches becomes
an object of religious homage.

The gods of the natives then are nearly as numerous
as their dead. It is impossible to worship all; a selection must be made, and, as we have indicated, each
worshipper turns most naturally to the spirits of his own
departed relatives; but his gods are too many still, and in
farther selecting he turns to those that have lived
nearest his own time. Thus the chief of a village will
not trouble himself about his great-great-grandfather;
he will present his offering to his own immediate predecessor, and say, "Oh, father, I do not know all your
relatives, you know them all, invite them to feast with
you". The offering is not simply for himself, but for
himself and all his relatives. We ask him, "What if

they quarrel with the other relatives about their share
of the feast ?" " Let them quarrel," he replies, " I have
given them enough."

Key to their view of the Spirit World.

We may think that the native chief in selecting
his predecessor alone, has left all the rest of the people
that once lived in his village without any homage.
Here we encounter an important native view that a
chief represents and is responsible for all his people. If
any one wish to treat with a native village it is with the
village chief that he must deal. If we give a present to
a village it is to the village chief that we must give it.
This does not prevent us from giving presents to any
other individual. So it is in the world beyond, which the
natives conceive to be peopled in the same way as this
world. There the old chief has his wives and slaves and
companions about him as of yore. To the natives death
is the time when they, in like manner, shall be literally
" gathered to their fathers ".

Nature of Offerings.

The man that makes an offering regards himself as
giving a present (mtuka) to a little village of the
departed which is headed by its chief. Those that are
best known to the offerer may get a present themselves,
but they will be expected to call the attention of
the chief when a public present arrives.

11.—LOCAL DEITIES.

We have seen that people residing in a village worship their deceased chief, but when their present chief dies he will become the principal god; more distant relatives give place to successors. But a great chief that has been successful in his wars does not pass out of memory so soon. He may become the god of a mountain or a lake, and may receive homage as a local deity long after his own descendants have been driven from the spot. When there is a supplication for rain the inhabitants of the country pray not so much to their own forefathers as to the god of yonder mountain on whose shoulders the great rain clouds repose. (Smaller hills are seldom honoured with a deity.)

The god of Mount Sochi is Kangomba. One tradition regarding him is this—When the Wayao were driving the Wanyasa out of the country, Kangomba, a Wanyasa chief, saw that defence was hopeless, and entered a great cave on the mountain side. Out of this cave he never returned; "he died unconquered in his own land". The Wayao made the old tribe retire before them, but the chief Kangomba kept his place, and the new comers are glad to invoke his aid to this day. Their supplication for rain takes the form (Ku Sochi, kwa Kangomba ula jijise) "Oh, Kangomba of Sochi, send us rain" The Wayao chief Kapeni often asks some of the Wanyasa tribe that can trace connection with Kangomba to help him in these offerings and supplications (7).

12.—SUPERIOR DEITIES.

Beyond and above the spirits of their fathers, and chiefs localised on hills, the Wayao speak of others that they consider superior. Only their home is more associated with the country which the Yao left; so that they too at one time may have been looked upon really as local deities. Among these other beings are Mtanga and Chitowe.

Mtanga some distinctly localise as the god of Mangochi, the great hill that the Yao people left. I regret much that I did not see this hill before leaving Africa, as I have heard so much of it. To these people it is all that the many-ridged Olympus was to the Greeks. The voice of Mtanga, some hold, is still audible on Mangochi. Others say that Mtanga was never a man, and that Mtanga is another word for Mulungu. He was concerned in the first introduction of men into the world (13). He gets credit also for supplying people with seeds, and making mountains and rivers. He is intimately associated with a year of plenty. He is called *Mchimwene juene* (very chief).

Chitowe (Siluwi) has not such a good character. He is associated with famine. He is often represented as having one leg, one arm, one side of his nose, and so on —the other half of his body being supplied by beeswax. He is invoked by the women on the day of initiating (kuumbala) their fields. The women of a village form a great procession when the new crop has begun to grow. They chant a hymn to Chitowe, imploring him on behalf of their crops. Chitowe may become a child

or a young woman.   In this disguise he visits villages,
and tells whether the coming year will bring food
or famine.   He receives their hospitality, but throws the
food over his shoulder without eating it.   Chitowe is a
child or subject of Mtanga, and some speak of several
Chitowe who are messengers of Mtanga.

Mpambe is often invoked by the Anyasa at great
supplications for rain.   This Mpambe in the Yao
language is " Njasi," in English " Lightning ".   The
Yao say that Mpambe is sent by Mtanga with rain.
This is a mythological expression of the fact that the
lightning in this quarter is always associated with rain.

This last example shows how natural it is for man to
deify the powers he sees around him.   At first he is
greatly touched with all the emotions of " wonder, love,
and awe," as he considers how much he is indebted to the
shower that makes his food grow.   He is ready to fall
down and worship.   What shall he worship ?   The
mountain whose lofty summit is clothed with the rain
cloud, or the lightning that springs from the cloud ?
He goes over everything he can fairly associate with
the rain, and still he is not satisfied—he craves for
something that can understand him.

He looks back to the days of his youth.   He remembers a grandfather who told how he had fled from the
face of an oppressor, how he had built his home far up
near the mountain top, and there brought up his family
in safety.   By and by as dangers passed away, this
ancestor moved farther down the mountain ; gradually
he increased in power, and in his old age found himself
the chief of a clan.   Yet he never forgot the days of

his adventure, and ever pointed proudly to the spot where he had first found a shelter; and his children's children, as they listened to the old man's tale, counted the ground holy. The days come when they can see the old man no more. "But does he not still exist? Yea—did we not hear his words as we listened to sounds that played about the mountain side? Did we not see him, though it was but for a moment, sitting beside his own home as he used to sit long ago? He wore the very same dress. Did he not appear to us in our dreams? There, too, we saw him moving beside his old home. Yes, he is living on our mountain still.* He is taking care of us. He knows when we need rain, and he sends it. We must give him something; when he had corn he always gave us. Now, the poor man has no crop; but perhaps his needs are many. We will give him food, we will give him slaves, and he will not forget us."

There is something full of pathos in the sight of

---

*This principle in human nature is fully recognised in philosophy. Butler in his ' Analogy of Religion' speaks of it as the principle of continuance, remarking "that we believe a thing remains as we left it, except where we have any reason to think it is changed". Dr. Bain recognises the same belief in our postulate that "nature is uniform," although he holds that the tendency in question gets its great value from "experience".

Beyond this there is a tendency to find a place, as we have assumed above, for anything that has passed beyond our ken. We saw this in the case of a little child that was separated from youthful playmates. When asked "Where's Nyama?" at first he pointed in a definite direction. As the journey proceeded he became quite at a loss, and shook his head over the question in sadness. Much farther on it was asked whether Nyama was not in yonder steamer, and the suggestion gave intense satisfaction, and ever after instead of shewing despair over the question he would brighten up and say, "She is in another steamer".

a man invoking his deceased relatives. He has got into great difficulty. None of his friends can assist him, they hardly sympathise with him. His thoughts turn to days when he had no difficulty, to the bright period of which, heathen that he is, he can say, " Heaven is about us in our infancy ". He is so sure that if he only had the grey-headed man that smiled on him then, all his difficulties would vanish. That man could understand him, and believe good of him as he did long ago. Could he but reach him across the portals of the grave all would be well. Thus, with great earnestness, the native turns to the spirits of his fathers.

13.—THE CREATION—COSMOLOGY.

The existence of the world itself is accepted as a fact not to be explained. But there are legends that explain the introduction of the sun, moon, and stars, clouds and rain; as also how mountains and rivers appeared on the scene. Man, or at least the father of these central tribes, sprang from a hole in a rock, from which the lower animals came also. Around this hole there were abundant footprints of all kinds of animals. It was closed by the people of Mulungu, and is now in a desert place 'towards the north' (kumpoto). Subsequent to the appearance of man, many changes occurred specially calculated for his benefit. Thus the mist was sent to keep the sun from burning up the crops—an arrangement that would readily commend itself to these philosophical children of the tropics.

Their legends go on to state that the Wayao, Anyasa,

Angulu, Awisa and others sprang from a common stock, and to explain how the tribes separated through one going to one side of the country and another to another. The chief cause of such separations is said to be war. The Zulus and the English belong, they say, to a different stock ; where they came from the natives cannot tell. They have a legend about Zulus (Mangoni) coming out in great swarms near a large river ; and another legend about a black man crossing a bridge, as he looked round he was greatly astonished to find that a white man (msungu) was following him. The white men are represented as having staid longer with the people of God (Mulungu), and learned more than the black men. With all due deference to the toothless old man who told me that the Zulus are different from the Yao, I am strongly of opinion that although their languages are not mutually intelligible now, there was a time when their forefathers played together by the same streams and hills ; but this time is more remote than his legend, which only explained when the Wanyasa separated from his tribe.

CHAPTER IV.

ON WORSHIP AND OFFERINGS—OCCASIONS FOR WORSHIP.

"None shall appear before me empty."—EXOD. 23, 15.

STARTING ON A JOURNEY (ULENDO), WAR, OR HUNTING EXPEDITION.

14.—PRAYERS AND OMENS.

When a man intends to set out on some expedition he goes to the chief of his village, and tells him. The chief presents an offering (mbepesi) to the spirit of his predecessor. This offering consists of a little flour, which he puts down very slowly at the top of his bed, or he may go to the verandah of the house of his deceased brother. As he puts down the offering he recites the words, "My son has come, he goes a journey, enlighten his eyes, preserve him on his journey, escort this child, may he return with his head unscathed (literally 'green,' wa uwisi). Please, please, let him undertake the journey, and be very successful."

If the flour do not fall so as to form a cone with a fine point there is a bad omen, and the journey is deferred. The remedy for this state of matters is to resort to the oracle (chisango) (I). It is seldom, however, that a bad omen is found at this stage, though some say it is possible. The oracle will explain what is the cause of the bad omen. Probably the man will be told to " try again ". If the cone form beautifully on this occasion, then it will be clear that the god wanted him merely to delay for a day or two, and for some good reason ; but if the cone still refuse to form, resort is again had to the oracle. The oracle sets to work, and finds that some deceased relative has a hand in this obstruction. This relative must be propitiated by an offering. Or it may be that a witch (msawi; Chinyasa, mfiti) is the cause of the trouble ; then it is the duty of the oracle to declare who the witch is. This leads to a serious state of matters, which will very probably end in the death of this witch.

A person cannot go to hunt with any assurance of safety till the witch has drunk the poisoned cup (mwai).

We were much affected by a case of this kind that came under our notice. A village chief, Matope, was led to believe that he was bewitched. First his principal wife became seriously ill—the disease was consumption—she was treated with the usual English remedies, and Mrs MacDonald made a bed for her, which took the place of the hard mat upon which the poor native lies down to die. As the native fare is hard as the native bed, and the poor invalid could not relish it, we sent her some soup every day, as well as sugar of which she was exceedingly fond. Ultimately the disease ran its course, going through the same stages as the terrible malady does in England. One day the husband came to

me and said, " There is mourning at our home ".   The
simple words revealed at once that the wife of the village
chief was dead.

We fully expected that, notwithstanding our remon-
strances, some one would be accused of causing her
death through witchcraft ; but perhaps owing to the
interest that we had taken in his wife all along, no one
was accused on this occasion.   He had four wives
besides, and he soon supplied the place of the deceased
by buying another wife, who was " very good to
her children ".

Then a little after, the son of one of his other wives
having gone out at midnight, a leopard came upon him
and caught his foot just at the door of the house as he was
running in.   The lad was badly bitten, and his mother
induced Matope to have resort to the usual methods of
detecting witchcraft ; the result was that Matope's own
mother was pronounced a witch.   We were very sorry
for the poor woman.   She lived in another village, over
the stream from her son's hamlet.   She had always
shown us the greatest kindness and hospitality.   She
was fond of joking and fun, but this sentence made her
an object of dread and aversion.   Every native now
shrunk from her, and her life became a burden.   We
tried to do everything for her ; we gave her presents ;
invited her to come and see us, and cautioned her against
drinking the poisoned cup.   We made the village chief
promise that it would not be administered.   The result
was that there was some delay in drinking the ordeal.
We made every use of this respite by talking on the
matter with Kapeni, the chief of the country, who was

her brother, and who promised to use every influence on her behalf. Her son, the village chief, was a very successful hunter. During the delay he could not go to hunt. The superstition was too strong for him. At the same time his mother was anxious to break the spell that bound him, she was so sure that she was innocent. She drank the dangerous cup and died, and however dearly the liberty was purchased, the hunter could now go forth to his usual pursuit.

So much for the danger of being suspected of witch-craft, a suspicion that might arise from flour not falling in the form of a cone. But it is seldom that a bad omen arises while the chief is in the mere act of putting down the flour. After the flour is put down, and has formed a shapely cone, he carefully covers it with a pot, and leaves it all night. During the night he may have a dream about the journey, and this will decide his course. But if he is still undecided he visits his offering early in the morning. Should he find that the cone of flour is broken down on one side (mbali jimo jiwalwiche), that it has not its proper point (lusonga), the omen is bad. The flour is thrown away in the bush, the journey is forbidden by the spirit, and cannot be thought of ; and the result is an appeal to the oracle (chisango). But if the flour has preserved its conical form the omen is good, the divinity has accepted the present and granted the request. The village chief tells his man to go forth with confidence.

The Wanyasa depend more upon the dream during night than the appearance of the cone. Some of them say, " Of course, the flour will form a cone if it is

put down carefully, and the cone will maintain its form
if the rats are kept away ". The Magololo chiefs would
not send their children to school until they dreamt.

When the chief has decided on the journey he gives
his man a thread (lupota), which is tied round some
part of his person, as a token that the god goes along
with the expedition. He may give an oil vessel (chisasi)
for a similar purpose. The man now takes the necessary
supply of food (inga) and fire-arms, bids his wives good-
bye, and sets forth on his journey.

15.—CEREMONIES OBSERVED BY THE WIVES OF TRAVELLERS.

The village chief may immediately call the wives that
are left behind, and advise each one to behave with
discretion during her husband's absence, as otherwise
she may mar his domestic peace, or even cause his
death (82). These wives must observe certain customs
during their husbands' absence. If at any time one of
them have a dream she must present a private offering.
(In describing the worship connected with a journey,
we have been assuming all along that the expedition is
of interest to the village chief. This is nearly always
the case, for one thing the chief wishes to pray that
his villager may be safely restored to him). Should a
man undertake a journey that is entirely private, then
he may perform the offering himself, or ask his wife
to do it for him. They would put down the flour, and
watch the formation of the cone as the chief does. All
the particulars connected with the success and failure of

omens are the same, and if they are relatives of the chief the god invoked is the same. If they are not related to the chief they may pray not to the god of the village, but to the god of their own family.

While a woman's husband is absent she goes without anointing her head or washing her face. She must not bathe, she scarcely washes her arms, she must not cut her hair. Her oil vessel (chisasi) is kept full of oil till his return, and may be hung up in the house or kept by the side of her bed. This neglect commences, according to some, as soon as her husband has gone. Others allow the moon " to die "; they wait for the new moon before they begin this species of mourning (kuwindika). It continues till the husband return.

16.—KICKING AGAINST THE STUMPS.

The expedition has started at last—surely all detention from bad omens is at an end. By no means. In a few days the leader of the expedition may appear at the village with all his men. He has hurt his toe on the stump of a tree (chisichi)! The natives, in preparing their ground for cultivation, cut down nearly all the trees. They do not cut close to the earth as an English forester would do. They find it much easier to cut the tree at a thinner part, and leave a stump. Such stumps are all over the cultivated land, and are often found on the footpaths. If a superstitious man strike his foot on one of these at the beginning of an important journey, he considers it to be ominous of evil.

When Julius Cæsar was landing in Africa with his

army, he stumbled and fell. This was an unhappy omen. But his presence of mind gave it another turn. He cried out, "Oh, Africa, I embrace thee". The less superstitious natives calm their fears by a similar method. While some speak with bated breath of the danger of picking up a buck that died of itself, others say "We always pick them up and eat them, and are very glad to have the chance".

If a superstitious man kick against the stumps, there is no hope for his expedition, he goes back, and the affair is referred to the oracle in the usual way.

A man whose heart is set upon a journey is sometimes wicked enough to disregard an unfavourable omen. His men call his attention to it, and he says "Yes, it is a very unlucky thing; we shall go to the oracle as soon as we return!" This is an evasion nearly as bad as that of the Roman General, who, when told by the soothsayer that the sacred chickens would not eat, said that he would make them drink, and kicked them overboard. Whether the consequences to the native that treats the omens in this off-hand manner are always as serious as they were to the Roman we have not heard. The native who has an unfavourable omen is not at ease in his mind; but we think that these superstitions will soon be overcome in the minds of future generations.

17.—ILL-OMENED SNAKES.

Some of the strongest superstitions are associated with snakes. If a snake of bad omen, as a sato (python) or a lukukuti, cross the path of a traveller, it is a sign that he will meet with disaster on his journey, and at once he returns to his home. But if the traveller is already on his return journey he does not go back, but goes on to his village expecting to find that everything has gone wrong there. This omen generally betokens a death at the village. If the snake is seen on the right hand, the omen betokens that there is some danger on that side of the road, and similarly if the snake is seen on the left.

Regarding this form of superstition, I once asked a native that strongly professed his belief in it, whether he would turn back on meeting a snake in his way if I gave him a letter for Zomba, and told him that it had to go on quickly. He said, " No ; he would not turn back when a white man sent him." Why ? " Because," he said, " you would laugh at me, and ask why I had not brought the snake home for a specimen !"

When a sungula (rabbit) crosses the path it betokens that the chief will die.

There is a great number of similar superstitions. But it is noteworthy that there is no such superstition about thunder as was among the Romans. To them thunder is ever welcome, associated as it is with refreshing showers.

When the men have been gone some days the villagers conclude that the journey is prospering—the god is accompanying the party. If the chief want to send out others before this party come back, he must send another spirit with them, and there will be no difficulty in finding several suitable escorts among the spirits of his deceased relatives.

After the caravan has been gone for some time the villagers begin to anticipate its return, and to talk of the wealth that it will bring.   It may be a hunting expedition, or a journey to the coast to buy beads and cloth, guns and powder, in exchange for ground nuts, slaves, or ivory.   As the caravan approaches the village, the news of its arrival goes on before quick as lightning.   All eyes are turned toward the direction where the long absent ones are expected to appear.   Already some of the villagers are rushing forth to meet them.   The returning party fires a salute ; the guns of the village reply. All are in ecstacies of joy.   The women run out with handfuls of flour, and sprinkle on the heads of the returning heroes.   The caravan goes on amid shouts of joy, straight to the village chief, and deposits the goods under his care.

18.—THANKOFFERING.

The chief immediately makes an acknowledgement to the spirit that escorted the party.   He goes to one of his wives and asks her for flour that he may present an offering.   He puts down part of this flour in the same way as he did when the expedition started.   Then he wets the rest of the flour, and puts it down beside the dry portion.   This water-and-flour is supplementary to the dry offering (mesi gakwe).   As he presents it he says, " Now we are happy, my children have come back, you have given us much."   When he has finished he claps his hands as a salutation to the spirit, and retires.   This expression of thanksgiving is generally made in a private manner.

PUBLIC REJOICING.

Now begins a season of public rejoicing. The whole hamlet makes high holiday. The women may now bathe, and cut their hair, and anoint their bodies with oil. So may their returned husbands. During their journey these men had refrained from using salt. They were afraid to use it (82), for they said, " Perhaps our wives are not behaving well in our home, and we shall die ". Now the chief prepares a great banquet, and calls a medicine man, who puts a charm into the food ; the travellers eat of this, and henceforth they may use salt freely.

A large quantity of beer is brewed, and as soon as it is ready the chief and all his visitors go to the verandah of the house of the deceased chief, where all larger offerings are presented. They carry flour and beer, and perhaps some such offering as tobacco. The chief is the first to invoke the spirit saying, " Please, please, Ching'ombe," or whatever the name may be, " here is beer for you, drink it, we want to live well at our village, and to drink in peace ". He will mention also the happy circumstances connected with the expedition, and hint mildly that when another expedition is necessary they will look for a similar service from the spirit. The sister of the deceased chief will also be an offerer, and any others who may be closely related. They first put down a little offering of flour, and then each takes a cup of beer to pour on the ground as a libation After the others have presented their offerings the chief finishes the worship by presenting all that is left.

Many guests may be invited. Any that happen to arrive before the offering has been given will accompany the party that goes to present it. All in the village may be present at this offering. It is a kind of public worship. Whatever may be the rank of his guests it is the village chief himself that acts as high priest. Even the chief of the whole country if present would only stand and look on. As soon as the offering is finished, the beer drinking begins. Great is the rejoicing in the village.

If an expedition were unsuccessful, if, for instance, some one died or goods were lost, instead of this rejoicing there would be a mourning. The god would be considered to have deceived them, and behaved very badly.

After the expedition has been the occasion of a public rejoicing, the god is acquitted of all blame. Yet, strange to say, many successful expeditions of this kind —especially when they have been to the coast with slaves and ivory—are the most unfortunate things that could happen to a district. Soon after the beer drinking is over, the goods have to be divided, and in a large proportion of cases so great contentions arise that the chief's kingdom is divided also.

Other occasions for approaching the gods occur in cases of sickness (19) or famine (20). On these we shall not dwell so long, as the foregoing principles generally apply.

19.—SICKNESS.

When a man is ill he puts down an offering to his deceased father or mother, saying, " I wish to give you a sacrifice ; can you tell us what you want? and I will bring it you ". He first gives this offering himself. He may say, " I am very ill, I wish you to restore me ; perhaps a witch wants to kill me, restrain this ". Then he looks for a good dream. An offering of flour is put at the side of his pillow to tempt the spirit to come. If the spirit come not, he tells the chief of his village, who may give an offering in like manner, or he may go at once to the sorcerer (mchisango) and say " We want to see the spirit that has been invoked ". After making inquiries, the sorcerer says the spirit wants such and such ; then the required offering is given. If the sick man recover, the matter rests there. In cases that are more serious, the sorcerer will tell him that bad spirits (masoka) have got into his house, that some one has bewitched the house and all his usual places of resort, that he must have another house in the fields. There are other manifest advantages attending this retreat from the busy village.

A house in the fields is built and prepared perhaps that very day We have not known many cases where the invalid ever returned. Sometimes a poor consumptive patient, when removed to such a house, is drenched with rain, as the thatch is not so good as on the other house.

REJOICING ON HIS RETURN.

Great is the rejoicing on the invalid's return to the village, if ever he return again.   Much beer is brewed. The usual sacrifices are given to his god.   The recovered patient says, " Now I am happy, I have health ; drink you this beer ".   Mats are spread out, he sits down upon one, and the physician (msing'anga) is called to his side. The physician pours beer on his patient, and after that, water, and then begins to shave his head.   The physician does not present any offering to the village god ; but he gives a thank-offering at his own home to his own gods.   He returns thanks that " he found medicine for yonder sick man ".

20.—PUBLIC SUPPLICATION FOR RAIN.

We have seen how the natives invoke the gods when they pray for a prosperous expedition (14) and for health (19).   We shall now see what they do when they pray for a good crop—which generally means, in their country, praying for rain.

When there is no rain at the proper season there ensues much distress.   Famine is dreaded above all other evils.   After private offerings have all failed the chief of the country calls a national meeting for supplication.   Much beer is brewed and offered to the spirit. The chief addresses his own god ; he calls on him to look at the sad state of matters for himself, and think of the evils that are impending.   He requests him to hold a meeting with all the other gods that have an interest or influence in the matter.   A council of the gods is

believed to be held, and if any god act as an obstructive
he is specially propitiated according to the direction of
the prophetess.

After the supplication there is a great dance in honour
of the god. The people throw up water towards the
heavens as a sign that it is water that is prayed for.
They also smear their bodies with mud or charcoal
to show that they want "washing". If rain do
not come they must wash themselves in the rivers or
streams. If rain fall, they are soon washed in answer
to their prayers. When the good crop follows, they
present as a thanksgiving the first heads of maize and
some pumpkins. Before they begin to eat the maize
themselves some of the cobs are roasted and offered
under the prayer tree (4). In smaller crops, as beans,
there is no special offering.

In the South of Africa the power of rain-making
has been claimed completely by the rain-doctors. Even
here the sorcerers have a great power. Still the chief
maintains what we think must have been his prerogative
in the earliest times. Does this not shew that these
races are a stage nearer the primitive manners than in
the South where such a priesthood has been developed ?

DREAMS afford another occasion for offerings (41).

THE NATURE OF THE OFFERINGS. GENERAL OFFERINGS.

21.—THE NATIVE FLOUR.

Of the ordinary offerings to the gods (which are just
the ordinary food of the people), flour is the commonest.

The natives eat it themselves in the form of porridge, but they never present it thus to the spirits except on the day of a person's death, or by special request. This offering, though common, is not made ready without a great deal of trouble. The poor native woman seems to be occupied at milling flour from morning to night. The process is like this—First, she takes corn from the cob, puts it into a mortar with some water, and begins pounding to remove the husks (maseta). These are separated by sifting (kupeta). She next puts the husked grain (msokolo) again in the mortar, and does as before. By this time all the husks are off. After this the corn is steeped in water for some time, when it is called mlowe. This she puts into a mortar without water, and pounds again. When the third pounding is finished, she resorts to another process of sifting (kusenyenda) and obtains flour, which may be broken down to any degree of fineness by repeated pounding. Many harder portions (lusenga) need pounding again.

This native flour is given to the spirits (misimu) either quite dry or with a little water stirred into it.

22.—NATIVE BEER.

The beer is made from maize or millet (D).

It is not like English beer. It is really a thin gruel, and serves for food as well as for drink. It is a very wholesome beverage for the natives, and it is well that they use it rather than other stimulants. The natives have a great desire for wine or brandy (they apply the

Brazilian word Kachaso to everything of this kind). We may illustrate how far this craving exists by mentioning how often chiefs and headmen request Kachaso. Sometimes we have prepared a little tincture of ginger, and seen it greedily drunk. Mrs. MacDonald was one day clearing out old bottles, a few of which contained lime juice in the bottom, and it was sad to notice how the persons that received these bottles were entreated by others " to give them some of the brandy ". When a person was thus entreated, even after he had tasted the old rotten stuff, he said he had only a very little for himself, and hastened away as if determined to enjoy it alone ! When we were on the Kwagwa River, a little above Quillimane, much merchandise was brought, and the first thing that was asked in payment was kachaso. The boatmen between Quillimane and the Missions were in danger of doing a great deal of harm in this way, as they brought up rum and such stuff, and traded on their own responsibility Chiefs can procure kachaso readily enough, especially from the slave traders. One time at Blantyre there was hardly a drop of wine for a whole year, but the chief of Sochi had obtained some, and sent a messenger to us to ask for wine glasses ! Another chief that we had opened up intercourse with, sent us a bottle of rum as a return present. Of course everyone gives things that have thus passed through the hands of the natives the cold shoulder, as it is not known what they are made of !

The temptation to drunkenness is one of the most terrible that the country can be exposed to. The natives go down before this temptation at once. A great deal of their drinking is an aping of the manners of Europeans as seen on the coast. We think that the civilisation of this race should be accomplished by total abstainers if possible. People who tamper with the natives by offering them brandy or by mixing wine and rum that they may make them drunk for their own amusement, are exceedingly thoughtless. In this country, unfortunately, any one can sell as much liquor as he likes without paying any license: and the effect of drinking brandy or such stimulants is sometimes very deplorable. One of the Magololo Chiefs or Headmen, as reported to me, seemed to go quite mad when he received a supply of brandy. He went about killing his people for the purpose of amusement, much in the manner of King Mtesa. On such occasions there used to be a great rush of people to the Mission, representing that their chief had drunk brandy, had killed very many of their friends, and wanted to kill them. They implored the protection of the Mission in the most earnest manner.

23.—THE EFFECTS OF NATIVE BEER.

But the native beer does not produce such serious consequences, although many fights and wars arise out of it. One must drink a great deal before it intoxicates, and by the time a man has consumed half a barrel of gruel he will be more inclined to sleep than to quarrel. Should he simply talk nonsense, his more sober friends pay little attention to him. At a great beer-drinking the guests may lie down and sleep where they were drinking.

What do the natives think of the crime of drunken-ness? When asked, "Do you say a man has a bad heart if he gets drunk on beer?" they reply "No; he may not have a bad heart". But on further question-ing they insist that such a man has certainly "a very bad head!"

24.—BEER AS AN OFFERING.

We have seen how the flour is used, both as an offering and as a sort of oracle according to the way in which it falls—according as it forms a cone or not. The beer may be used in the same way, both as offering and oracle. If when poured on the ground it sink into one spot as it would do in sandy soil, then the deity receives it, but if it spread over the ground there is a bad omen. Beer-drinkings may be held on the conclu-sion of favourable journeys and on many other occasions. Besides there may be beer drinking without any special reason, as when a man wants to treat his friends : but even in this case there is an offering.

As soon as the beer is ready the man goes to the village chief and carries some with him. The village chief presents this offering to the village god. There is no special prayer, except " I want that my beer may be sweet". After the village chief comes back from the offering he drinks some of the beer himself, and declares the feast open. Among others the custom is simply for the brewer of beer himself to put down a little in his own house, with a prayer to the spirit that his beer may be sweet.

25.—SPECIAL OFFERINGS.

All the offerings are supposed to point to some wants of the spirit. If a spirit were to come saying, "I want calico," his friends would "just say that he was mad," and would not give it. " Why should he want calico ? What would he do with it ? There was calico buried with him when he died, and he cannot need more again." But if the request is at all reasonable (as when an old hunter asks animal food), it will be quickly attended to, and personal taste carefully consulted. In cases of this kind they may anticipate his wishes. When a deceased smoker wants tobacco his worshippers put it on a plate and set fire to it. If a spirit ask a house they will build him one.

It is a general rule that these special offerings are in answer to special requests, and such special requests are made known either by the oracle (chisango), or by dreams, or by the prophetess. The requests of a more serious character, involving the sacrifice of human beings, are made known chiefly through the prophetess (5, 3).

Near Lake Moere the people have idols that represent a departed father or mother. They present them with beer, flour, bhang, and light a fire for them to smoke by. —(Livingstone).

We shall now say a little about such special offerings and the way of presenting them.

26.—OFFERING OF A FOWL.

They generally kill the fowl by wringing its neck. Some speak of cutting its throat, and making the blood

flow down. This is akin to an Arab method, but as the
natives practice their offerings this custom is neither
essential nor common. When the fowl is killed they
simply lay it down at the prayer tree (4). If it be taken
away during the night the spirit has accepted it. If it
be known to have been carried away by a leopard, the
leopard was commissioned by the spirit, or if the
deceased was a hunter he may himself have taken
the form of a leopard. The fowl may lie till the ants
eat it, and the offerers are quite satisfied. This fowl
may be given uncooked, or it may be either roasted or
boiled as indicated in the request made for it.

27.—OFFERING OF A GOAT.

A goat may be offered in the same way, only it is not
likely that the whole animal will be given, unless the
offerer is very rich. One leg is usually sent to the spirit,
while the remainder is eaten by the villagers themselves.
In conversing with natives on these offerings, we have
often inquired whether the person that advises the
offering may not sometimes appropriate it, and thus
cheat the spirit for whom it was intended. We have
often thought that the bones of these offerings might
play a great part in the superstitions connected with
cannibalism and witchcraft (107). The same might be
said of the bones of human beings (28) that are thus
sacrificed ; but the bones of the lower animals would do
as well for imposing on natives, who are not anatomists
enough to know the difference.

It is not considered necessary that these offerings be

taken away by the spirits. It is sufficient that they are placed there, and that the spirits may come and lick them.

28.—OFFERINGS OF HUMAN BEINGS.

Sometimes the prophetess will announce that the spirit demands the offering of a man or a woman. As soon as this intimation has been given all set upon the victim that may have been indicated. If wanted for a deity residing on a mountain, the victim is stripped, his garments are cut up into narrow bands, with which the legs and arms are secured. The victim is not killed, but tied to a tree. If a beast of prey come during the night and devour the unfortunate being the deity has accepted the offering. Where wild animals are not abundant a little house is built on the hill side, and the person with his legs and arms securely fastened, is put inside and left to die of hunger.

If the deity live beside a lake or river, the man or woman, after being stripped, and having the legs and arms securely fastened, is tied to a large stone and thrown into the lake or river. The crocodiles may seize the offering at once, but in any case death is the certain result, as the stone prevents the victim from swimming.

The victims in such cases are usually slaves ; but if a freeman were to set fire to the grass or reeds beside a lake, and cause a great conflagration close to the chosen abode of the deity, he is liable to be offered up to the god that is thus annoyed ; but if he be the owner of many slaves he can easily redeem himself, one of his slaves will be offered instead, and something paid to the prophetess to facilitate the transaction.

The vast immolations of human beings made at the grave of a chief we shall consider under another heading (32).

Chapter V.

CEREMONIES CONNECTED WITH DEATH.

" Qualis vita Finis ita."

29.—TRANSITION FROM THE SUPERNATURAL.

We have now spoken of the gods—their nature and number—their prophets and priests, the occasions of their worship, and the nature of the offerings. This finishes what we have to say on the supernatural. Before descending to the natural, we shall cross the dark border-land that lies between.

This border-land is Death (30-43). By and by we shall reach what we may call the Natural (44 and seq.) By the time we reach section 103 we shall have brought before the reader many things that he may class as the Unnatural.

To shew that there is nothing so very unusual among these African tribes, let us remark that in that model of ancient civilisation—the Roman Republic—prisoners were slain at the tombs of heroes that fell in battle, and slaves were sacrificed at the funerals of all rich people. The advance of civilisation allowed such victims to kill each other, when the custom gave rise to the exhibition of gladiators.

30.—ILLNESS.

We have seen already (19) that a sick man may be removed from his village to a solitary hut in the fields, and that he may return in good health ; but very often when a man leaves his village for this solitude he never comes back. We have mentioned that the diviner or oracle-man may be able to cope with the witch who is the main cause of the man's illness, but very often the diviner fails entirely, and the disease takes its course.

There is another man, the herbalist or physician (jua sing'anga) that is often called in, and to whom we have already alluded ; he carries on his cures by the use of charms, which in many cases are really medicines (I). When a person is sick his friends go in search of a physician.

They generally carry a present for him. He considers for a little, and gives his answer which may be, " I refuse to attend this patient ; I cannot do you any good. The witch that has taken him on hand has medicine more powerful than mine." On other occasions he is more hopeful, and will try. He goes to the woods and the fields and searches for medicines, and then comes with them to his patient. If the patient recover the mediciner gets a large fee, but if the patient die he gets nothing ; on the contrary, an unsuccessful physician may be accused of murder, and we have known a great fine paid for the crime. We only knew of one case of this kind, and the victim was an English doctor. We do not think the occurrence is at all so likely in purely native cases. But in other parts of Africa a mediciner may pay for the patient's death with his own life.

All the natives soon become very disheartened when they fall sick, chiefly owing to the fear that they have become the prey of some cruel witch.

31.—DEATH.

Every charm has failed, the attendants see that the end is near, the sick man too is aware that he is leaving this world. In civilised countries many a man toils for fame. He would regard himself happy if he were sure that he would be remembered after death. The dying man before us has this fame ready made for him. He knows that after his death he will be worshipped as a god. Does this make his death bed happier? Do his last thoughts turn with delight to the prospect? Alas, no! The poor man would live longer if he could, and the last desire he expresses is generally this, "You will take care of my children when I am in the grave," then he enters on the dark journey alone.

32.—SLAVES ESCORT THE DECEASED.

Did we say he went forth alone? This shall not be, if his friends can help it. His death must be concealed for a few minutes. If he be a man of some property in slaves, and belong to a certain family of the Wayao tribe (say to the Abanda or the Amilansi), he will have a great many slaves to accompany him. Some of the attendants leave the dead man at once. If any of his

slaves are sitting outside the house they are told that
their master is better, that he is doing well ; but
suddenly a capture begins, and many slaves of the
deceased are made fast in slave sticks. When their
master is buried they will be put in the grave along
with him.

This terrible custom does not prevail among all the
families of the Wayao tribe, but where it does, as many
as ten slaves may be killed to follow an important chief,
and rather fewer to accompany one who is not so rich.
Kapeni, a chief that belongs to the Abanda family, told
me that he was going to give up this custom now
because of the English ; but not a few of the slave
refugees at Blantyre have run away from his dominions
to escape the dreadful fate. Though the chief were
opposed to the practice himself, he would not regularly
interfere between his people and their own slaves or
goods. It is said that the slaves must be caught before
they have taken part in the mourning. This furnishes
one escape for them. If they run away and stay till
the funeral rites are over, they will be comparatively
safe on their return. But they are liable to be sent
after their master (28) if he should ask for them.

The practice of sending messengers to the world
beyond the grave is found on the West Coast. A chief
summons a slave, delivers to him a message, and then
cuts off his head. If the chief forget anything that
he wanted to say, he sends another slave as a "post-
script".

33.—WAILING AT THE DOOR.

If the man do not belong to the families that require an "escort," the mourning begins as soon as he is dead. There is no stratagem practised for catching slaves. One of his wives has likely been in attendance, and she will raise the sad wail, which is heard afar off, and is easily recognised. A great assembly of mourners is soon collected. The mourning consists of plaintive chants, drumming, and dancing. If powder be available a great many guns are fired that people at a distance may say, "there is a mourning in yonder village". This is called the "mourning at the door" of the house (ku mlango), and continues until the deceased is buried, which may be in one or two days. In the case of an important person, the mourning at the door may be continued for five or ten days, or even for a month. In mourning the Wayao put flour on their heads, the Achikunda, I have observed, doing this at what was quite an ordinary dance, so far as I could see. The Anyasa put strips of bark round their arms and various parts of their body. If it be a chief that has died they use strips of cloth instead. One time we tried to buy some badges of mourning, made of plaited grass, but were told that the wearers would not part with them. They are worn till they fall off.

34.—THE UNDERTAKERS—THEIR DUTIES AT THE HOUSE.

Soon after life is extinct the undertakers (awilo) are sent for. They are generally two in number. As a rule they are not relatives of the deceased, though from the derivation of their name I think they may have been so originally (kuwila, compare juakuwilwa, bereaved). Some make it a point that the undertakers must not have seen the deceased during his illness, but this is not universally observed. In some families the slaves of the deceased are the undertakers, and the slaves of a deceased chief may invest his successor with the insignia of office.

The undertakers wash the body (mtembo) of the deceased. For this purpose they use water from the stream—the ordinary water used at the village (if the deceased be a woman her body is first partially washed by female attendants). They close the eyes ; some fail in this, and are considered unskilful. They dress the body in calico, covering it all except the eyes and the upper part of the face, which may be left uncovered until they are on the point of carrying it to the graveyard. They tie up the deceased in a mat, the very mat which was his deathbed. The Wayao are buried with the legs bent, the Wanyasa with the legs straight. When all these ceremonies have been finished, the undertakers come out of the house and wash their hands, not in ordinary water but in water of medicine, " because they handled a corpse ".

35.—PROLONGED WAILING.

If the wailing is to continue for a long time they procure the bark of a large tree and encase the body therein. The body is then set in a position nearly upright ; a hole is dug in the floor of the house so that

the putrid matter may drop (kusulula) into it. Should
the body be in an advanced state of decomposition, they
burn Indian hemp (chamba), and carry beside it on the
way to the grave, this is done to neutralise the smell.
But in cases of prolonged mourning the deceased is
often buried in his own house.

36.—DEATH IN WAR.

If a man be killed in war, his friends, if they can
procure his body at all, do not " show it at the village,"
but bury it on the war path. If his enemies find the
body they disembowl it and cut off the head, taking
certain parts for charms. Enemies allow no burial, but
cast forth the mangled remains to the vultures and
other carrion eaters.

When a man is wounded in an engagement he is
carried back, not to his own dwelling—there are bad
spirits in it—but to a little hut made ready for him in
the bush (19) at some distance from the village.

If a person die through drinking mwai (and this con-
stitutes an enormous percentage of the older natives),
he is denied the ordinary rights of sepulture. Several
years ago the burning of witches was practised. At
present this would not be done unless the witch refused the poisoned cup, which she is, on the contrary,
most eager to drink to show her innocence.

37.—JOURNEY TO THE GRAVE.

When the 'mourning at the door' is finished they
proceed to the grave. A large bamboo is passed along

the body, and projects beyond the coffin or mat (ugono), both behind and before, and the body is carried shoulder high.   One of the undertakers carries at the head, and the other at the feet.   The undertakers have the charge of carrying the body to the grave, although others may assist, but there is not so much changing as is seen in Scotch funerals.   A large procession of men and women now set forth to follow the deceased to his last resting place.   They have a drum with them, and march to certain very plaintive and not unmelodious chants.

Some of the men carry hoes to dig the grave, and a small bowl or basket (chiselo) to throw out the earth. They carry also an axe to prepare palisades for the sides of the grave.   The women follow in the rear, carrying some porridge, with the usual relish (mboga), as also a pot of beer.   It is not every one that is allowed to follow the funeral procession—a person that has not been at the mysteries may not go.   Thus a boy of six years may have a brother or a playmate die, but he will not be allowed to accompany the funeral party.   No one that is very closely related to the deceased will go to the grave.   A father will not go to the funeral of his child, nor a husband to that of his wife ; but, in cases of poverty where there is difficulty in employing under-takers, or if the death take place on a journey, the nearest relatives have to be present at the funeral rites ; but in ordinary circumstances, if they follow the remains at all, they turn back at the chikomo, that is, the path that leads from the village to the main road. A mother is allowed to go to the funeral of her child

only if it die in infancy.   One reason why the chief
relative of the deceased does not go to the grave is that
he has to prosecute the witch that caused the death :
going to the grave would unfit him for the task..

38.—DIGGING THE GRAVE..

The grave is not dug nor marked out at all, till the
funeral party arrive.   On their arrival the body is laid
down on the ground under the shade of a large tree, and
the grave-digging begins.   As hoes are the implements
used, the process takes a long time.   It often begins
about noon, and is not concluded till night.   No one enters
the grave except the undertakers.   After a sufficient
depth has been reached they bring forward the body to
measure whether the size and shape of the grave will
exactly suit.   After this measuring is completed the
body is again laid aside out of the hot rays of the sun.
By and by other men are at work with an axe cutting
pieces of trees to form a kind of palisade round the
inside of the grave.   The shaping of these sticks takes a
long time.   The structure when finished resembles the
piling used to keep the banks of a river from falling in
or being washed away.   It forms the sides of a strong
wooden house which is erected over the body.   When
these posts have been securely fixed two forked sticks
are driven into the ground, one at each end of the
grave.   The body is then lowered, and the forked sticks
receive the projecting parts of the bamboo that carried
it to the grave.   The body when lowered is suspended
between these forked sticks, and remains hanging with-

out touching the ground. Other logs are put above so as to form the roof of this strong wooden house, and afterwards the earth is filled in ; only before filling it in they have certain articles to bury with the deceased.

The wooden house is for the purpose of keeping away the witch who caused the death, and who now wishes to eat the flesh of her victim. It serves to keep away carrion eaters of all kinds, for the witch may assume the shape of a hyena.

39.—OFFERINGS AT THE GRAVE.

Along with the deceased is buried a considerable part of his property. We have already seen that his bed is buried with him, so also are all his clothes. If he possesses several tusks of ivory one tusk or more is ground (siaga) to a powder between two stones and put beside him. Beads are also ground down in the same way. These precautions are taken to prevent the witch from making any use of the ivory or beads.

If the deceased owned several slaves an enormous hole is dug for a grave. The slaves that were caught immediately on his death are now brought forward. They may be either cast into the pit alive, or the undertakers may cut all their throats. The body of their master or their mistress is then laid down to rest above theirs, and the grave is covered in.

After this the women come forward with the offerings of food, and place at the head of the grave. The dishes in which the food was brought are left behind. The pot that held the drinking water of the deceased and his drinking cup are also left with him. These, too, might be coveted by the witch, but a hole is pierced in the pot, and the drinking calabash is broken.

The man has now gone from the society of the living, and he is expected to share the meal thus left at his grave with those that have gone before him. The funeral party breaks up ; they do not want to visit the grave of their friend again without a very good reason. Any one found among the graves may be taken for a cannibal (107). Their friend has become a citizen of a different village. He is with all his relatives of the past. He is entitled to offerings or presents, which may come to him individually or through his chief. These offerings in most cases he will share with others, just as he used to do when alive (10).

40.—TAKING DOWN THE HOUSE.

" It is unclean. And he shall break down the house . . . and he
shall carry them (the stones, timber, and mortar) forth out of the
city into an unclean place."—LEV. xiv., 44, 45.

The day after the remains have been committed to the grave the undertakers see to the destruction of the house that was occupied by the dead man. The house of the deceased is always taken down whether he died in it or not. No one will live in that house on any consideration. The spirit (Mulungu) of the deceased would be very angry with the man who did so, and would say, " This man is glad that I died that he might enter my house ". If he possessed a great many houses it is the house of his principal wife that he is most identified with.

Her house is taken down, and the houses of his other wives are left.

The fabric is demolished very effectually. The foundations are dug out of the ground. Any remains of the deceased man's food, the ashes of his fire, and the thatch of the roof are carried away and burned at a cross road (malekano) that the spirit of the deceased, or the evil spirits that caused his death, may enter some of these paths.

When the house is broken down, the parts of it not carried away are buried, the place where it stood is swept all over, fresh earth is put on, the spot is considered sacred. All the children are warned that they must not play on this ground. A pot is put down to receive offerings of beer, and when any special offering is given to the deceased it is usually presented here (4). If this place become too public (as when children play near and send dust into the pot), the pot will be placed under a tree at a little distance from the village.

The man may be buried in his own dwelling. In this case the house is not taken down, but is generally covered with cloth, and the verandah becomes the place for presenting offerings. His old house thus becomes a kind of temple (chilisi cha nguo). There may be cases also where the deceased is buried in the village, although not in his own house. In such cases a new house will be raised above the remains.

When the house is taken down the funeral rites (mtembo) are finished.

An important feature in these observances is that the relatives of the deceased have their heads shaved. There

are a great many absurd regulations that could not
be published, with reference to burying the hair. Some
of it is buried at the place where the house of the
deceased stood. A second shaving takes place after
their hair grows again (43).

When a chief or headman dies the village is often
entirely forsaken.

41.—CANONISED.

The deceased is now in the spirit world, and receives
offerings and adoration. He is addressed as " Our
great spirit that has gone before." (Msimu wetu woku-
lungwa ulongolele).

He has now a certain power over the lives and desti-
nies of his surviving relatives. If any one dream of
him it is at once concluded that the spirit is " up to
something ". Very likely he wants to have some of the
survivors for his companions. The dreamer hastens to
appease the spirit by an offering.

42.—CONTINUANCE OF MOURNING.

But the mourning, as distinct from the funeral rites,
is not yet finished. The surviving relatives do not wash
their faces or anoint their bodies with oil, neither do
they cut their hair until the great day of the second
shaving (43). Sometimes they eat no salt, use no
warm food, and drink no beer. Cases of this kind are
among the nearest approaches to fasting that we met
with in the country. If a friend come to see them he

will get his porridge warm, but the mourners wait until
theirs cool. On the day of the wailing at the door the
undertakers may give a dispensation from some of these
penalties by putting salt in a common mess of food. If
a man have been absent from this dispensation he must
follow customs like the above.

The duration of this mourning may be two months,
or even more. The chief of the country, especially if
related to the deceased (which he may well be if the
deceased was a man of great influence), may have a voice
in determining how long the mourning is to continue.
In more humble life the relative of most influence would
be consulted.

43.—END OF MOURNING.

After two or three months have passed, there is a
great gathering. This is the day on which the mourning is formally ended. Already you hear them beginning to sing "Iya! iya! ungolele ukana;" to which the
response is, "O manja o," while the undertakers respond, "O Kangolele." This is, in fact, quite a drinking
song, like "Willie brewed a peck o' maut," and shows
that the party are not to sit and mourn for ever. On this
day much beer is brought, and the deceased's spirit is
especially remembered, and is considered to partake in
the festivities.

The undertakers come back. One of their duties is to
see to the second shaving of the heads of the dead man's
relatives. They take off a little of the hair in the front
and a little on the back of the head (kukawa), and others

complete the shaving.   The hair is buried again at the house, where the deceased relative receives his offerings, or in the bush.

ENTERING ON INHERITANCE.

On the day of the second shaving the successors of the deceased enter upon their inheritance.   They take possession of the deceased man's wives and whatever property he may have.   This day is a great marriage feast in one aspect.   Now the services of the undertakers are at an end ; they have been feasted sumptuously throughout, and are now paid.

Chapter VI.

CHILDHOOD AND YOUTH.

44.—BIRTH.

When the time of a child's birth draws near, the mother does not stay in her house, or even in the village. Accompanied by one or two female friends, she goes forth to seek the retirement of the great forest. As a rule she will soon be able to return, but if the delivery be protracted it is usual to apply to a physician, who sends a medicine to drink, which is viewed as a charm. Though the native women are generally hardy, it would not do to assume that they are entirely made of iron. Many poor women suffer severely, and die in the bush, the child being generally unborn.

45.—THE INFANT.

On the birth of the child, one of the female friends takes it and carries it to the village. The mother is able to accompany on foot. In the case of a first-born child, the party is met with considerable rejoicing, in which the grandmother of the child takes a prominent part, and raises the song, Ngwete chisukulu none sechelele, "I have got a grandchild, let me rejoice".

On arriving, mother and child are put into a house, where they stay from three to six days. No one enters their abode except the elder women (achakulungwa).

After this there is the ceremony of introducing the child into the world—bringing out the little stranger to public notice. The head of the mother is shaved, as also the head of the child. The child is now named. Both mother and child come out of the house, and are received with rejoicing, at which the elder women are present. The mother has received a medicine or charm, in which the child has to be washed for a great many months to come.

If the child should die before being brought out of the house it receives no mourning. The relatives do not shave their heads on account of it, nor do they present offerings to its spirit. But if it has been brought out of the house, even if it should survive but a very short time, the usual mourning is held, and offerings are presented to it, especially by the mother. Such a denizen of the spirit world is supposed to be able to affect the fortunes of the survivors ; besides, it may be very powerful in interceding with the older spirits (10).

Several African customs with reference to young children remind us of the well-known superstition about "Changelings".

46.—NAMING.

The child receives a name, which it retains until it goes to the mysteries. The name is given by the relatives : if a female child is betrothed she may be named

by her future husband. The name the child receives
may be determined by some circumstance connected
with its birth, as in the case of Jacob or Joseph, or such
Scripture names. Sometimes it is named after other
relatives of the family, as is the custom in Britain.

The person who receives a name at the mysteries
has some choice in determining what he will be called.
We knew a boy who assumed much at his own instance
the name of Kalikalanje, the hero about whom there
are so many native tales, reminding one of the class
of tales that Jack the Giant Killer belongs to. All the
names of the people are significant. Every name may
be assumed to have originally had some meaning, very
much as every effect has a cause.

47.—NAMING EUROPEANS.

One point where natives show a great deal of cleverness
is in giving names to white people. They never talk of
a white man by his own name, which is generally un-
suited to their pronunciation. They have an invention
of their own, and the new name is generally very happy.
It hits off some peculiarity in personal appearance, and,
over and above this, it aims at pointing to some mental
habit. After seeing a few efforts of their naming, we
almost become prepared for the theory that physical appearance is a reflection of character.

Thus they meet with a man who is a miser, they
regard his miserliness for some time in silence ; at last
they begin to take a look round him. They wish to
discover some of his physical peculiarities. He cuts

his hair very close. " Ah! we have it now," and they call him " The close shaver ! " When an Englishman with any marked pecularity arrives among them he generally creates a profound impression. The natives, like the Greeks of old, are fond of hearing some new thing. It is often very trying to one's sense of the ludicrous to go about the country with English companions and hear the remarks and criticisms, while the new comers are quite unconscious of what is being said, and feel sure that they are complimented. If one do not make progress in the native tongue, he may be in the country for as long as five years without knowing his native name, although it is a household word all over the place, and no one speaking to the natives would ever think of using anything else.

Some names, again, are general designations, not so much of the individual as his work, and in this way they may be modified, so that the original meaning is lost. One man had besides his own proper name the name of Kasisi or priest. This word means originally shaven, or without hair (kabe sisi, or kalibe sisi). It was first applied to the monks with reference to their shorn heads. There is a rock that is seen on the Zambeze at the Lupata mountains, which, at a distance, looks exactly like a monk. The natives call this rock Kasisi. A clergyman will get the name applied to him, and that although there be no baldness in the case. The word is used too of Makukani, who acts as the priest of the Magololo, especially when rain is required. But it was entirely unused in the native language till the first man with a tonsure appeared on the

Zambeze. He would get it as a nickname, or rather as a name (for they would not necessarily want to make fun of him), and the word would linger after the monks disappeared, and would be applied to any that resembled them in other particulars.

Visitors sometimes throw a great deal of responsibility on those that are in the country already. The latter are asked to tell all about them, and if there be anything peculiar the danger falls on the old settlers. It is a rule in Africa that where a stranger pays a visit and gets into trouble in his friend's district, the whole responsibility lies on his friend; the same rule is generally applied when travellers are following a guide. Though it may seem strange, yet the appearance of many people is apt to be deemed "uncanny". The phenomenon of a person without an arm, of people able to change the colour of their hair, or "to take out their teeth and put them in again," though easily turned to a laugh among friendly natives, especially the young, is nevertheless felt to demand explanation, and might cause serious results among natives disposed to quarrel.

48.—THE DESTINY OF THE CHILD.

In civilised countries the destiny of the new arrival is left to unfold itself gradually. No definite course is chalked out. In the life of the civilised infant there is consequently a great amount of uncertainty and plot interest, especially with reference to marriage, as every romance bears witness to. Here this is not the case. Take the instance of a little girl. All the lovely day

dreams, all the pleasures of hope and pictures of
fancy are rudely set aside long before she has reached
sweet seventeen.   While the child is yet unborn she may
be sought in marriage.   This is often done.   Very
usually the ardent suitor will wait until it is known
whether the child is to be a boy or a girl.   Then
he begins at once to ask for her.   He goes with his suit
to the Surety (Angoswe), whose name we intended to
translate "undertaker," only the Awilo (34) usurped
that word.   The Surety promises to attend to it, and
tells him to come back soon.   When he returns in a day
or two, if he has not been forestalled, the Surety refers
him to the mother.   The first comer is almost always
successful, especially if he bring a decent present, and
the infant is at once betrothed.   When the mother's
consent is given the future son-in-law offers the present
which he has taken with him, and promises to keep the
little girl supplied with clothes.   Her clothing, of course,
is nothing but a scanty loin cloth.   It is the acceptance of this cloth and the wearing of it that is the great
token of betrothal.

The same word that is used for betrothing a girl is
also applied to the selecting of a piece of ground for
hoeing.   A person who wants a new farm goes forth and
makes his selection.   After doing so he takes bunches of
long grass and ties round the trees in that field.   Everyone that passes knows by the grass put upon the trees
that the field has been taken possession of.   Anyone
that interfered with it would be liable to have an action
brought against him.   In the same way the intending
husband points to the cloth that he has given to the

girl, and says, " She is mine ". If any one interfere with her the intending husband may put him to death.

A boy may also be betrothed in his early days. His guardians will try to secure a girl about his own age, by arranging with other guardians that may have a female child to dispose of.

If a girl have a husband betrothed to her she often cooks food for him. But her claim on him is not of an exclusive nature, as he may have more wives than one, while the misfortune of an unhappy union is more bitter to her, as she is excluded from others that she might prefer.

In the Mission School at Zomba there were many couples of twelve years and under, that were engaged to each other. The boys could tell what girls they were to marry, and the girls could also point out their husbands. The marriages of the natives are generally very happy. This result gives some countenance to Dr. Johnson's view that there would be more happiness if all marriages were made by the Chancellor of the Exchequer. The parents seem never to doubt that they know the "minds" of their sons and daughters better than they can do themselves. At the same time I have seen many cases where the girl would have done anything rather than marry the man that had been assigned her.

49.—INFANCY AND CHILDHOOD.

While the mother goes about her ordinary pursuits she carries her child upon her back. Native children learn to walk and to talk much sooner than white children do. They are put upon the ground at an early stage; little supervision is exercised, and they are accustomed to eat handfuls of mud. There seems to be no very good food for young children, consequently they are suckled for a long time. By and by they get a species of thin porridge (likoko). No cradles are used; the child sleeps on a mat. Very often it will be asleep on its mother's back as she is hard at work under the tropical sun.

It is not common to see a mother beat her child; in fact, there is very little occasion. There are no clothes to soil, no house to spoil, no windows to smash, no dishes to break, no spoons to lose; the child may play with anything that it can find; it may go where it likes without going into much danger, and without destroying flower-beds or favourite plants!

50.—BOYHOOD.

As the child grows, his life is equally wild and free. He has to pay no penalties to the requirements of polite society, he has to go through no ordeal of being taught to sit properly at table, to hold his knife and fork properly, and such things—Simple child of nature, thou hast neither table nor chair, knife nor fork!

He has no School Board to confine him, his time is all his own; he goes forth to swim in the brooks, or play in the woods. There is no clock in the hall that will tell tales about his long stay; he watches the course of the great clock in the face of the heavens, which he

learns to read with astonishing accuracy. As darkness
sets in he must go home (from danger of wild beasts),
and may be seen returning to the village. Perhaps he
carries a great bag full of beetles or of field-rats, which
are to serve as a relish (mboga) to his evening meal.
Possibly he is laden with wild fruits ; in any case he
has the appearance of brightness and buoyancy that an
English child has when returning from a pic-nic. He
carries his little bow and arrows, and is accompanied by
two or three companions like himself.

Apprenticed to no trade, he is left to acquire what
he wishes at his own discretion. Still he has some
duties. A very common occupation is to watch the
baboons (majani), and keep them from eating the corn.
All this time the boy is picking up a great deal of information. He hears the talk of his elders as he sits with
them at their meals, or when they are engaged in public
counsel ; and by and by, for amusement in the first
instance, he will take to some little occupation himself.
Of course, in this country he can live and become rich
(as a native counts riches), without learning any trade.
Hoeing comes naturally to him, but his wives will hoe.

51.—AMUSEMENTS (1) TALES, AND CONUNDRUMS.

I was once walking along a native path with a little
boy, and when the conversation began to flag I proposed
a native riddle for him. He turned round with a very
peculiar look, and asked me if we recited riddles at our
home. " Yes," was the reply, " and you do it too."
Then he asked, " Do you do it at mid-day ?" And by

and by, after smothering many conflicting thoughts and some irresolution, he began to explain that the old people said that "if boys recited riddles at mid-day, horns would grow on their foreheads!" Tales and conundrums are generally recited after sunset. While asleep, as our companions thought, in a tent beside the camp fires, we have often lain almost bursting with suppressed laughter, as we listened to the tales and conundrums that went round. Natives have plenty of such traditional literature, which, accompanied by their shrewd observations on men and manners, makes their society highly interesting.

(2) A very simple method of amusement in the villages is for the children to dance or skip along the roads, singing simple songs and choruses (Cf. chilewe).

(3) The out-door games are numerous; (indoor games will not be looked for when we remember the size of the houses). One of the commonest is playing at ball (kung'anda mpila). In the usual game there are two sides : the players mix with each other, and the object of each is to throw the ball so that it will always be caught by one of the same side. If one of the other side catch it, the ball changes owners, and the side that originally had it must try to recover it. The side that keeps the ball longest is victorious. It must be thrown up as soon as it is received. Sometimes the time of throwing is regulated by beating a drum.

(4) TOPS.

They set up maize cobs (isonde), which represent soldiers. The player on one side has the same number

of "soldiers" as his opponent. Each discharges tops
(njengo) upon the opposing army, and the man that first
demolishes those of his opponent is victorious. Another
amusement with tops is the same as in Britain, and consists in merely trying how long they can make a top spin.
They often shout or sing something as it revolves.*

(5) DRAUGHTS (NJOMBWA).

A game reminding us somewhat of draughts is very
common. Little holes are dug in the ground, the
players have a certain number of plums. The
object of one player is to take possession of all the
plums of his opponent. We have seen regular boards
used for this game about the size of a draught board, but
with little holes like those in a bagatelle board.
These holes are in four rows or lines (nyili). The
councillors of Malemya, the chief of Zomba, are very
fond of this amusement during their beer drinkings.

(6) SKIPPING ROPE (CHIWEWE).

They tie a large bunch of African grass (like a bunch
of hay or straw) to the end of a rope. One man swings
this rapidly in a circle of which he is the centre. The
skipper stands within this circle, and must jump over
the rope each time it comes round. If he cannot clear
the rope in time it " ties his legs, and he falls and gets
laughed at ".

All these games are for the boys, but they do not
forget them when they grow up; in fact, the young

* East African Tales, by Rev. Duff Macdonald. (Blackwood) Page 9.

men seem to be the most zealous players. The girls have not so much time for play; they are kept constantly pounding at corn as soon as they are able to lift the pestle.

(7) Both boys and girls have games, in which they imitate the graver pursuits of their fathers and mothers (kulinganila misingu jao). They build little houses, where they go to dwell during the day. Girls in their play often break down soft stones between harder ones, after the fashion that women grind flour. Boys go about with miniature bows and grass arrows (sugumbe). Playing at war and stealing slaves is a common game. In teaching young natives substraction, the illustration found simplest was like this : given a village with 30 people, the slavers catch 11, how many are left ?

CHAPTER VII.

MYSTERIES.

52.—"LITTLE-GO" FOR THE GIRLS.

When a girl is very young, scarcely approaching the age of puberty, she is taken to one mystery called unyago wa chiputu. The Wanyasa girls are a little older when they go to this ceremony. Girls until this ceremony are called "uninitiated" (wesichana); after it they are "initiated" (wali). The same terms are applicable to boys and young men, although more commonly applied to females. The girl may have been living with her husband even before this mystery. In such cases she gets a special charm at the ceremony. The mystery is a very great occasion among these tribes. Long before the time a great deal of food is prepared: the women may be seen pounding maize for about five days before. It begins at new moon, and continues for a month or more. The children to be initiated stay in booths away in the bush. Thousands of people collect from all quarters. There is a great deal of dancing and singing.

The girls are initiated by a female, who is called the "cook of the mystery" (mtelesi wa unyago). Among other things this "cook" gives an exhortation in which they are told to be obedient and respectful to their elders, and to avoid making any disturbance in the village. Towards the close of the ceremony the little girls are put under a roof, which they can carry on their heads. Ten may be under this at the same time. A great part of the exhortation has reference to the customs of the tribe, especially with reference to marriage duties, and advice is given in a great many absurd details. Each little girl is told that she must be faithful to her husband, otherwise he will kill her. Although the adultress is liable to punishment by death, this threat goes perhaps a little beyond the truth. But it is considered prudent to impress the mind of the child by warning her of the extreme danger that such conduct might incur. The heads of the girls are shaved, and their bodies anointed with an oil which contains various charms. One hurtful superstition is that when the girl is initiated she must find some man to be with her on her return otherwise she will die. The same superstition is implicitly believed with reference to the boys' ceremonies. It reminds us a little of what Herodotus relates of certain Asiatics. When the girl comes back to her home her name is changed, and must not be again mentioned.

The ordinary fee for this initiation, payable by the guardians of the girl to the "cook," is about four fathoms of cloth. This is a heavy fee—about a month's wages of a native workman.

"LITTLE-GO" FOR THE BOYS (NDAGALA).

The boys go through a similar ceremony. First there is a dance (kwina) at a place cleared of the small trees and bushes (lupanda). This dance lasts for two or three days. After this they pass to the initiation (ndagala). Here they stay in booths made of cut trees, grass, and bamboos, for about a month and a-half. The ceremony begins at new moon, and continues until next full moon; but anyone may be initiated sooner if there be a cause for speed. (The Anyasa do not make their males go through this ceremony; but an Anyasa slave taken by the Wayao is put through it even if he be an old man and married.)

The candidates carry their beds with them. They provide themselves with sticks like ramrods (mbininga), which are thrown at any one that may intrude on their retreat; and if a person should thus be seriously hurt there is no redress. This reminds us of the

Odi profanum vulgus,
Et arceo

of Horace. When they leave the ceremony great care is shown in destroying or disposing of these sticks: some are put together at a "cross-road".

The chief figure in this ceremony is a man called the "rattler of the tails" (juakuchimula michila). Tails are possessed of great power as charms. A chief who goes to war seeks for such medicinal tails; the sick are restored by them. A house in which ivory is to be stored must first be swept by tails. Belief in their virtues is not confined to one tribe. Pictures of the

Zulu witch-doctors represent these personages as fully
armed with tails, and there are many other instances in
Africa. The man that rattles the tails communicates to
the initiated all information with regard to the customs
of the tribe, and special observations connected with the
sexes. He delivers lectures and is said to give much
good advice. A person that has not gone through this
ceremony is laughed at as being uninitiated (mwisichana). The lectures condemn selfishness, hence when
one man refuses to share with another a piece of meat
he is called mwisichana.

No one must call the initiated youth (wanachikopoko)
by his previous name. "What would happen if any
one were to forget this, and call the youth by his old
name?" "Why, he would kill you." It is a terrible
way of teasing a Wayao to point to a little boy, and
ask if he remembers what was his name when he was
about the size of that boy. Some would not mention
their old name on any consideration.

53.—THE "GREAT GO" (UNYAGO WA CHIMBANDI).

There is another of these mysteries. It must be remembered that the foregoing mysteries are great occasions among the natives, and this one, though in some
respects less public and more a family matter is no less
so. When the "greater mystery" (unyago wokulu),
as the Anyasa call it, is to be held, a quiet and peaceful
village is converted into a scene resembling an old feeing
market or a penny wedding. The ceremony is held

when a young woman is with child for the first time; it is attended only by women that have borne children themselves. Other women are banished from the village, and all the males except the husband of the young woman, who must be present if he has not been initiated before.

The day before the ceremony women may be seen pounding corn for the occasion, as they have been doing for several days. A preparation is made that might do for a marriage feast. The young woman that is to be the subject of the mystery is seated before the door of her hut, and her head is smeared over with castor oil. The "Cook" seems to superintend this operation, although other women assist. They take the thinner end of their razor (lukwangulo), and keep poking all along her head while the girl sits quiet and gloomy. That day her head is shaved. Next day there is the mystery proper. The Surety (48) has gone to invite other women. The "Cook" also invites her friends. The young woman herself (achakongwe wene) invites some. There is a very imposing gathering of matrons; songs and dances of the usual indelicate character are the order of the day. One of the most conspicuous parties is to be seen with an enormous pumpkin tied under her dress. The young woman is anointed with oil and red ochre (ngama). The ceremony is finished towards night and inside the house. The fee to the "Cook" is two bushels of maize. This is the last of these mysteries. The advice given to the young woman (and her husband) is not deficient in quantity; but on its quality we prefer to be silent. To the natives themselves it appears ridiculous as soon as they become critical.

We have met a Yao far from his own home, and once or twice, in order to find out at what age he had been carried off in slavery, we have asked whether he was at the mysteries; the very mention of the subject nearly put him beside himself with laughter. He looks back to the matter as a comical experience of his life; but at the same time he is rather ashamed, especially when he thinks that a European knows about it. The following from the Zulu tales of Bishop Callaway illustrates a similar practice in the South of Africa :—" When young men come to the Umgongo where the ceremonies of puberty are being performed (for when a damsel is of age it is then that the filthy custom is practised of all the young people going there), the house is now a house of sweethearts and damsels where all kind of evil will be spoken; modesty is at an end at that time, and all fearful things are mentioned, which ought not to be openly mentioned, and which, if a man mentioned them by name, he would be regarded as mad. There then all become mad, for there is no one of authority to say, ' Do not mention such things'."

On this whole subject writers are divided. Some say that the mysteries include circumcision after the Jewish or Mahommedan custom. Others deny this. The subject has its difficulties, as these rites are supposed to be inviolably concealed by the initiated, who often say that they would die if they revealed them. Mr. Rowley, in his book on the "Universities Mission," makes the remark that the Wayao circumcise. From one native I gathered that such was the case ; but on subsequent inquiry I could not verify the statement. The Mahommedans, who are pressing into the country, have, according to Senhor Nunes, a missionary spirit about them, but even at Quilimane the administration of circumcision is confined to their prosy-letes. The general character of the mysteries is as we have described above. We may also point out that in the initiation of males, figures of the whale (nyamgumi) are made on the ground, and in the initiation of females, figures of leopards, hyenas, and such animals as are seen by those that never leave their homes. Flour is sprinkled on the top of these figures ; if it fall off soon, there will be war in the country. Some of the advices given to the Namaquas at similar ceremonies is that they must not any longer suck goats !

At initiation the Bechuana girls are put under the authority of a stern old woman, who sets them very severe tasks in order to teach them to undergo pain and fatigue. One of their duties is to hold a piece of hot iron in their hands for some time. We have often been astonished at the manner in which the natives about us used to handle fire. It seemed to become quite harm-less in their fingers !

The boys in some Bechuana tribes have an ordeal still more severe. A number of questions are asked, for instance, " Will you herd the cattle well ? " When the boy says " I will," he receives a stroke which inflicts a deep gash in his back. Another question is put to him, which is impressed on his memory by another terrible blow. If he were to wince under these inflictions he would fail to "pass". The boys generally acquit themselves marvellously. The cuts inflicted are said to be from 12 to 18 inches long. Few Europeans would survive the initiation.

Few things better shew the degradation of the African heathen than the fact that instruction at the Mysteries is the only kind of formal teaching to be found in his country.

Chapter VIII.

MARRIAGE.

54.—Ways of procuring a wife.

(1) We have already seen that a little girl may be betrothed very early. After she is grown up, even before she has attended the mysteries, she may go to live with her husband.

(2) If a man succeed a relative that possessed five wives, every one of these women passes over to him by inheritance.

(3) If a man make a raid on a neighbouring village, and carry off some girls, they will become his wives, unless redeemed.

(4) Another way of procuring a wife is simply by buying. Two skins of a buck is a fair price in the Mangoni country. Similarly wives may be paid over in settling debts.

(5) Young men are sometimes presented with wives by the masters or guardians of the latter.

(6) The case of wooing is treated below (56).

When a man's wife dies he gives an offering to her spirit (cf. 41), and goes to seek another to fill her place. A wife whose husband is dead may not get another so

quickly lest he should die also (82).   There is nothing
to prevent a man from marrying his sister-in-law ; but
no man may marry his sister, a fact that is brought out
very distinctly in a common native conundrum, which
might be rendered, " What is the fruit that you must
not pluck, however sweet it may be ? "

A couple may marry though they belong to different
tribes, and can hardly communicate except by signs.

55.—RANKS AMONG WIVES.

As a rule a man has one wife that is free, while
the other three or four are slaves.   If he be the
chief of a village his wife also gets the title of msyene
wa musi, or " possessor of the village ".   His other wives
are not called slaves, but ladies of the harem (akusyeto),
although their status is really that of slaves.

The chief wife is generally the woman that was
married first.   There may be exceptions.   For instance,
if the principal wife be betrothed in infancy to a full
grown man, this man will take a female " to fill the
place of the betrothed infant ".

After being married for a year or two the husband
is almost expected to get junior wives.   These the chief
wife, as a matter of courtesy, calls her younger sisters
(apwao).

We have seen instances, however, when a great strife
arose on the introduction of the other wives, and where
the chief wife would threaten a separation, and carry it
out too.   But these were instances rather of self-will
than of conformity to the customs of the country.   It is

an object of common aspiration to be possessed of five wives.

The chief wife has the superintendence of the domestic and agricultural establishment. She keeps the others at their work, and has power to exercise discipline upon them. The punishment she inflicts for laziness is to banish junior wives from meals until hunger bring them to their senses. When a junior wife is very obstreperous her superior may put her in a slave stick. The authority of the chief wife is not a matter to jest with. I knew a case of a junior wife that had her infant child promptly put upon the fire by this terrible overseer.

When a man is severely pressed by some legal action and has to pay heavy fines, he begins by selling off his junior wives. When reduced to one wife he has reached the highest point of distress. His free wife he cannot sell, as she is under the protection of her surety (60).

Plurality of Free Wives.

A man may procure more than one free wife, by inheriting an elder brother. In this case he may often become the possessor of another village, and thus his free wives need not come into collision. His late brother's wife may live at her old home, at which her new husband will dwell on stated occasions; at other times he will live at his own village, where his other free wife continues to reside.

56.—ADULT MARRIAGE.

It is not easy to explain in a short form all the customs with reference to marriage. They are so different from what we are familiar with that, to make the description less tedious, we shall suppose a case of *adult marriage*, which may easily happen, notwithstanding the custom of betrothal, as a marriage here is not necessarily a union for life.

A man sees a young woman who has apparently no husband; he wishes this young woman to be his wife. He may talk to her privately, and ask her sentiments. If he be favourably received, he will tell his wishes to his surety (48)—this may be his father or uncle, or elder brother, or the chief of the village in which he lives. This step is very prudent, seeing that at marriage the man leaves his father and mother, leaves his own home and country, and goes to stay with his wife.

The woman takes no steps whatever, she returns to her home and says nothing—wonders whether the man is in earnest; by and by her suitor, after receiving the sanction of his surety, goes to the country of the woman and asks formally for her hand. The woman's surety tells him to come back again, and meanwhile communicates with the woman. Next time the suitor comes, perhaps in a day or two, he engages his bride. She is at once his wife.

The man immediately leaves his own village and proceeds to build a house in the village of his wife. As soon as he has finished the door, and perhaps before the roof is on, she enters it and lives with him.

Day of entering the house.

There is no ceremony on the day on which she enters the house *(lia kwinjila nyumba)*. The elders may be present on this day, and a rich man may signalise it by having some beer ; but the rule is that what would be the marriage day with Europeans, passes by without receiving any distinction. The woman simply enters the house that her husband has built at her father's home, and takes with her, pots, baskets, a bed, and some flour to make their simple meal. The axe and hoe belong rather to the man's outfit, although the woman will use them oftener than he. One of her first duties is to plaster their house.

57.—WOMAN'S KINGDOM.

The wife has the chief part of the hoeing and *cultivation* of the soil. The husband cuts down trees and may also hoe with her if he have not many wives, in which case he has less occasion to work. She has also to go to the forest with her axe and cut *firewood (ngwi)*. The husband may go with her. It is interesting to meet a couple returning from a journey for firewood. The man goes first carrying his gun or bow and arrows, while the woman carries the invariable bundle of firewood on her head. Mrs. Macdonald used to amuse such parties by taking the wife's load and putting it on the husband, telling him 'this is the custom of our country'. It is also the wife's duty to go to the field for the supply of beans, potatoes, or pumpkins.

One of the hardest parts of the woman's work is the *pounding* or milling of the corn. She breaks it down in a mortar by means of a large pestle, which is a weight in itself. The work is certainly hard and tedious, but results in the formation of a very fine flour.

She looks to her husband to find her in clothing. When her clothes are torn it is his duty to sew them, and a very serious thing it is for a husband to neglect this work. It may cause a separation. But he finds that her wardrobe is not expensive. If he can get calico at 3d. a-yard she will really cost little more than 2s. per annum. No wonder that she expects her husband to show her some little attention since she does so much for him. The wife may be described as performing nearly the whole of the ploughing and sowing, the whole of the reaping and ingathering of the crop, the whole of the milling, the whole of the brewing, and the whole of the cooking, including the carrying of fire and water.

When a woman has cooked her husband's meal she does not sit down to enjoy it with him except they be quite alone. If they sit down together and a male stranger arrive she retires and takes her food apart, and he may do the same when a female comes to visit them (67).

58.—MARRIAGE CONTRACT *(chikulundine).*

We have seen that there is no marriage ceremony on the day that they enter their house (56), but some-time after, perhaps when they get the first produce of their new field, there is a meeting to lay down certain rules as to their behaviour in their new relationship (*kuwika chikulundine*). The wife's surety comes to ' settle' her (*ne kuja angoswe kwatula alumbuwao*).

The young wife ' cooks' (*kuteleka*) or brews a great quantity of beer. Two pots are prepared for the surety or sureties of her husband, and two others for her own surety or sureties. Then there is a great feast at which these personages are present to offer their instructions. The sureties of the husband (*angoswe wa chilume*) may kill a cock, while the sureties of the wife (*angoswe wa chikongwe*) kill a laying hen. Very often a part of such fowls is carefully carried to an old surety that has not been able to come.

These marriage rules (*chikulundine*) prohibit the wife from adultery, and bind both parties to resort to the medicine man (*mchisango*) in case of sickness or misfortune.

In Deut. xxiv. 5, it is said, ' When a man hath taken a new wife he shall not go out to war, neither shall he be chargeable with any business, but he shall be free at home one year, and shall cheer up his wife whom he has taken'. So certain Africans will not go on any warlike expedition or act as undertakers (34) when they have a young child.

59.—SEPARATION.

The husband and wife may separate if they can show some reason. The reasons for a separation are such as these : (1) If the wife commit *adultery*, for one offence she may get off with a reprimand, especially in the case

of a poor man ; but the repetition of the offence
generally insures dismissal, if not death.   If she be free,
she goes back to her surety, if she be a slave, she will
likely be sold.

(2) If either speak disrespectfully of the other's
friends there may be a separation.

(3) If a woman's children all die her husband may
leave her.

(4) Where the husband neglects to sew his wife's
clothes, or where the wife will not hoe diligently, there
may be a divorce.

(5) In cases where they do not please each other, a
separation may be arranged.

When they separate, the wife takes away the few
domestic utensils which she brought with her, none of
which are used by the man.   If he gave her, occasionally, pieces of cloth to wear she does not pay them
back, because she was the " cook of his porridge for
him ".

In all separations, except for serious cases like adultery, the one party gives the other a token *(msimbo)*,
which may be cloth, arrow-heads, beads, or some such
current money.   The one that begins the strife *(juaku-
tanda)*, and is the cause of the separation, pays the other.

Very often a husband leaving his wife will give her
a male slave, while a wife leaving her husband will give
him a female slave.

Marriage with Slaves.

If one of the parties be a slave to the other, the
marriage bond is not so readily dissolved.   Slave spouses

must listen to the dictates of their partners, and where there is practically only one will there can be no collision. The free spouses when tired of their slave partners, or offended by them, can dispose of them just as in the case of other slaves.

We have known many cases of slave wives running away from husbands, but we have not known instances of slave husbands running away from free wives. We might think that where the wives have the upper hand in marriage relationships, there is not such a risk of strife as in the ordinary arrangement; only the proportion of free wives with slave husbands is small.

In no case can a woman, even if she possess many male slaves, have more than one husband. If a wife with a male slave marry a free husband, her male slave is discarded; and if again she should fancy another man, she must devise some reason for separating from this new husband. There can easily be found cases where it could be said to a woman, "thou hast had five husbands," although they would not be contemporaneous.

The husband on the other hand may have as many wives as he can secure. Very generally the head of a village, instead of appropriating for himself every woman that he might have, gives over certain for his younger brothers or male slaves. A Yao Chief is content with ten to twenty wives. Some of the Magololo have 170.

I have been often asked how a man can *maintain* the scores, and even hundreds of wives that Africans are allowed to have. The man finds no difficulty. The more wives he has, the richer he is. It is his wives that *maintain him*. They do all his ploughing, milling, cooking, &c. (51). They may be viewed as superior servants who combine all the capacities of male servants and female servants in Britain—who do all his work and ask no wages.

60.—PECULIAR POSITION OF A FREE WIFE.

In the case of a free wife the husband is not responsible for her debts, if he were so, it would go hard with her, as she might be sold off to pay a " legal action". When a woman gets into trouble the accuser does not go to the husband at all, but to the surety (48). Suppose a woman is accused of theft, it is no matter for her husband. The accuser goes with some evidence before the surety. If the evidence be exceedingly little, no notice is taken, but if the accuser has a chance of incriminating the woman, the surety will call her, and she must respond, whether the husband be willing or not.

If she confess to the charge, her surety pays the fine. If she deny the charge, she will appeal to the poisoned cup (*mwai*). If she drink it and survive, she is innocent, and receives a fine which is paid, not to the husband, but to the surety. When the plaintiff has to pay three slaves, the surety will retain two of them, and out of kindness give one over to his relative whose life has been endangered by the ordeal; thus the accused woman has a kind of solatium. If she die, her guilt is proved : the plaintiff is entitled to restitution of the stolen goods or their value, and a fine as well. All this is paid by the surety ; the husband has nothing to do in the matter except to observe the customary mourning (33) when she dies, but of course the unfortunate woman that dies of the poison is only entitled to mangled funeral rites (107).

Family Relationships.

We may here mention the great difficulty we have at first in understanding their relationships. The modern European family is founded on marriage, but the time was, even in Europe, when it was founded as much on power. The single fact that families may be founded on other grounds than marriage will give the ordinary reader an idea of the difficulty. A native child sees nothing wonderful in claiming to have two or three fathers, and as many mothers. If a man have several younger brothers their children are called his sons, so are his own grandchildren. But the children of a sister are called his nephews. This naming fits very well with their system of inheritance (97). If a man have a brother and a sister, he is called one thing by the brother, but quite a different thing by the sister. Again, we cannot give a literal translation of " Joseph and his brethren": we require to say " Joseph and his elder brethren and his younger brother ".

Chapter IX.

SOCIAL LIFE.

61. MAN IN SOCIETY.

HITHERTO we have looked at the native as an individual or as a member of a family and have spoken of his birth, training, marriage, and death. Now we shall view him as a member of society.

Rarely does a native live a hermit's life. We did know of men that forsook their relatives and lived alone, but they were considered mad. Not unfrequently, however, a man and his family live entirely by themselves, independent of the rest of the world. Such cases occur where invading tribes have overrun a country and driven out its people. After the invaders retire, the old inhabitants are afraid to go back, and an enormous tract of country is left desolate. Still, in some inaccessible nook there is often found a solitary family—a remnant either of the invaders or of the invaded. Usually the natives live in small villages containing 10 or 12 huts, occasionally in larger villages containing three times as many. They do not like to pack themselves closely. In times of peace few villages contain more than 100 people. Owing to the native method of cultivation (64), the inhabitants of a large village soon find themselves too distant from their farms. On one small island in Lake Chirwa, people are massed together to the number of 4000, but they subsist by fishing, and are obliged to live there for protection from slavers.

62. FOUNDING A NATIVE VILLAGE.

A man wishing to found a new settlement, first takes steps to get out of the village he belongs to. He goes to the village chief and says " I wish to leave you and form a hamlet of my own ". Should the latter object, he remarks, " Remember, I am not your slave ". In times of peace it is inconvenient to crowd people together, and the chief's consent is readily obtained. In times of war no one cares to form a small settlement which might become an easy prey to the enemy. In a populous district the founder of a new village makes arrangements with his neighbours regarding the fields he is to farm. Then he chooses the ground and betrothes it (tomela). When ready to remove he takes his axe and his grass-cutter and marches to the site of his new home, accompanied by his family who are able to carry all the furniture at one journey. In a single forenoon they erect temporary dwellings for themselves. They then begin to clear away the bush, the man cutting the trees, and his wives doing the hoeing while the children play beside them. The party find themselves in a pleasant little world of their own where no one inter-

feres. Their method of manuring the ground by burning the trees on it, makes sad havoc of the beautiful
woods. After the hoeing is well advanced they think
of erecting a house. During his wood-cutting the man
sets aside the trees that are suitable for building. He
also lays past some of the grass for thatching. When
the erection is finished it is carefully plastered by the
women, and then we have before us the house or hut
which is the chief material constituent of the native
village. Separate houses for fowls and bins for corn
may next be erected (c).

63 INCREASE OF VILLAGE.

The single family may rapidly become a large state.
A man with three daughters, one of nine years, another
of five years, and another of five days will soon have
three able-bodied sons-in-law added to his village. The
girl of nine years likely has her husband already, who
now comes and builds a house at her father's abode,
while his young wife tries to look as important as she
can. The girl of five years may also have crossed the
Rubicon, otherwise her husband, if a lad of sixteen
summers, will be counting the weary days of single
life, and looking forward to the time when he may go
to dwell with his bride. The girl of five days, if she
have not a presumptive husband already, will be given
to the first applicant, and he will in due time be added
to the colony. Since a husband, instead of taking his
wife from her home must leave his own abode and go
to dwell with her (56), daughters are the great hope

of a rising village. Sons do not cheer their father's
heart in the same way ; for their marriage removes them
from his settlement and adds nothing to his splendour
as a village chief. The sons-in-law have all separate
dwellings. However large the settlement may become,
the man that is first in the field is the chief or headman.
In course of time he adorns his position by acquiring
wealth. He may shoot some buck and get possession
of their skins. With these he goes to the Mangoni
country and buys slaves. An old person he obtains for
a single skin, but a young slave costs two ; and women
cost much more than men. The female slaves thus
bought are his junior wives, and he keeps them busy
in hoeing the farm, and all such female duties. The
male slaves he employs in farming, building, making
baskets, sewing garments, and such masculine pursuits.
He keeps all these persons strictly at their duties, and
at the same time welcomes an opportunity of selling
them at a profit. The gain thus realised he lays out in
purchasing more people. If his daughters were un-
married, he would give them slave-husbands. The
natives aim at "replenishing the earth and subduing
it ". As it is no expense for them to rear families, they
are all desirous to have many children.

Besides this increase of the village from the chief's
own resources, there may be an accession of freemen.
After the settlement is begun, a man may come to its
founder and say, "I wish to live with you ". The village chief gives him permission and calls him " younger
brother " The new comer brings his family, builds a
house, and cultivates a farm in the same way as his chief.

A freeman may leave his present chief and take up his abode with another, whose subject he becomes. His former chief has no longer any authority over him whatsoever. But a man often decamps by night taking with him many slaves belonging to his fellow-citizens ; he then goes to some influential chief who may be only too glad to give the fugitive ground, and to establish him as a sub-chief. Freemen who thus leave are detested by their former chief, who welcomes every opportunity of shooting or capturing them.

To retain a runaway slave is to proclaim war with his owner. A chief though not bound to catch a runaway and hand him back, may do so in order to show friendship to the slave's master. A fugitive slave when recaptured is treated unmercifully, hence he almost chooses to die rather than to be sent back.

64. VILLAGE LIFE AND WORK.

As we take a journey into the country we come on a path quite new. Curiosity prompts us to follow it. Our natives exclaim, " Oh, when did this new settlement begin ? How quickly it has sprung up." We quench our thirst at the beautiful stream, and then advance towards the village green. The hamlet is already large, but we find only two male slaves sitting manufacturing a bed. " Where is the chief ?" " He has gone to drink beer at Masangano's." " Why did you leave your old home ?" " Chikumbu is killing people, and we wanted to live nearer the Mission." " And where is little Mpakata that used to come to school?" "His father sent him to watch the monkeys, but he takes his book with him and reads." "Where are all the rest of the people?" "They have gone to carry food from our old fields." When villages are small we find them in the forenoon entirely deserted, and all the doors barred on the outside. In the first year of a settlement the farm is just at the door. Each year it moves farther off, for instead of hoeing the old fields, the natives go beyond them, and without remorse cut down more of the beautiful trees. Thus they advance year by year till they reach the boundary of another farmer. From him they get permission to go right beyond his farm and hoe on the other side. The new fields they plant with their corn and principal crops; the old fields they think fit only for beans and crops of small importance. When they have in this way exhausted the soil in their neighbourhood, they remove altogether, and build a new village in some uncultivated spot.

65 THE WORKERS.

The wives and slaves of a village chief do the greater part of his hoeing (62). His sons-in-law are also required to assist. Should a slave son-in-law refuse to comply with this custom he is liable to be driven from his wife: a free son-in-law would get off more easily. It is not common for the man's own sons to contribute their aid, but they may do so out of kindness. The freemen that settle with a man, and own him as their chief, are under no obligation to do his farming; they have fields of their own : but it is common for a farmer to be assisted by all in his neighbourhood through what is called a *chijawo*, which resembles a hoeing match, only there is no competition. The farmer brews an enormous quantity of beer. All his friends turn out with hoes, and work hard till midday; after that they drink the beer.

66. A DAY'S WORK AND A DAY'S FARE.

The natives rise at daybreak (6 A.M.) and go off to their fields without any food. They work till noon, and then come back to breakfast. Their day's work in the field is now over, and in the afternoon the village so recently empty is full of inhabitants. The women are occupied in preparing the second meal, while the men may do some of their more artistic work (H), though among tribes that have been hitherto hunted from their homes every twenty or thirty years no high art is to be expected. As the shades of evening gather round the hamlet (6 P.M.) the villagers partake of their second meal, and soon after retire to rest.

67. COOKING AND MEALS IN COMMON.

Though each family has a farm of its own, no family eats its food apart from the others. All the inhabitants of a small village take their meals in common. They manage in the following way :—One night Mrs. Kumlomba supplies all the flour, and takes her share of pounding and cooking. Next night Mrs. Chipaliko does the same, and next night Mrs. Chendombo. As soon as the food is cooked, it is taken to their husbands and all the other males of the village, who wait for it in the forum. Part is reserved for the women themselves, who along with the female children must eat in a different place. A large village is divided into several messes, one part of each mess consisting of the males and the other part of the females.

CHAPTER X.

GOVERNMENT AND ADMINISTRATION OF JUSTICE.

68. VILLAGE POLITICS.—THE HEADMAN OR VILLAGE CHIEF.

THE inhabitants of a native village live together on well-understood principles, whatever may be said of their practice. The village headman is their Governor, or rather their "Father". In describing how a new settlement is founded (62) we supposed that a man went forth alone, and was afterwards joined by others, who were called his "younger brothers". But often the founder is from the first accompanied by several friends. Now, all these "younger brothers" form a kind of Parliament. The founder of the village, or in other words the village headman, presides over this body, but is not obliged to follow its instructions. Slaves cannot be members of Parliament, neither have females any voice in the council. So much is this last fact recognised, that when a mother is asked whether the infant in her arms is a boy or a girl, instead of saying "It is a girl," she will reply, "It belongs to the sex that does not speak!" —an answer which strikes us as implying an unusual

definition of the female sex. A headman does not con-
vene his parliament except when he sees occasion. If
he think, for instance, that some of his people are
becoming too rich, he transfers their goods to himself
without making any fuss about the matter. But if he
wish to engage in war, he considers it necessary to
assemble his parliament. In the same way if he desire
to carry out any public work, as surrounding the village
with a stockade, he summons his people to consider the
proposal and assist in the undertaking. The headman,
however, cannot make his villagers hoe his farm for
him, or do any such private work (65). Neither does
he exact tribute from them—for who would tax his
"younger brothers?" Still he expects them not only
to stand by him in war, but to support his government
on all occasions, and to render special assistance in the
trial of judicial cases. After such cases have been
debated by his parliament, it becomes his duty to give
decision. He may pronounce a capital sentence, or
order as large a penalty as the fine of four slaves—especially if he be a higher headman (72). But his judgment
may be complained of by any of his free subjects (only
such appeals are rare, unless by parties that want to
leave his village altogether). His decision may be
revised by some other headman, as the ruler of the village from which his own settlement broke off (62); but
the ultimate appeal is to the chief of the country.
While the village headman settles all smaller disputes
without troubling his chief, he usually reports graver
cases. Where he has any difficulty in administering
justice he appeals to his chief for aid, and if such aid

were refused, he would have sufficient reason for re-
belling.   The headman is called the "owner of the
village," and when he dies his position is taken by his
heir (97).

69. THE KING OR CHIEF OF THE COUNTRY,

The chief is called the "owner of the territory"
(msiene chilambo), and has supreme power over every
one that dwells within his dominions.   It is true that
he does not personally interfere with all his subjects,
much less with their slaves, but he holds the headmen
accountable for the government of their respective villages.   He lives in what is called the "capital" (kum-
bala), which is inhabited mainly by his wives and
slaves—a man's greatness being always measured by
the number of these.   If he have ten wives, he must
have ten huts for them ; and he requires other huts for
his older children and his slaves.   These items alone
make his village large, and he may have many people
besides.   He maintains no special army, for every man
in the country is supposed to be a soldier.   He rules
his own village in the same way as an ordinary headman would do.   He often gives considerable authority
to his principal slave, who may be as important a functionary as Joseph was with his Egyptian master.   In
and around his own village the chief of the country is a
terrible power, and his government is supported by the
most prompt and severe punishments.   But in distant
parts of his dominions, where influential headmen live,
he may be little known, although as a matter of theory

he is supposed to settle all graver disputes even in
remote villages.   When an appeal comes up from a
headman's village, the chief generally decides it himself,
but he may refer it either to this headman again or to
some other headman in whom he has confidence.   In a
dispute between the inhabitants of different villages, the
respective headmen represent their own subjects, and
the chief is appealed to.   All his decisions are final.
Still the chief may often have less influence than powerful headmen, and we have known cases where he simply
contented himself with grumbling when his headmen
acted contrary to his desire ; and in many criminal trials
he is eclipsed by the sorcerers and pounders of poison.

70. GOVERNMENT OF THE COUNTRY.

The chief governs his whole territory on the same
principles as a headman governs a village (68).   He
presides over a parliament composed of his headmen,
and he deals with this body in the same way as the
headmen themselves deal with their own village parliaments.   Order is maintained among the various classes
of his subjects as follows :—(1) Slaves are entirely under
their own master—they are his " goods " ; (2) Freemen
are under their elder brother in the first instance, but
they may carry their cases to the headman of their
village, or even to the chief of the country ; (3) Headmen are under higher headmen and the chief.   Where
a chief sees occasion to interfere with his subordinates,
he generally consults his own interest.   He will say to
a headman, " I see that you have been behaving badly

to that subject of yours. You cannot get on with him; he must leave you and come to dwell in my own village!" The chief thus secures another servant.

71. HEADMEN.

Headmen are of various classes. Some are the chief's blood-relations and are called his 'younger brothers'. But just as in a village, there may be free-men not related to the headman, so in the chief's country there may be headmen not related to the chief. They may have come over with a large following from a hostile chief, in which case they are called "settlers," or "refugees" (alambi). Or they may be men that have gained the chief's favour by their services, and been sent to occupy new spots in his kingdom. Again, when a large village increases, and sends forth smaller hamlets, new headmen arise; but some of these may carry all their trials to the mother village, and in this case they are still the subjects of their "elder brother"

When a person has acquired several villages (97), he becomes a higher headman, intermediate between the chief and the owner of a single village. Each headman lives in the village he likes best, and leaves his "brothers" to manage his other villages. But a headman of great ambition often places "brothers" all around him, decides their cases, and practically governs a small kingdom of his own. If he live far from his chief, one might suppose that he was quite independent. When a quarrel arises between the chief of the country and an important headman, the latter may rebel, and found a new kingdom, thus depriving the old chief perhaps of one-third of the villages in his dominion. On the other hand, a headman may keep up the chief's authority in a district that the latter could not otherwise hold.

72. DUTIES OF HEADMEN TO THE CHIEF.

In all public transactions the headman represents his village. He receives the chief's orders and sees them carried out. When he kills an elephant he sends one of the tusks to the chief. Should he kill twenty elephants he is not expected to give up twenty tusks— two or three would be sufficient. If he shoot a large buck he gives one haunch of venison. For all such tribute he expects to receive a return present (generally of a little powder). It is customary for him to invite his chief to a beer-drinking, at least once a year, and the latter accepts the invitation. He is expected to attend the chief's parliament, unless he is under an elder brother, in which case he is not allowed to speak, except when specially commissioned. Headmen are expected to report all cases of war, but they often attack enemies without telling their chief beforehand, saying, " Let him hear of the enterprise when it succeeds ". Yet this is dangerous unless they are sure of success, and well acquainted with the chief's private sentiments. On reporting the attack they present the chief with part of the booty. In times of war each headman when summoned, must follow his chief's flag, otherwise his village is burned down, and all that fail to escape are killed or enslaved.

73. COURTS OF JUSTICE.

Courts of justice are held in every village for trying
cases that occur among the villagers.   These courts are
identical with the village parliament (68), and the
members discuss the cases, some taking one side and
some the other.   The supreme court is regularly held
in the chief's village, and tries graver cases.   It is
identical with the supreme parliament of which the
village headmen are members.   Although the village
headmen and the chiefs of the country preside over
these courts, yet in many trials their influence is less
than that of the sorcerer or the pounder of poison.
Since the natives neither divide their days into weeks
nor number the days of their "moons," they have no
stated time for holding courts, they just call them as
occasion requires.

74. TRIALS.

In a trial the accuser speaks first, and the accused
replies.   Afterwards the various members of the
council (68, 70) give their views.   Throughout the
speeches there are expressions of approval at the close
of each sentence, which serve to mark the punctuation.
One man keeps crying out, "Amao! Atati! Nangolo!"
"Mother! Father! Parent!"—words extolling the
wisdom and experience of the speaker.

The chief or headman on settling a fine does not
claim part of it.   The whole is paid over to the ag-
grieved persons, but if they thus obtain several slaves,

they will present the chief with one in consideration
of his services. The idea of friends paying each other
is not agreeable to the native mind. Professional men
such as sorcerers and physicians are paid, but transactions between a superior and his younger brother take
the form of presents. The natives show here a beautiful delicacy of feeling that we are apt to overlook, amidst
their obtrusive greed. An unsophisticated chief will give
a goat as a present, where he would scowl very much at
the idea of selling it, although it is true that he expects
the return present to be greater than the proper price.
The services of a judge are not such a hard task in this
country : as there are no newspapers the chief and his
companions feel the need of something to talk about.

75. EVIDENCE.

Though witnesses are appealed to, it must not be
imagined that cases are decided by their testimony as
in England. Let a man be accused of theft, and though
six witnesses declare that they saw him steal, the case
may be as far from a settlement as if there had been
no witness at all. The accused cries, " I did not steal,
give me the poison (mwai) and it will prove my
innocence ". If his friends think him innocent they
support his demand, for an innocent man (they believe)
will vomit the poison, and thus become entitled to
receive a fine. But if they think him guilty they will
rather not appeal to the poison, for a guilty man will
die in great pain,[1] and his representatives must make

---

[1] When mwai is not vomited it is fatal, and the symptoms that
appear in such cases, are said to resemble those of dysentery.

full restitution. The accusers of course, insist that the
goods should be given back at once. They do not
wish to run the risk of the ordeal, for if the thief
vomit, they must pay him a fine, besides losing their
goods. All the natives believe that mwai is infallible, while they well know that the testimony of their
countrymen is not so. Were a judge to attempt to
decide a native case by ordinary evidence he would
produce the strangest results. The prosecutor would
come with hundreds of his friends prepared to swear
to anything that was wanted. The defendant would
come in like manner with all his friends ready to swear
against everything said by the opposite party. Even
though the alleged crime should be of the most secret
character, none of these persons would hesitate to swear
that he had been an eye-witness. To crown all, each
man would attend the trial, "armed to the teeth".
But when cases are decided by the poisoned cup, the
natives feel that an element of quiet solemnity is
introduced. They see one of their fellow creatures
brought face to face with death. Here we encounter
the most deeply rooted faith that these tribes have.
If they believe in anything, it is in this ordeal. I
once asked Kumpama of Cherasulo, "What would you
do if a man stole ivory and vomited the mwai, but was
afterwards found selling the stolen ivory?" His reply
was, "If the man stole the ivory he would not vomit
the mwai, the mwai would kill him". I have made
similar suppositions to many natives, and though I carefully concealed my *petitio principii*, they at once pointed
out that I was supposing cases that could never occur.

76. DISCOVERY AND GENERAL TREATMENT OF CRIME.

Since evidence is of such small importance, how can
the natives ever discover criminals ? They cannot use
the poisoned cup for mere discovery, because no freemen
can be compelled to drink it without a reason. They
encounter a peculiar difficulty here, but they have a
peculiar remedy. Their method may be explained by
showing how it works in the case of theft. When a
man finds his goods stolen and can get no trace of the
thief, he applies to the sorcerer. This personage takes
up the case, inspects the dry bones in his calabash, and
in a short time is able to declare the thief. The sorcerer
usually trusts to his calabash alone, but occasionally he
makes men lay hold of a stick which after a time begins
to move as if endowed with life, and ultimately carries
them off bodily and with great speed to the house of the
thief. When his divination is completed, the sorcerer
announces that he has " detected " (kamula) the thief
and then formally names him to the owner of the stolen
goods. The latter goes to the alleged thief, tells him
that he has been detected by the " oracle " and boldly
charges him with the crime. When the theft is proved
either by the thief's confession, or by the ordeal (75),
the pursuer demands his goods and a fine besides, and
holds the headman of the thief's village responsible. It
is always assumed, and generally correctly, not only
that the headman knows[1] of every theft committed by

[1] It is characteristic of Native Law that it throws all responsibility
on Superiors. In illustration of this principle I may mention an
application of it that occurs very naturally to these natives, and which

his villagers, but that he has even received part of the plunder. Where the accused party, in spite of the verdict of the oracle denies the crime and survives the poisoned cup, the result brings discredit on the sorcerer. As the poison is the infallible test, the sorcerer is proved to have " detected " the wrong party. He accordingly loses his fee, and the pursuer is not likely to put confidence in him again. Should the pursuer still hope to recover his goods, he applies to another sorcerer, but the latter must not " detect " the party that has just been accused. A person cannot be asked to drink poison twice for the same charge.

Caught in the Act.

When a criminal is caught stealing in a man's house, the course of justice is more speedy. The owner may kill him on the spot, and he has the sanction of the law for doing so. The friends of the criminal cannot complain. The thief deserved his doom for he was behaving like a bewitcher—he had put himself beyond the pale of human rights, and was in the position of a lion or a leopard. This holds good whether the theft is by night or by day, whether the criminal is killed in the house or after a long pursuit. The thief is generally well armed—a circumstance which makes his capture more dangerous. But the injured party, for the purpose of extorting a great ransom, often tries to secure the

they have urged upon me again and again. When I spoke to them of a day of judgment they remarked, " On that day we shall plead that we are the white man's sons, and you, father, will not forsake your children ".

criminal. On succeeding, he puts the captive in a slave-stick and sends a message to the headman of his village, who will be glad to pay several slaves in order to redeem his "brother". Should the headman refuse to pay the ransom the unfortunate "brother" is left entirely in the hands of the prosecutor, and is liable to be killed, sold, or retained as a slave. When it is known to what village the stolen "property" was taken, as in cases of kidnapping, the injured party applies at once to the headman of the guilty village, and if he can get no satisfaction, there arises a state of war. The prosecutor captures the very first inhabitants of the guilty village that come into his power, and then he keeps them in slave-sticks until compensation is made. Here is a case where a lingering imprisonment falls on persons that are entirely innocent, the only thing against them being that they belong to a guilty village.

SUMMARY.

As native law is rather intricate, we give the following summary of ordinary procedure in criminal cases.

Detection.

The criminal (1) may be caught in the act, (2) may be known to have the stolen goods in his possession, (3) may be detected by the sorcerer, or (4) may be convicted on the confession of himself, or (5) the statements of his accomplices and others. This last case (5) shows that, after all, the natives cannot exclude testimony, and even in case (3) the sorcery must derive all its value from ordinary evidence. The sorcerer has, doubtless, many agents that are more useful than his calabash, although it is for his interest to represent that all other evidence is of little value as compared with his own inspiration.

Proof.

In cases (1), (2), (4), no trial is needed. In cases (3) and (5) the mwai is appealed to.

Punishment.

The criminal is either killed or fined ; imprisonment is rather a preliminary step. In some cases, as in the poison ordeal, a fine is demanded over and above the death. For all fines the headman of the criminal's village is responsible, but he can repay himself either from the criminal or his relatives. He may even pay the criminal over to the injured party, but in this case he loses a subject who may be related either to himself or to some influential man in his village.

The demand of compensation over and above restitution seems to spring from the constitution of human nature. A little child deprived of a toy is not content to threaten or revile (or whatever the infantile manifestation of feeling may mean), while the toy is in the hands of the aggressor. He pours out the same torrent of hostile feeling after the toy has been restored. Besides, there are cases in which *mere* restitution would not be sufficient compensation for the injury sustained.

CHAPTER XI.

PERSONAL RIGHTS AND OFFENCES AGAINST THEM.

77. PERSONAL RIGHTS—SLAVERY.

"For he (*i.e.*, the slave) is his money"—*Exodus* xxi. 21. "If his master have given.him a wife, and she have born him sons and daughters, the wife and her children shall be her master's."—*Exodus* xxi. 4.

I ONCE heard a native remark in a village assembly, "A fowl is a fowl, a goat is a goat,—well, what am I?" It is often maintained that among savages no rights are recognised except rights of property. But although native jurisprudence deals mainly with questions of property, here was a savage using as strong an argument for personal rights as any philosopher could employ.

There is a great difference between the treatment of a free-man, and the treatment of the "thing" or "flesh" called a slave. The following sections (78-102) apply chiefly to freemen, and many points have no application to slaves, for instance, the goods of a deceased slave (if "goods" can be said to possess goods), do not go to his brother but to his master.

The word for "free" (mlukosyo) literally means "belonging to the tribe or family," and shows how slavery was originally viewed—the slaves did not belong to the "family". A freeman becomes a slave when *captured*. He may be captured by an enemy or by one that has a quarrel either with himself or with the village that he belongs to. Freemen may be *enslaved by relatives* or by superiors. Often a man will pay a debt by giving up his own kindred to his prosecutor. Those most liable to this treatment are his sisters, after that his daughters, then his brothers, and then his father and mother. In clearing off a heavy debt a native first pays over his slaves, next his inferior wives, and then his relatives in the above order. Sometimes one pawns his relatives only, if he cannot redeem his pledges promptly, he may find them sold. A freeman may become a slave *voluntarily*, as when he is in want during a time of scarcity. A man may also become the slave of a master that possesses many females in order to get a wife from him. A person may be a slave by *birth*. If his parents be both slaves he belongs to their master. When a female slave bears a child to a freeman, the child belongs not to its father, but to its mother's master.

Slaves become free when redeemed or when their master grants them liberty. Persons that have been long in slavery may be redeemed by relatives. Some say that a slave may redeem himself by presenting to his master another slave whom he may have bought or captured in war. Other native authorities, especially the older men, deny this most strongly, and no doubt correctly, as everything that a slave can possess belongs really to his master. But the older views are now being modified by contact with English Missionaries. Before the arrival of the missions, slaves could obtain nothing except from their master himself, who supplied them with clothing ; when the missions came they had an opportunity of working for pay.

When a slave earns wages, his owner may no doubt claim the whole of it, but some masters among the Yao are said not to exercise this right to the full extent. They allow the slave to retain a great part of his earnings, so much so that he will occasionally remark, " Ah ! my master is poor to-day, I must give him some cloth ". Such masters look with satisfaction on the increasing hoards of their slaves in the same way as an English employer delights to see his labourer in a con-dition of comfort. They will even boast of the rich slaves that they possess. Every owner of property finds slavery the most profitable investment. One of the slave's duties is to procure other slaves (*i.e.*, more property) for his master. Each male slave is allowed to build a house for himself. He may also get a wife (59) who, however, may be taken from him again. He is politely called his master's " child " (mwanache), the more offensive word "slave" (mkapolo) being seldom used. Still the time, the talents, and the very lives of slaves are entirely in their master's hand. However great a ransom they may offer, if the master refuse to take it, no one in the country can legally set them free. The master's power is absolute. The only check that he feels is this,—he says, " If I treat my slaves badly, one day they will find me alone, take courage (mbilimo) and kill me ". But a slave would think twice before adopting such a desperate measure. If he murdered a freeman he would run as fast as Moses ran to Midian, and with as good reason.

78. KILLING SLAVES OR WARDS.

If a master kill one of his slaves, no one can bring a complaint against him. People that hear of the matter merely say, " That man is very stupid to destroy his own property ". The companions of the deceased—his fellow slaves—may venture to plead, " Why did you kill him, he did no adultery ? " but the master silences them, by pointing out that the deceased was his " goods " (chipanje), or his " flesh " (nyama). But after killing a slave, the master is afraid of *Chilope.* This means that he will become emaciated, lose his eyesight, and ultimately die a miserable death. He therefore goes to his chief and gives him a certain fee (in cloth or slaves or such legal tenders), and says, " Get me a charm (*luasi*), because I have slain a man ". When he has used this charm, which may be either drunk or administered in a bath, the danger passes away. In the same manner, if a man kill his younger brother, or anyone under his charge, there is no case against the murderer. For one thing, there is no prosecutor, and moreover, relatives may be treated as slaves (77). If a man have a fatal quarrel with his ward, he finds it a sufficient excuse to say, " The deceased began it ". But if his ward or even his slave be killed by another party, the guardian at once becomes prosecutor, and does not rest till he obtains the fullest compensation.

79. KILLING ENEMIES.

When an enemy is killed, there is a desire to secure portions (*ikawo*) of his body (36), which is mutilated accordingly. The parts [1] generally taken are the eyebrows, nose, little finger or toe, and the pudenda. If there be no danger of interruption, the man or woman thus mutilated, will be also disembowelled and the heart plucked out. The portions thus cut from a body, are roasted or burned till quite reduced to ashes (*sile*). They are then used as charms in various ways. The savage makes tatoos (*malaka*) in his arm and rubs the ashes into them. Or he cooks gruel (likoko) and stirs the ashes into it. This dreadful mixture of flour and flesh, must be lapped with the tongue, as it would be " unlucky " to eat it with the hands. There are several devices for facilitating the lapping process, such as pouring the mixture from one dish to another and licking the bottom of the emptied dish. Another way of using this weird and awful charm, is as an amulet (njilisi)—the ashes are mixed with castor oil and sewed up in a small bag, which is worn round the neck or

---

[1] Stanley in *How I Found Livingstone*, mentions that the natives in Unyanyembe, on killing an enemy, eat " the skin of the forehead, the lower part of the face, the forepart of the nose, the fat over the stomach and abdomen, the genital organs, and a bit from each heel ". Hence we see that African tribes, although living far apart, practice similar forms of mutilation.

about the loins. I knew one headman whose great
success in war was attributed to the fact that he had
eaten "the whole body of a strong young man". But
if he had not been protected by powerful charms, such
cannibalism might have been dangerous to him. The
person that eats a human being is believed to run a great
risk. Even the person that kills a human being, though
the victim be only a slave (78), must take certain steps
to quiet his conscience. In most cases the murderer tells
the chief of the country who procures a charm from
his medicine man. Of this charm the chief himself
also partakes that he may not be unlucky " because of
the blood that has been shed in his land". If the
chief sent the person to kill the deceased, he now
presents him with a slave or some such reward. So
when a headman makes an attack and kills a party
on his own responsibility (72), the chief if approving
rewards all that went on the expedition. He also kills
a goat for them. At this feast they must not eat salt
until a charm is first put in the food. If the chief dis-
approve of the attack, he exacts a heavy fine, which he
usually settles as follows :—When the injured parties
retaliate, and kill or capture some of the chief's subjects, he makes this headman pay the relatives for
their loss. So when the chief wants to dissuade a
headman from dangerous wars, he says to him, " Remember you will have to pay for all the slain ".

80. PUNISHMENT OF MURDER.

If one man slay another, the friends of the deceased
are justified in killing the murderer on the spot (76).

But if they catch him alive they put him in a slave-stick, till compensation be made by a heavy fine of from 4 to 20 slaves. When the fine is paid the life of the murderer is not demanded, but several of the slaves obtained in compensation are killed to accompany the deceased (39). The rest of them are retained : indeed, the friends of the murdered man look not so much to his sad fate as to the possibility of making gain by it. If the murderer escape, some one connected with him is captured, and a message is sent to the friends in this form, " You have slain our brother, we have caught yours, and we will send him after our brother unless you pay a ransom ". The ransom is expected to include some slaves to accompany the deceased. The captive if not redeemed is entirely at the disposal of the injured party and that for life or death. The above applies to murders occurring among parties friendly toward each other, and living perhaps in the same village. But should a man go to another village and commit murder, the act, if no explanation be granted, is held to be a declaration of war. When the injured village is strong, the other villagers will all be killed or enslaved without delay. Where the village is not so sure of its strength, its headman goes to the chief of the country and presents him with a slave, saying, " I desire your help, I want to punish that other village ". If the chief has already failed to bring the aggressors to reason, he receives the present, promises help, and soon the guilty village is annihilated.

81. PUNISHMENT OF HOMICIDE.

The natives are aware of the difference between murder and homicide, but the punishment of the two crimes is often the same. A man enters a village, puts down his gun which goes off and kills a person. The gun is claimed by the friends of the deceased. It is worth several slaves, and the owner may be as anxious to redeem it as he would have been to redeem his brother. When there is no gun to pledge, the homicide is put in a slave-stick and retained just as in murder (80), and the surviving relatives are equally anxious to slay persons to accompany the deceased. Some native authorities take a more lenient view of homicide. Instead of seizing the party or his gun, they pronounce him quite blameless, and go to the sorcerer to discover the bewitcher who has been the real cause of the death. They hold that it is this being that must bear the whole of the responsibility. They use a simile here that is borrowed from hunting customs. The hunter that first wounds a buck claims it, even though it be ultimately brought down by another man. The man that brings the buck down is only the finder, as it were, of another man's game (juakupakanila) : so the homicide only found or brought down the victim that the witch had already destroyed; he is not the cause but the occasion of the death. Some insist that although the homicide may protest his innocence and affirm that he is the victim of some witch, he must pay damages all the same. I once saw two men tried for a disturbance committed while they were drunk.

The person that had supplied them with beer was also brought up, and was afraid that he should be supposed to have bewitched the beer. A still deeper terror hovered over his speech, "Perhaps he himself and his beer were both bewitched, and used as a cat's paw by some other person".

82. PUNISHMENT OF UNCHASTITY.

We already mentioned (56) that a man may have an opportunity of contracting a marriage with an adult female and that he may ascertain her sentiments privately. Long ago I was told by one qualified to speak on African customs, that a native man would not pass a solitary woman, and that her refusal of him would be so contrary to custom that he might kill her. Of course, this would apply only to females that are not engaged. A girl with no claim upon her readily agrees to marriage, and the man will marry her although he have several wives already. But if a betrothed girl be seduced, the crime is treated as adultery and may be punished by death. Her intended husband has a right to kill the guilty man. In cases of adultery the injured husband may in like manner kill the seducer. As for the woman, her first offence may be condoned, but subsequent offences cause divorce or death. When a wife has been guilty, her husband will die if he taste any food that she has salted. As a consequence of this superstition a wife is very liable to be accused of killing her husband. When women are preparing their husband's food they may ask a little girl to put the salt in it.

With a faithless wife the husband cannot live until a third party (mjinjila nyumba) has been with her. The name of this party is concealed from the husband who, from jealousy, might kill him. After the ceremony, the husband and wife may live together again. Several of these observances are explained and enjoined at the mysteries (52). As adultery is a crime not easily proven, the native appeal to the sorcerer, or the ordeal in such charges has a peculiar significance—it always leads to a definite decision.

CHAPTER XII.

RIGHTS OF PROPERTY AND OFFENCES AGAINST THEM.

83. PUBLIC PROPERTY.

In Britain, the land belongs to a proprietor, so that if another person go into the woods and cut a tree, he is trespassing and damaging property, if he shoot a deer he is a poacher. But among these Africans one may cut as many trees as he wishes, and hunt as long as he chooses. This is not because the land is common property. In the Yao language the chief is expressly called the " owner of the soil ". It is rather because trees are so abundant and grow so fast that the natives are anxious to keep them down. In the same way deer are plentiful, and it is better to let man feast on them than to leave them for the lion or the vulture. The natives seem to be placed on certain spots for the purpose of subduing the country and maintaining their right to exist against the wild animals around them, and this must have been so to a much greater extent at the time when these tribes formed their 'social contract'.   Even as it is, man looks a very puny object when placed amidst the vastness of the African jungle.   Human beings are quite lost among the grass, not to mention

NATIVES IN THE AFRICAN JUNGLE.

the trees and bushes.   Hence "to catch a man among the grass" is a proverbial expression which means to do one an injury in secret.

I shall make a few remarks, first on various kinds of public property (84-91), and next on private property.

84. LAND.

A man may hoe as much land as he pleases, and for any purpose. He may make trenches for entrapping deer, he may cut up the ground for great distances in search of moles for his dinner, or he may begin to plant and make a farm (62). He must never cultivate ground that has been betrothed by another party. But as soon as he hoes a field the ground is entirely his own. He hoes, and plants, and builds, without paying any tax or rent.

It has been said with reference to various parts of Africa, that the soil belongs to the tribe and that, according to the native idea, no chief has a right to make grants of land. But I found chiefs always willing to grant as much land as they were asked for. It would be more correct to say that these natives do not know what can be the use of Perpetual property in land : when *their* fields are farmed for two or three years, the soil yields a poor return, and they find it necessary to go to new ground.

85. TIMBER.

One may cut wood wherever he chooses. I knew a chief ask strangers to pay for trees that were cut to make canoes ; but he let his own subjects fell the largest trees without demanding any tax.

At the time of the Mission's arrival, the Blantyre district was covered with a dense jungle, which contained not only an impassable mass of young trees, but also a sprinkling of old ones. About twenty years before, the ground had been farmed over by natives who had then cut down the timber for manure and firewood, sparing only those larger trees, some of which had been the prayer trees of their old villages.

86. ROADS.

Any person may hoe up a public road. Many a time have I found it difficult to keep the path after a new village had risen in its neighbourhood, although I had been familiar with the king's highway before. When the owner of a farm puts a bunch of thorns on a path, every bare-legged native understands the signal. Still the road cannot be closed altogether, it will take a graceful curve round the side of the new farm. Where it passes through the centre of a large field the farmer leaves it alone. It is so hard that he prefers to try his hoe on the surrounding soil.

87. MINERALS.

Where one has a right to hoe at all, he has a right to all the minerals that he may find, but if he dig much iron and make many hoes, he is expected to present some to the chief of the country. No one in this district knows about gold or silver. A piece of calico is more valued than all the coins of the Bank of England would be.

88. BUILDING MATERIALS.

Grass, reeds, bamboos, and other materials used for erecting huts may be cut anywhere. In the dry season the country is covered with grass of from two to eight feet high, according to the richness of the soil. This mass of vegetation will make an enormous blaze. Some set it on fire to catch deer or buffalo, others to catch field-mice, and others for mere sport. Anyone may burn the grass, but if the flames spread to a village or a corn field, the fire-raiser is responsible for the consequences.

89. STREAMS AND RIVERS.

In this district one may draw water, bathe, or catch fish anywhere. When a number of men have to cross a stream at a place where they see women bathing, they shout out "Travellers! Travellers!" (alendo). So when a woman comes to a stream and sees a man approaching, she will often turn back with her water-pot, saying, "Perhaps he wants to bathe". There are certain superstitions also, and it is very common when walking along a stream even in the morning (when no one bathes), to see women emerge from a village and retreat as soon as they observe men advancing. As to fishing, there is no restriction, and the natives use the euphorbia tree (mtutu) which kills fish much as lime would do.

90. HUNTING.

Any resident or traveller has a right to hunt. On shooting a large buck or an elephant, he is expected to send the chief a present. But if he be far from the chief's principal village he seldom does so. A company of native travellers who shoot a buffalo out in the bush far from the abodes of men, will use the whole of it themselves. Strangers may be imposed on by head-men, who, although loud in making demands, have no right to such a present. But their claiming it, shows how much they regard themselves as being separate kings. English hunters used to obtain a great amount of ivory not far from Blantyre, much of it being shot in No-man's-land. The Mangoni first drove off the Yao, and then receded themselves, leaving the country unoccupied.

91. TRAVELLING.

As a matter of theory, a person may travel in this part of the country without asking permission, but unless well acquainted with the chiefs and the people, a foreigner will find it awkward to go without a guide. It is easy, however, except in times of war, to get a guide from one chief to the next. The right to travel naturally implies the right to hunt; arms must be carried for protection and may be used to obtain food.

92. PRIVATE PROPERTY.

Were a native to count over the items of his pro-perty he would give a list like this:—(1) His chief wife, whom, however, he cannot sell (60). (2) Inferior wives (masulila) with their children. (3) Female slaves not related to him (achambumba pa mlango pao), who may be given as wives to his male slaves. (4) Male slaves (achachanda), who, although valuable in times of war, fetch lower prices than females. (5) His money, *i.e.*, cloth and beads (which except in the neighbourhood of the Mission are small items of native property): arrowheads, hoes, and indeed most articles are used in bartering. (6) Implements and weapons—axes, hoes, mortars, baskets, guns, spears, &c. (7) Houses, crops, fowls. In this list he may include his sisters or other relatives, who are to a great extent at his disposal (77). If rich, he may possess also a tusk of ivory, or a few goats. When an attack is made a native that saves his life has little to lose. The greater part of his property can run with him and carry all his moveables. Each wife takes a child on her back, and a basket with all her goods on her head. The houses are left, but the party can make a shelter in a few minutes. The crop is the man's greatest loss, the roots and leaves of the jungle do not taste so well as his porridge.

93. BORROWING AND LENDING.

The natives are fond of borrowing from each other. If a school-boy possèss an unusual dress, it goes round the whole of his companions. Often a native begs for cloth, and when told that he has enough, he replies, " All that I am wearing is borrowed ". Likely this statement is false, but the custom of borrowing is so common as to make the falsehood plausible. If a woman at Quilimane lend a pot, she expects on its return to receive something for the use of it, but the more primitive natives about Blantyre lend " hoping for nothing again," in the shape of interest.

94. PETTY THEFT.

Many cases of pilfering dealt with by village headmen we might call petty thefts.   Natives possess so
little property that nearly all stealing from them comes
under this head.   Plucking the ears of corn in a field
is not criminal.   The person that takes a cob of maize
leaves the stalk so as to convey a well-known meaning
to the farmer, who as he looks at the signal is able to
say, "Oh! it is a poor man that has eaten because of
hunger," or "It is my friend that has helped himself".
But if the smallest article be taken by an enemy, a
disturbance arises.   Natives are fairly honest among
each other.   When one is plundered by a companion he
exclaims, "If you had stolen from a white man, then I
could have understood it, but to steal from a black
man——".   Several articles were once carried off from
the Mission Station.   As a rule, when theft is mentioned, the natives say stealing is "very bad," "some
black men do not know how to steal, other black men
are very bad".   But one little fellow, on this occasion,
took a milder view of the matter and said to his
instructor, "Black man very poor, ma'am".   Among
the older natives, however, a tendency to extenuate is
seldom found, and often we see cases like that mentioned
by Livingstone, where a person had to drink mwai for
taking a few ears of corn.   One circumstance that
makes even petty theft very heinous in the eyes of
the native is that the thief is identified with the Bewitchers (106).   He uses "medicine" like them, and
employs "horns" in the same way.   He has a charm

(chitaka) that enables him to go to a sleeper at night and ask, "Where are your hoes? Where are your beads?" So complete is his power over his victims, that he makes them answer all such questions without waking, and so secure does he feel that he cooks porridge and takes a meal before leaving the plundered house. So much is thief-medicine believed in that few venture to steal without seeking the proper charm. Hence it is that a thief becomes an object of disgust, and may lose his life for taking a few articles which he might have got by simply asking the owner. The native view about witches modifies the whole civil code. Any offence may be brought under the terrible crime of witchcraft. If a wife run away it is easy to convince her husband that she would not have done so but for powerful "witchery" used against her.

The following statement sent me by Mr. Buchanan of Zomba will further illustrate the law of theft :—

After mentioning that "a man found stealing is in the position of a baboon, hyæna, or hog, etc., and is as liable to be shot down as any of these animals," Mr. Buchanan says, "Kasanda, one of my gaffers, had charge of a gang of women who were carrying clay from a swamp about a mile distant, and I allowed him a gun partly because kidnapping was rife at the time, and partly because he had seen an eland as he went to the clay hole the previous day. When returning in the evening he heard a crashing noise in a clump of sugar cane just over the stream. Crossing as quickly and as quietly as possible, he reached the spot unobserved, and found a man tying up a large bundle of cane. He challenged the thief, presented the gun, and had the case been his own, or had he been serving a native chief, he would most undoubtedly have given the rascal its contents, but knowing that the English discouraged such customs, and doubtful how I would look on such an act, he allowed the man to escape. The following day I sent for Kalimbuka, showed him the bundle of cane, and stated what had happened. Several of his counsellors accompanied him, and all were unanimous in asserting that according to native law Kasanda had committed an egregious blunder in not shooting the thief dead. While strongly objecting to this mode of procedure, I earnestly enquired if such was really the law of the country, and found that it was. I remember too that when Mr. Macdonald and I went to visit Malemya, his prime minister told us of an instance in which this law had been carried out to the bitter end. A man from Chikala had stolen yams belonging to Malemya's people, the owners lay in wait, and the thief returning a second time was shot dead. But when a man detects a thief in his field during the day, and knows the thief well, he need not shoot or capture him unless he likes. He may march to the man's village, ask the chief to turn out his men, and then point out the depredator, who, if not redeemed, becomes the lawful property of the man who owned the stolen stuff (it matters not what it be)."

95. THEFT AND ROBBERY.

All the above-mentioned classes of property (92) are liable to be pilfered, and among these tribes it is perhaps human beings that are oftenest stolen. We do not now dwell on theft as we have taken it to illustrate the general treatment of crime (76). When the injured party demands redress, the refusal is a declaration of war. Robbery with violence and bloodshed is a declaration of war almost under any circumstances.

96. MISCELLANEOUS CRIMES AND PENALTIES.

Besides direct breaches of the 6th, 7th, and 8th commandments of the Decalogue, which are all punishable by death, there are many other crimes recognised and punished by native law. Burning a neighbour's house, setting fire to the bush and destroying his crops, and trespassing so as to cause damage, are instances that have suggested to the native the *lex talionis*. To the question " What would you do if your neighbour destroyed your crop?" comes the prompt reply, "I would take his," and many injuries or accidents that result in the loss of property are settled accordingly. Abusing another person—defamation of character—is also paid back in kind, unless the stronger party give the other a beating to the bargain. To be called a liar is rather a compliment, but to be called a bewitcher is much resented. When a woman charges another with adultery, the fight is often furious; they bite and scratch each other till they are covered with blood and the dust or mud of the highway.

Fines may be paid in slaves or any other kind of property except ivory. An offender may be bound over to keep the peace. When convicted of some misdeed, he presents his superior with a spear, saying, "Kill me if I offend you again ". The token is common between slaves and their masters. In reviewing native punishments we find that almost every offence may be punished by death, but when an offender is not redeemed, the particular punishment is left to the headman of the injured party. For instance, if a headman of Kumpama's go and say, " Chenyono has killed a subject of mine ; I have caught a subject of his and want to kill him," the chief's answer will be, "He has done you wrong, do according to your heart " (poli mtima wenu). The punishment is thus inflicted not by the criminal's own chief but by the injured party, and it may fall, not on the guilty person, but on one connected with him. It is when a man transgresses against his own village-chief that *personal responsibility* is brought home to him. When he transgresses against another village, his own chief pays for him. Of punishments inflicted for small offences by superiors on their own wards, imprisonment in a slave-stick is common, and may be inflicted by a husband on his wives, or by the chief wife on her subordinates. *Beating* is another punishment. When a slave is sent to keep off the monkeys, and lets them eat the corn, he will taste the rod : so will a child, or even a younger brother. These beatings when inflicted are very severe, but they are rarely needed, slaves being generally obedient, and young people respectful. *Justice is evaded* by running to the country of a hostile chief. It is common (as it is prudent) for a fugitive to steal something from his present chief as a gift to the man that receives him.

CHAPTER XIII.

INHERITANCE AND INTERNATIONAL LAW.

97. INHERITANCE.

" . . . the wife of the dead shall not marry without unto a stranger; her husband's brother shall go in unto her and take her to him to wife."—DUET. xxv. 5.

WHEN a man dies, part of his goods is buried with him, part goes to pay the precentor at the wake, and to feast the undertakers and friends. Besides these and such like funeral expenses, there is the cost of the legal investigation into the cause of death, and this item if not repaid by damages from the bewitcher (107), will be the most expensive piece of mourning. The remainder of his property (92), including his wives and children, passes on, without any government tax, to his heir. The nearest heir is his eldest brother, who obtains complete possession. This is no hardship to younger brothers, who will succeed in their turn. Failing a brother, there comes the eldest sister, not indeed herself but her son, so that the next heir after a man's younger brother is his nephew (mwipwagwao). By this custom a man's own children are purposely set aside. When we tell the natives about the English law of succession, they say that it is "very stupid". They want to be sure that the heir really has the family blood in his veins, and they cannot trust that a man's sons answer to this description. The same laws of inheritance are found in various parts of Africa —as for instance among the Ashanti on the Western Coast. Any will that attempted to strike at this custom would be at once set aside. Where writing is unknown, written wills are impossible, but no will would be recognised except perhaps in the case of some trifling matters. If the rightful heir be a minor (*i.e.*, a mere child), some one takes the inheritance till he comes of age. The first-born always has the precedence, the younger brother being nothing while the elder is alive. We saw an amusing illustration of this in the case of our own two children. On the birth of the first, the relatives of the chief Kapeni patronised him and even proposed a wife for him, while all the natives called him little Kapeni. But the second child they took no notice of, he was merely "the younger brother of little Kapeni". The heir pays any debt that may be on the inheritance, he also takes the risk of the "witchcraft" trial. If his predecessor died by witchcraft, he receives a large fine from the bewitcher's estate, but if his predecessor died by the poison (mwai), he pays a fine to the bewitched persons, or their representatives. The great majority of the natives are the victims of witchcraft one way or other. They either die of witchcraft themselves (106), or are poisoned because they bewitched some one else. On the day of entering on his inheritance the heir marries not only the inferior wives, but the chief wife of his predecessor (43). Should she have property her sureties look after her interest. A married woman, if free, may have property—she may be a herbalist, or a "cook" at the mysteries, or she may make money by her flour and fowls. When a wife dies possessing wealth, her husband to keep off the "surety" (48), asks a younger sister to marry him, and take charge of (kwachinga) the children. If he cannot succeed in this, the goods may be divided, part going to the husband and part to the sureties of the wife.

98. SUCCESSION TO THE CHIEFTAINSHIP.

The order of this succession is the same as in ordinary inheritance. The chief's nearest heir is the eldest of his brothers (97), who will be younger than the chief himself, otherwise he would have had a prior claim to the title. Next to younger brothers come nephews, but not the sons of a brother, who are really reckoned the sons of the chief (60). Occasionally natives set aside this order of succession. The parties concerned are—(1) The deceased man's slaves. (2) His wives and children, many of whom are also slaves. (3) Headmen related to the chief. (4) Headmen not related to the chief. The 3rd class are not impartial judges, because some of them may be candidates for the throne. The 4th class, however, often do much to settle disputes. But strange to say, it is the slaves and wives, the 1st and 2nd class, that raise the loudest voice. They are a numerous and powerful body, and

may contain some of the old chief's best fighters. On
the death of the former Malemya of Zomba, there
survived a younger brother Kumtaja, who, so far as
birth went, was the rightful heir; but there was also
a nephew called Kasabola. Kumtaja urged his claim,
but the slaves (achachanda) disliked him, and so did
many of the headmen (alambi). Moreover, all the
wives of the old chief desired Kasabola, and quoted
a saying of the deceased chief in his favour. The
Alambi said, " If Kumtaja enter Malemya's village,
all that reside there will run away," and accordingly
Kasabola was made " Malemya". Still it is dangerous
to tamper with the law of the land. Kumtaja set up
an independent kingdom, taking to him such headmen
as would go; and had there been a division among the
wives or slaves, he might have claimed all that wished
to adhere to him.

At an installation there are several ceremonies, which,
however, vary among different tribes. The new chief first
gets a severe lecture, in which he is told that he must
be hospitable and not beat his people too much. Afterwards he is formally installed in office (34). His
temples are girt with the brow-band (ndawila), which
he will henceforth wear on every formal occasion. He
is then called by his new name, and received with
songs of rejoicing. His assumption of the name is
much dwelt on. When old Kapeni of Sochi became
chief in the distant Yao country, before his tribe
migrated, the songs and the response, " Awo Kapeni
'wo" (that is Kapeni), produced an impression that is
fresh in the memory of his people to this day. The

chief may appoint a high priest (jua mbepesi) of his government, who is also called his captain. It is the duty of this man to carry the chief's banner and lead his army. The chief seldom goes to battle ; " he stays behind to supply powder and deal with deserters". Another duty of the high priest is to find out whether war is to be successful, but if he fail to get a favourable answer, the chief himself presents the offering, for just as every headman is the priest of his village (7), so the chief is the real high priest of the country. If the army go forth and be thoroughly defeated after the offerings declare victory to be certain, the people simply say, " Our God has deceived us ". When the chief has a beer-drinking, his priest or captain brings out the beer to the guests, and tastes it to show that it is not poisoned. In the case of English visitors, the Mago-lolo headmen taste all the food themselves, but at Kapeni's capital his priest generally performs the cere-mony. When there is a witch-dance at a place where the chief cannot attend, the priest is sent to represent him, and takes a prominent place in beating the drums. Many ceremonies seen at a chief's installation are ob-served when any one succeeds to a village. Moreover, since it is only certain families that have brow-bands, a headman may wear the badge where his chief has no right to do so. Headmen don it when presiding at trials, or when they go to a beer-drinking in full dress !

99. INTERNATIONAL LAW.

Disputes between a master and his slave, between a governor and his ward, between a headman and his

villager, or between a chief and his headman, are easily
settled by the power of the Superior. But disputes
between different villages are more puzzling. If a man
of Chingota's kill a man of Matope's in Chuma's village,
the three headmen may be involved only, when all
belong to one chief, reference is ultimately made to him.
But when they belong to different chiefs the case is
rendered more dangerous, as their respective chiefs may
become parties. The following instances show how cases
between chiefs are settled. If a subject of Malemya be
killed in a village of Kapeni's by men of Kumpama,[1]
Malemya expects Kapeni to catch the criminals and
hand them over to him ; and Kapeni must do so, otherwise he becomes a party to the crime. Kumpama sends
a message to Kapeni asking, " Where are those men of
mine that went to your territory ? " and Kapeni refers
him both now and in all subsequent steps of the dispute
to Malemya. The chief of a country thus takes cognis-
ance of crimes committed in his land not by punishing
the guilty parties himself, but by handing them over
to the injured. Again, suppose that Malemya's men
when carrying goods for Kapeni were plundered by
subjects of Kumpama, if the deed be done in Malemya's
territory, Malemya takes the matter up, but if the
goods be once out of his territory, Kapeni becomes
prosecutor. In either case Kumpama is asked to sur-
render the thieves, and is liable to punishment, either
because he is a party to the theft, or because he fails to
govern his kingdom in the proper way.

[1] These names happen to be real, but are used only as counters.

100. GENERAL REMARKS ON NATIVE LAW.

As law is a subject of great complexity in all countries, it must not be supposed that we have settled every question. In a native dispute difficulties may arise regarding the form of prosecution, the form of evidence, the proper court, the position and members of that court, and in short at every step. These *special* difficulties are settled according to the merits of each case : and cannot be here solved without treating the subject with a minuteness that would be too tedious for the most ardent student of African customs.

101. WAR.

As war may begin in Africa without any provocation at all, trivial reasons are quite sufficient to produce bloody feuds. Hence, quarrels that in civilised countries would be mere law suits become occasions for war. A chief *declares* war by killing or kidnapping some of his enemies. He may either find them on a journey, or send an expedition to their villages. Deeds of this kind proclaim that a messenger sent to the aggressor will be either slain or sent back mutilated, the two parties are now declared enemies, and all friendly intercourse is at an end. War may be declared on a travelling party by simply calling out " ngondo " (war). The natives *conduct* war by making a series of attacks in order to plunder or to destroy by fire and sword. The Yao chiefs say that they do not attack by night—" to attack by night is a sneaking piece of conduct fit only for the

Anyasa and the Achipeta ". But they can explain with
great relish the method of night attack. A band of
men go to an enemy's village when the people are all in
bed. They carry sticks finely sharpened at the point
(songa), and place them in the ground right before the
hut doors, and in such a way that a native coming
hastily out of the house in his usual dress will run one
of them into his body. After setting this trap, the
invaders apply fire to the various houses, and then look
on with loaded guns. Sometimes they tie up the doors
before setting the houses on fire, but unless their ani-
mosity be very deadly, they will not burn all their foes.
It is more profitable to capture the women and children
for sale. The boldest of their enemies will be the first
to rush forth to investigate the disturbance, and once
they have impaled themselves on the sharp-pointed
sticks, their wives can easily be captured.

A war may *end* in various ways. One of the parties
may be entirely broken and driven from the country,
their wives and children becoming slaves. Or the
weaker may succeed in buying a peace. Two hostile
chiefs may continue beside each other for many years,
afraid to risk anything more serious than kidnapping.
Since the natives trust greatly to war medicine, a small
chief that long maintains his position against a stronger,
and occasionally gains a battle, is believed to have a
powerful "medicine," and is feared accordingly. Native
wars frequently cause more deaths through famine than
through actual slaughter. All natives confess that war
is "bad," but strangely enough each race values itself
upon its military powers. Even the Achipeta, although

they have been completely vanquished by the Mangoni, will boast, " In our country we know nothing but war".

Natives jump and swing their guns about by way of making a war dance, but these evolutions being originally adapted for their long spears, are unsuitable for guns. The Mangoni, like the Zulus, have a special training for war.

Native fights remind one of the days of Homer. A good tongue is as essential as a good spear. So long as a combatant has courage to demand his rights, the fact that the enemy has " eaten " a number of his followers is regarded as mere by-play.

Chapter XIV.

A SLAVE GOVERNMENT.

102. THE MAGOLOLO.

As an illustration of a Slave Government, we shall
here insert a few remarks on the Magololo, who are half-
a-dozen men that came with Dr. Livingstone a journey
of "many moons" from the south of the Zambeze—from
the land, which on maps of Africa is marked Makololo.
Hitherto we have spoken of chiefs and headmen ruling
among free people. The native word for "free" means
"belonging to the tribe," and implies that persons falling
into the power of another tribe lose their rights. The
Anyasa under the Magololo are in the hands of aliens,
by whom they are consequently treated as if they were
captives. When not promptly obeyed, a Magololo cries,
"All the Anyasa are my slaves"; hence although he
has many good points about him, his government is
severe, and he is more suspicious than the Yao chiefs
who rule their own kinsmen. "The Magololo," according to Mr. Rowley (277), "sprung all at once from a
condition little removed from bondage to that of lords
of the creation. When left by Dr. Livingstone, they

had little but their guns and ammunition. With guns
they knew themselves to be formidable. They hunted
the slavers far and near, released captives and took the
plunder. The women thus released they took for wives,
the men and boys they kept for slaves. They had no
sheep, goats, nor corn, but the Anyasa had, and as in
their own country, the possession of cattle by a neighbour is a good *casus belli*, they were prepared to make
war on the Anyasa for their flocks and corn, if the
latter did not yield them without resistance. The
Anyasa yielded, and thus arose the bleating of sheep
and goats, the cackling of fowls and the well-stocked
houses of corn in the Magololo habitations." "It was
a great mistake on the part of Dr. Livingstone to leave
the Makololo at Chibisa's unprovided with everything
but arms. They were identified with the English—
they adopted our name in their raids." The remark
that these men are identified with the English holds
true to this day. Chiputula, one of the Magololo, was
viewed by Matekenya as a " child " or " subject " of the
English, and Matekenya often put the question, "What
will the English do if I kill Chiputula ? " The latter
used to be constantly entreating us to send messages to
Matekenya : and Dr. Macklin once brought up a " son "
of Matekenya to conclude a peace with Chiputula.
" Mangokwe talked of driving them out of the country,
but they would have driven like sheep five times the
number of Anyasa that Mangokwe could have brought
against them, and so he appeared to think . . ."
(2nd edition, p. 278). "They had plundered the
country on all sides, and so great was the terror of

them that the Anyasa were afraid to come to us with
food.   It was necessary, therefore, to take vigorous
measures, and catching one of them (in the act of
stealing), I laid hold of a stick and gave the fellow a
good thrashing."

The writer describes how they continued amenable to
the authority of the English.   When the Scotch Missions
settled in Central Africa, these Magololo readily sent their
sons first to the Free Church Mission, and subsequently
to Blantyre, which was nearer their home.   This was
due to their previous acquaintance with the "English".
Some Magololo children came to Blantyre about a
month after my arrival.   But I wrought steadily in
school for three years afterwards, before Kapeni, the
Yao chief, sent his sons.

During the time of flight and famine, the beginning
of which is described by Mr. Rowley, some headmen of
the Anyasa fled towards Tete, but the most important
died.   People died without any reason (lulele), there
was quite a dying (chaola) among the race.   Then the
Magololo "got in their fingers" (kwinjila yala).   They
took possession of the children of the deceased, they
killed others and took their families also.   They had
no right to act in this way, but they relied on their
power, which increased every day till they could claim
all the Anyasa on the lower Chiri for their subjects.
These helpless people have suffered exceedingly from
war, and have been enslaved in all directions.   Near
Blantyre many of them reside as slaves among the Yao.
At Zomba there is an important Anyasa headman who
although possessing several villages, is under a

Machinga chief. Even on Lake Nyassa (Nyasa) itself, most of the unfortunate tribe are under Yao or Machinga rulers. On an island in Chirwa many of them are packed together to escape slavers (62).

103. GOVERNMENT OF SLAVES.

In their normal state, the Anyasa have the same customs as the Yao (1-102), but under the Magololo they are governed like prisoners of war. In a Yao village the people are ruled by a headman of their own kindred (62), who has power to try all village cases. Among the Magololo there are no such headmen, the leading man in the village is merely a sort of overseer or taskmaster, put there by the chief and possessing no civil or criminal jurisdiction. While the Yao are not compelled to hoe their chief's fields, the Magololo villagers cannot begin to cultivate for themselves till they have first "finished the chief's farm". After doing this, the overseers and the villagers under them may begin to cultivate ground for their own sustenance. At all times they may cut trees for their own fires. When they make canoes these are not for themselves, but for the chief. While the Yao have village parliaments, the Magololo are autocrats, who keep their people at arm's length. A subject of the Magololo, on killing a buck carries the whole animal to the capital. He gets back two legs, and the chief keeps the rest. The chief in like manner takes all the ivory, and gives the poor hunter only a small present of cloth. While among the Yao each woman has a surety (48), the

Magololo dispose of female children as masters dispose
of slaves (59, 92). They even try to make all the
children of their subjects live with themselves—a
measure which alienates the more respectable of their
people. By the Magololo all refugees are expressly
received as slaves even though they were free before.

104. PROOF AND PUNISHMENT.

Ordeals.

The Magololo prepare mwai, call their people in great
numbers and command them to drink it. Several die
in one day, who were therefore bewitchers and deserved
their fate. I have seen so many who have drunk mwai
with the Magololo and recovered, that I am inclined to
think either that the poison is of a milder type, or that
it is not fairly administered. Although the Yao are not
compelled to drink it, except for strong reasons, among
them the chance of recovery is smaller.

Investigation by torture is one of the saddest things
that the Magololo practise. It is often employed in
cases of alleged adultery. When a Magololo suspects
his wives of this crime, he places a stone in a jar of
boiling water or oil, and orders them to fetch it up with
their bare arms. He then judges of their guilt by the
amount of injury they sustain. When a woman is thus
convicted, he makes her confess who seduced her. In
vain does the helpless creature protest that she is innocent. Notwithstanding that her arm is severely scalded,
she is subjected to the most cruel torture by a kind of
" thumbscrew " (mbanilo) which is applied to her head.

A small tree (katela) is partly divided along the middle, the skull of the poor woman is inserted as if it were a wedge for splitting the tree still farther. Great pressure is exerted by forcing the halves of the tree together with the aid of pulleys. The instrument works like a gigantic nut-cracker, and during its operation the chief and his assistants look on with calm satisfaction, and suggest the name of her seducer. When the woman, under this torture, indicates that the man is guilty, he is put to death without a trial. Should he plead that he knows nothing of the crime, the chief takes no notice of his protestation. Perhaps the woman herself is quite guiltless, and has been convicted solely by the ordeal. The Yao used to apply this method of torture (kuwana) to a bewitcher in order to extort a confession. The bewitcher was first proved guilty by the oracle, and then had his head squeezed till he told where he had buried his horns. But now the detective both proves the guilt and finds the horns (107). Among the Yao at present this process of torture is seldom applied to free people.

Even in serious cases the Magololo may refuse to give any trial " because the accused was their slave ".

Crimes and Punishment.

Petty theft, as of a fowl, is punished among the Magololo by flogging with whips of elephant hide. There is no formal trial. If the criminal says he has not stolen, the chief says he is a liar, which, to do the chief justice, is often the case. Cropping a thief's ears, and cutting off his fingers, are also practised. Few Yao take such decided measures even with their slaves. For *theft* of anything more valuable the punishment is death. A man that steals a sheep or a goat is stabbed and thrown into the river. On other occasions he is flogged to death with whips of elephant hide. "But do they always want to kill a thief when they flog him?" "No, sometimes they stop before he is dead, and then the man's companions remark, 'You have been very fortunate to-day!'" At other times a thief is made a public *example*, in which case he has his hands and his feet, or one or more of these members, cut off, and is placed in the forum for "two days". After this he is killed and thrown into the river. We asked, "But does not the man bleed to death in a short time?" "Not always," was the reply, "but the place where he sat is covered with his blood, and the chief kills a goat, which is disembowelled on that spot". The Yao do not often kill or mutilate in this way except in cases where they can get no compensation: but when they catch an enemy, they cut off his hand and tell him to go home and show how he has been received.

Adultery with their own wives the Magololo all punish with death. But when the crime is only among their people, their punishment is not uniform. Chiputula inflicts capital punishment on all adulterers, remarking that "next day they would interfere with his own wives". Makukani, when one of his men complains against another, may order the accused to hand over his wife for a week or more to the accuser.

When one of these chiefs wishes to make an example of an adulterer, the method is as barbarous as can well be conceived. The victim has his hand or some other part of his body cut off, and he is then compelled to eat it. I was unwilling to believe this, till I met men that had been eye-witnesses on several occasions, and then it appeared that the custom was notorious. We asked, " Why do the criminals consent to eat part of their bodies ?" The reply was, " The chief persuades (nyenga) or cheats them to do so. They think that if they eat, he will allow them to live." But in all such cases execution soon follows.

The practices of the Magololo not only furnish an illustration of how individual slaves and captives are treated, but show how a strong government in a barbarous land may " grind " its subjects. After a chief has been successful in many wars, he begins to think that both his slaves and his own kinsmen derive all life and property from him, and hold these privileges during his pleasure.

Chapter XV.

WITCHCRAFT.

105. THE POISONED CUP (MWAI.)

THE poison so often referred to in connection with native trials is made from the bark of the mwai tree, which grows plentifully throughout the country. The dose is about two gills, and is prepared by a pounder of poison (1). The accused, it is said, has a voice in the selection of the pounder, but so implicitly is the ordeal believed in that the natives think it is of little consequence who "pounds" it; still most tribes seem to have a milder concoction for trivial offences. The drug may be taken by proxy—it may be administered to a dog or a fowl or some animal representing the accused. In this case the animal is tied by a string to the criminal. If it survive, the accused is innocent, if it die, he is guilty. This method of administering the ordeal is more humane, and is allowed in smaller offences. It is much used by the natives that live near the coast. Indeed, the inhabitants of Quilimane believe in the ordeal as implicitly as the tribes of the interior, and although they have been in contact with

Europeans for centuries, they were accustomed when
called before a Portuguese judge to swear on the mwai
instead of the Bible.

106. WITCHCRAFT (USAWI.)

We have now described so many native customs that
it is time to set our examination paper that the reader
may satisfy himself as to his progress in African lore.
We therefore propose the following question, " When
a man is killed by a wild beast, do the natives think he
died by the hand of God ? " If the reader can answer
this, he has studied the subject with profit, and he
would be able to answer many similar questions. For
those who are doubtful we shall submit our own view.
In the first place, the question as Christians understand
it, is quite unintelligible to the native. We have reason
to believe that in the times of his philosophising, the
idea of a Supreme Being rises before his mind, but that
Being is to him "a God afar off" who takes nothing to
do with the ordinary course of events, and from whose
hand, therefore, death or misfortune never comes. We
must try then to interpret the question as the native
does (3), and we are thus led to enquire whether death
comes from the hand of the Departed Spirits. Now
undoubtedly these spirits have great power. Under their
auspices journeys are successful, by their assemblies
famine is averted, through their influence death is
driven away. Yet it is not so much their business
either to cause evil or to prevent it, as to indicate
whether evil be coming. The departed spirit may have

to answer a question like this, "*If* Saul come down, and *if* I remain here, will the men of Keilah deliver me up?" Now by giving a false answer, the spirit may bring about the death of his worshippers. Yet it is not the spirit that kills them—the real cause of all such mischief in this lower world is the Bewitcher. When we remark that the god is quite as much to blame, the natives say, "There is no use of blaming the god. *He did not set the horns.*" It is on the Bewitcher therefore that all responsibility lies.

The word "Bewitcher" (msawi) carries with it two ideas—the person so called (1) has power or knowledge sufficient for the practice of occult arts, and (2) is addicted to cannibalism. The second meaning is the more prominent. Let a person eat a morsel of his deceased friend, and though he be the feeblest and dullest-looking creature in the world he is msawi. This throws light upon the native view of witchcraft. Witches kill a victim for the purpose of eating him : not only so, but every man that dies even what we call a natural death is really killed by witches. These terrible beings visit their victim when asleep (94) and instil a powerful poison into his ears. They carry out their infernal tricks chiefly by means of horns (misengo.) Of themselves these horns may be harmless, being merely the horns of small buck, and if a bewitcher were to die after burying these weapons, they would have no evil influence. But as a matter of fact, such horns are always dangerous, for the witches hold a council beforehand with regard to killing their victim and sharing his flesh, and although the witch that buries the horns may

die, the survivors are able to carry on the plot to its
termination.

Hence when any native dies, his friends are certain
that he has been slain by witchcraft, and at once call in
the witch-detective, who will discover the guilty witches
and remove their dangerous horns.

107. THE WITCH-DETECTIVE (MAVUMBULA).

Although a male detective has appeared in the past
history of these tribes, all the witch detectives that I
have seen were female. They are in one aspect the
most important personages in the country.   At present
two reside at Lake Chirwa ; they belong to the same
fraternity, one is called Chipembere (Rhinoceros), and
the other Tambala (Cock).   Many speak as if the office
now belonged entirely to females. A native in ordinary
conversation often remarks, " If I have any misfortune
I will go to the woman," and when pronouncing a
person guilty, the terrible functionary ends her speech
with the words, "Thus saith the woman".   The detective when called to investigate a case of death,
appoints a day for the ceremony.   She goes with a
strong guard of armed men, and although her meetings
are frequent, people crowd to them from great distances.
Her approach causes as much excitement as a public
execution would do in a quiet English town, with this
difference, that the assembled multitude cannot tell
who will be the victim.   At sunrise the drums begin
to beat and are heard over the whole country side ;
about three hours after, all the villages in the district

are deserted. Their inhabitants, men, women, and
children, are to be seen hurrying to the "witch dance".
On arriving they sit in a circle, and leave a large space
in the centre for the "Woman". She is waited for
with breathless anxiety. After a time wild screams
are heard, and there rushes before the spectators the
maddest-looking person conceivable. A stranger con-
cludes at once that one witch has been captured already
and is now driven before the detective. The wretch
looks as if she were haunted by all the Furies and
Demons of Pagan Mythology. Her face, breast, and
arms are marked with patches of blood-red. Her
head is covered, not with short negro wool, but with
snaky tresses which hang down her back. Her loins
are girt with leopard skins. Her legs are overhung
with "rattles," which sound at every step. In her
hand she grasps a scourge of tails, which she waves
wildly about her. Her eyes roll and stare in her fierce
frenzy. She is evidently surrounded by fiends, which
though invisible to others, are dreadful realities to her.
With them she maintains a desperate struggle, ever
trying to beat them off with her scourge. After wrest-
ling thus she utters shrieks of the most unearthly character, and with a terrible bound dashes into the circle,
and we have before us the witch-detective herself. Once
in the middle of the crowd, she shouts and rants, sings
and dances, eats grass and chews branches for several
hours. Of her chants some are common in the district,
others in the Walolo language, contains a sound of the
letter *r* that the Yao cannot pronounce. She chaffs
them for their awkwardness, and notwithstanding the

grave nature of her ceremony, she succeeds in drawing smiles from the multitude. In some of her chants she boasts of her power. "Let the bewitcher become a leopard or a carrion crow yet," she cries, "there can be no escape." A large part of the crowd are in a state of terrible suspense. Each person knows that from three to five people will be "detected," and what if he be among the number? The first time I was at a witch-dance I was not free from concern! The bewitchers, however, will either be relatives of the deceased or persons that have had a quarrel with him.

As the decisive moment arrives, the detective asks the hand of every one in the crowd as she chants the appropriate words :—

> "Pasa manja Chipembere (Give Chipembere your hand).
> Pasa manja Chipembere."
> > *Response.*—"E, e, e, e, e, e, e."

The instant she touches the hand of a bewitcher she leaps back with a terrible start and utters a wild scream. Another method of detecting is by smelling, and this she brings into use at various stages of the investigation. Soon after feeling the hands of the spectators, she retires from the scene literally drenched with sweat. She has found out the whole secret. But the triumph of her art is not yet fully disclosed, and soon she proceeds to reveal where the witches have hid their horns. Taking a hoe and a pot of water, she marches off for the purpose, followed by hundreds of the crowd whose curiosity is most intense, and who begin to share her savage manner. She goes to the forum, to the stream that supplies the villagers with water, and to their various houses. At a spot where she wishes to dig she pours out water to soften the ground. During her digging, she groans, shrieks, and gesticulates, in the most frantic way. She succeeds in finding the horns most readily. One set she digs up at the stream, "they were placed there to bewitch the water drunk by the deceased". Another bunch she finds under a tree in the village. She looks up, and pointing to some fading branches at the top, she exclaims, "No wonder that this tree has begun to wither". Every spectator is dumb with astonishment and terror. No one will dare to touch these horns. It would be fatal to do so. They were buried by the bewitchers, and are the very means by which the deceased was killed. All are greatly relieved when these potent spells are removed by the "Woman," who will doubtless find them useful on another occasion.

The witch-detective always spends one night at the village where she is employed. She is then permitted to wander about at midnight, under the pretence of going to watch the graves. Should she find any one out of his house at that hour, she catches him and brings forward this suspicious circumstance against him. To be found at night by the witch-detective is one of the most unfortunate things that could happen to any man. Even if he has not been already recommended as a victim, he is certain to be now among the guilty. While the detective goes about at midnight among the houses, she is supposed to be unknown to the witches. Sometimes she begs for food, and the witches, thinking she is one of their own fraternity, give her some human flesh. This hospitality she ungratefully rewards, for the flesh said to be thus procured she produces as evidence against the person that gave it.

Besides horns, the detective may dig up arms, legs, and other portions of human bodies in suspicious places in or near the houses of the witches. The whole process of unearthing is of a nature to satisfy a craving for magic, and if more harmless, would be intensely humorous. There is no saying what the witch-detective may " find," and she seems as much surprised at her discovery as any of the spectators !

Midnight Feasts.

Any witch may join in eating a person that has been killed by the agency of others ; indeed, most of the witches in the country are believed to come to a great feast when one of their number has robbed the grave of its prey. Here is a description of such midnight feasts translated from the very words of a native :—" They cook the body at night, when everyone is asleep, in a pot with water and salt. They eat it with their porridge as a relish in the same way as they would eat a fowl. They go and bury the bones. They take the head and singe off the hair, and go to the stream and wash it with water and take out the brains and cook them. They disembowel the body and eat all the entrails after washing them at the stream." If a body is kept in a house until putrefaction has done its work, " the witches are cheated of their meat ". This is one reason why the body of a person of rank is kept in the house for a long time after death. The witch-detective, or rather the mwai, kills only the person who bewitched the deceased and those that consented to his death before-hand. Those that partook of the feast are not so guilty, but they generally come with a present to the detective and justify themselves by saying, " We only followed the meat ". One of the exploits of witches, according to Kapeni, is to make milk come down a straw in the inside of a house. We mention this because it resembles witch-stories in other lands. When witches are caught by the detective, no one will speak to them. Generally they are some helpless creatures whom a relative wishes out of the way. They must soon drink the mwai, which is certain to prove fatal to some of them. The credit of the witch-detective would suffer if they all survived.

Death by mwai.

The person that dies by mwai, whether the crime be theft, adultery, murder, or witchcraft, is denied the ordinary funeral rights. The body is either cast into a cave, or hung on a tree for the vultures. No coffin (34) is allowed, and the ordinary grave-cloth is denied. Much of the effects of the deceased goes to paying the prosecutor, who has a large account with the witch-detective. It may, however, be the prosecutor himself that succeeds to the bewitcher's inheritance. This whole superstition casts a dark shadow over the closing days of the poor native. If we pass over slaves (who may be killed to escort their master) and young children, we do not hesitate to say that in many districts one half

of the natives are killed by mwai. On every occasion
of what we call natural death, there is at once an investigation by the witch-detective, and the result is that at
at least one individual dies.

Towards the last year of my own residence in Africa
there occurred ten deaths of persons that I was well
acquainted with. Of these, four died by violence, three
by natural causes, and three by mwai. Of the three
that died by natural causes two were living with the
English, and their friends were not allowed to be
avenged on any bewitcher, so that we believe that the
proportion of deaths by mwai is really larger. We have
sometimes wondered that the chiefs did not check the
operations of the sorcerer, but the following from Lady
Barker will throw much light on their position. A
Kafir chief said, " You ask me to put down the witch-
doctors, but you forget the circumstances of my country.
You Englishmen have gaols, policemen and soldiers ; I
have none of these things, and if I were to prohibit
' smelling out' there would be no check whatever upon
the criminal classes."

On first finding myself face to face with the above
agency of heathenism, I began to reason against it. In my
first efforts I took very strong ground, not only deny-
ing that witchcraft was possible, but asserting that I did
not believe in cannibalism. I even ventured to argue
that when these tribes spoke of " eating each other "
they " did not and could not mean " that a man literally
ate his fellows. But it is a dangerous thing to give a
native lessons in his own language, and I was soon convinced that they " did not and could not mean " any-

thing else.   But they were generally very fair in
controversy.   They were unanimous in rejecting my
views about cannibalism—"was not human flesh as
sweet to the bewitcher as monkeys, beetles and caterpillars were to other people?"   But they were willing
to admit that the detective while prowling about at
midnight might busy herself in burying horns, and they
laughed heartily when I volunteered to unearth as
many horns as they wanted if they allowed me the
same privilege.   I am not without hope that the deception may soon come to an end, for the little boys and
girls that lived with us used latterly to get up a mock
witch-dance for their own amusement, and they acted
on hints most willingly given by the " white man," and
implying that the witch-detective buried the horns
herself.

Divination.

The following method of divining as described by Mr.
Buchanan may conclude this chapter :—

" A common custom amongst the Machinga is divination (kupenda).   Few will venture to go a distance of
ten miles without first assuring themselves that no
danger is to befall them on the way.   Men going from
Zomba to Blantyre seldom forget to try the 'Chipendo'
before starting.   One mode of divining is by means of
the root of a small bush.   This root is about the thick-
ness of a pencil, and three bits of it about two inches
long are usually employed.   Most men carry these lots
or roots with them when on a journey, and carefully

preserve them when at home. A man wishing to know whether he may proceed in safety takes these bits of root and lays them carefully on the ground, placing the third above the other two. He then declares his intention of going to a certain place, and asks whether there is any hindrance. After retiring a few paces he returns to take his answer from the position in which the roots are now lying. If they have remained as he placed them his journey is to be prosperous, but if they have been separated it is to be unsuccessful, and he will not set out. Or the diviner may use only two roots—a method often resorted to by a traveller who comes to cross roads. He places his knife in a horizontal position, and lays the two roots against the blade. The traveller then stands pointing to one of the roads and says 'Shall I take this one?' and if the roots remain still fixed he takes it, but if they fall to the ground he chooses the other path. In the event of a man being without a knife he may use the palm of his hand or the side of a tree.

"Another and more complicated method consists in boiling the roots and mixing the entrails of an adder with the water."

This use of the entrails is suggestive in an ethnological point of view.

Chapter XVI.

AFRICAN ETHNOLOGY.

In trying to settle whether tribes are of the same race the Ethnologist turns his attention to such points as (1) their language, (2) their customs and beliefs, and (3) their physical characteristics. Though in this chapter we refer only to the second of these particulars, we may remark that on the evidence of language alone we can decide that the Wayao, Walolo, Anyasa, Achikunda, Machinga, Mangoni, Makua, and others in their neighbourhood, are sprung from common ancestors, and that all these tribes are of the same race as the majority of the tribes found south of the Equator, which have been grouped together as the Bantu.* The other important inhabitants of South Africa besides the Bantu are the Hottentots and Bushmen, who again have been often classed together. The Hottentots and Bushmen seem to have been first in the Continent. Then the Bantu came into the middle of them, and split them into two sections. One section (Hottentots and Bushmen) is

---

* The word for *people* is among some of these tribes *antu*, among others *wandu*, among others *abantu*, &c., hence has arisen the word Bantu.

found in the South, the other section (represented by tribes like the Akka) is found in the North. As to the time when the Bantu established themselves in South Africa there is little to guide us. It is said that the Kafirs were forcing their way down by the West Coast at the time when the Portuguese were settling on the East Coast. It seems clear that Santos on one side of Africa and Merolla on the other both mingled with this great people.

African Ethnology is a vast subject, and in treating it some have been led to maintain that there was once a continent to the east of Africa, which has become submerged. The traditions common among these African tribes to the effect that the Bantu came from the North tempt us to look northward along the map of Africa with the view of discovering whence they came. On examining the tribes of Northern Africa, we find that one obstacle has been put before the Ethnologist by Mahommedanism, which, pressing into the country by the seventh century, changed the ancient tribal customs. On the other hand, the customs of certain ancient races like the Egyptians have been preserved by history.

Putting aside language for the present, we shall note the customs of various African races. This besides pointing to certain ethnological conclusions, will throw light on the customs that have been laid before the reader, and may increase the interest in those tribes. Taking our stand in the Nyassa region, we shall, after glancing at customs of Eastern Africa supplied by earlier missionaries, look towards the South, the West, and the North in succession; and then conclude the chapter

with notes on ancient races that might have had contact with the African Bantu.

EAST CENTRAL AFRICA.

*Santos** (1586) remarks : "The people bewail their
dead by dint of drumming, and desist from leaping
and dancing only when fatigue obliges them to cease
(33). They regard their king as the favourite of the
souls of the dead, and think that he learns from them
all that passes in his dominions (1). The Portuguese
delivered from their dreadful slavery a number of
women and children whom this wretch kept with a
number of men in pens for the purpose of killing and
eating them in succession (79, 106). They acknowledge
a God who, both in this world and in the world to come,
measures retribution for the good or evil done in this."
[This looks, I fear, somewhat like reading our ideas into
their language. Still, natives might easily fancy that
the old chief to whom they go at death will treat his
subjects much as he did in this life.]

The Rev. H. Rowley, of the Magomero Mission, gives
an account of a public supplication for rain amongst the
Anyasa (20). In conducting war, "The Yao," he says,
" left their camp before daybreak, marched direct to the
principal village, destroyed that, and fired the others
which lay in their line of march home. The difficulty was
to get messengers to the Yao. . . . When we asked

---

* These statements do not occur consecutively in the authors
quoted.

our own men to be the messengers, they put their hands instinctively to their throats " (101).

In a case of accidental death " it was difficult to convince one party that it was an accident, and both that witchcraft had nothing to do with it " (86).

SOUTH AFRICA.

The Zulu and Kafir have customs so similar to the Yao that I refer only to a few, some of which are quoted on account of the difference.

They do not eat fowls, ducks, or eggs, lest they should be barren (D). They conceal birth-names (52). A man must not see the face of his mother-in-law. The eldest son succeeds his father. They bury in a circular hole, placing the body in a sitting posture. On returning from a funeral they get a charm administered to them. A spirit may come back as a snake (5). Their Witch-doctors and Fetishmen are more set apart from the people than those in Eastern Central Africa. Feathers, claws, teeth, pieces of wood, &c., are charms. Prophets smell a person to see whether he speaks the truth. The witch is believed not to eat the body taken from the grave, but to use it as a charm.

A recent account of one of the southern Bantu tribes, the *Amandebele*, which was formed of 30 or 40 smaller tribes, is given by Thomas, from which we take the following customs :—

The first to " bleed " a field with his pick possesses it (48). Soldiers going to war charm themselves before and after the expedition (14, &c.). An invalid is removed from the village to a field (19). At funerals there is an offering of cattle, and the deceased is introduced to his father, grandfather, and others. In cases where the spirit of a deceased friend enters an invalid, this spirit gets a sacrifice : sometimes the particular animal wanted by the spirit is named. The dead may be changed into elephants, buck, lions, snakes, &c. Hence offerings are given to such animals.

Mr. Thomas carefully distinguishes two classes of professional men that are often put together : one is the class of diviners, each of whom is trained by an older diviner. The other class is the common *izinyanga*, and includes self-taught physicians and those doctors that are priests as well as physicians (1). Witchcraft is carried on and punished in ways similar to what we have described (107), and yet with important points of difference. Their traditions on cosmology state that when men came out of the earth they found the animal and vegetable kingdoms prepared for them, and that they received the opposite messages of life and death. This last statement refers to the chameleon legend common among the Bantu (*Appendix*, Tale 15).

WEST CENTRAL AFRICA.

Merolla (1682) says :—" The people ate serpents. They had an oath by which a person's limbs were bound tighter or looser to force out the truth. [In § 104, we saw this principle applied to the head]. They did not approve of marrying in *facie ecclesiæ*, for they must be satisfied before marriage whether their wife will have

children, and whether she will prove diligent in her work
and obedient. When the fault proceeds from the wife's
side, the present that was made by the husband is
restored; when the fault is on his side, he recovers
nothing (59). When the father receives the present he
complains not even if it should be small—for that would
look like selling his daughter; but he asks in public
beforehand how much the man will give. [This is more
like the Kafir custom than the Yao (48)]. Sometimes a
man leaves a concubine to his kinsman (54, 43). The
wife waits at table on her husband; after he is satisfied
he gives the rest of the food to her, and she shares it
with her children (67). Whilst children are young they
are bound with superstitious cords made by the wizards
(45). They are put down naked on the ground; when
they can move, a bell is tied to them, to show where
they have gone. The fields are planted round with
stakes, which being bound with bundles of herbs by the
wizards, will kill any thief (K). When they have private quarrels, they do not decide them singly, but each
man gets as many friends as he can. The parties meet,
begin to argue quietly, proceed to invectives, and lastly
they fall to it 'helter-skelter'. [We could give no better
account of many native trials in Eastern Africa.] On a
death, the kindred collect: hens are killed; they be-
sprinkle the house of the deceased with the blood, and
throw the carcases on the top of the house, to prevent
the soul of the dead from coming to give Zumbi to any
future inhabitants (40). The dead person is believed to
summon others out of this world (41). They weep over
the dead, if not naturally they hold Indian pepper to

their noses, which causes the tears to flow plentifully. When they have howled and wept for some time, all of a sudden they pass to mirth, feasting at the expense of the person that is nearest akin to the deceased (43). Many abominations take place after these feasts. The Giaghi offer human sacrifices to the dead (28). Burial places are in the fields, and have something placed over them—*e.g.*, horns or earthen pots (39). The poorer people wrap their dead in straw mats. All are given to 'idolatry' and the eating of man's flesh (106). If any person whatsoever pass by where the guests are eating, he or she thrusts into the ring and has an equal share with the rest (D). Their wives work in the fields till noon, and must get their husbands' food ready, and wait till he finish " (57).

Battel (1590—Angola and adjoining countries) writes: —" The Gagas ate their captives, except those under fourteen years of age. The women draw out two teeth above and two below (A). A dead man has his hair dressed, and is put on a seat in a vault dug in the ground. Two of his wives are put by him with their arms broken, then the vault is covered up. The greatest part of his goods is buried with him (39). Every month there is a meeting of his kindred, who mourn and kill goats and pour the blood and palm-tree wine on the grave. [The Yao have dances every month, when the moon is full ; on other occasions there would be difficulty in lighting their great ball-room.] They suffer no white man to be buried in the land. The body is thrown into the sea about two miles from the coast. [Unless where the English possess land,

or are well known, this custom can be traced in East
Africa. On Lake Nyassa, at least one English body had
difficulty in obtaining a grave. In the same way some
of the deceased Magomero missionaries were exhumed.
In keeping with this is the custom of carrying about
bodies for long distances, as in the case of Livingstone
and some Portuguese.] If a person denies a charge, he
drinks a root (Imbando), which kills him if he is guilty.
*No one on any account dies but they kill another for
him.* They believe that some one bewitched the deceased (106). Many times 500 men and women come
to drink Imbando" (104).

Bosman (1700—Bosman's Guinea) mentions 5 classes
of people : (1) kings, (2) chief men who take care of a
city or village, (3) those that have got riches, (4) the
common people, (5) slaves. [This exactly applies to
the Eastern tribes.] In their salutations the first question is, " How did you sleep ? " to which the reply is,
" Very well " (G). At Fida, if any visit his superior,
he falls on his knees, kisses the earth, claps his hands.
[Here we find kneeling and clapping the hands.] The
women suckle the infants for two or three years. Child-
bearing is not troublesome ; here is no long lying-in nor
expensive gossiping or groaning feasts (44). The chief
handiwork is smithery. They have no notion of steel.
A hard stone is their anvil, and they have a pair of
tongs, a small pair of bellows, and three or more pipes
(H). When they begin a war, drive a bargain, travel,
or attempt anything of importance, their first business
is to consult their false god by means of their priest,
who may tell them to offer sheep, &c. [14. Another

resemblance to the Zulu and Kafirs. Among the simpler
Yao, a man may be his own priest.] Questions may be
put to the idol, which are answered in this way :—About
20 bits of leather are shuffled by the priest ; if those
indicating success come much together, success is an-
nounced (1). Public general religious exercises are
customary on account of great drought (20). They kill
a cock or a sheep to their god in words alone : for when
it is dead they immediately fall upon it, tearing it to
pieces with their fingers (27). Most of them believe
that after death they live in another world in the same
character as here ; but they have no idea of future
rewards or punishments (10). They drive devils out of
villages (107). Children don't inherit their father's
goods (97). If a woman is with child for the first time,
rich offerings are made to the false god to obtain her
safe delivery (53). They call in medicine men when
sick, who prescribe offerings to deities. They have
medicaments of the roots, branches, and gum of trees,
and about 30 different herbs (1).

From various other writers on Western Central
Africa we gather the following facts :—

When a child is 7 days old, the parents make a
small feast, imagining that the infant is past its greatest
dangers ; and in order to prevent evil spirits from doing
it any mischief, they strew all the ways with dressed
victuals to appease them (44).

If a man like a virgin, he tells the most considerable
among her relations, who goes to her house and asks
her of her relations, who, if she is not before promised,
seldom deny the request : then the bridegroom clothes

his future bride with a rich suit of clothes and ornaments (48).

A man contracts with his wife when she is under age (48), and afterwards carries her forcibly to his home amidst her struggles and shrieks. A dower is reserved for her, so that, in case of widowhood, she may be able to buy a husband (59). When a present is paid to her parents, the bride is led to her husband's hut, and he sends her for water, wood, and other necessaries. One of the wives is the superior (55). Adultery is punished by selling both offenders. The husband may turn off an unfaithful wife at pleasure ; he makes her take all her children with her, unless he want to keep any himself (59). Wives do all the hard work, do not eat with their husbands, and are in great subjection. They name the child by shaving its head and rubbing it with oil (46). The women carry the children on their back as they go about their ordinary work. Many writers "impute the flat noses and pot bellies to this mode of carriage". As soon as a person dies the neighbours are collected by loud cries and lamentations. They cry over the dead for several days. They give the deceased about a twelvemonth's provisions, and make a point of securing the body from carrion-eaters (38). The brothers, sisters, and relations take possession of the goods of the dead man, and leave little to his children (97). If the deceased be a man, his wives shave their heads. [40, 43. All the Yao shave the head for any deceased relative.] If they drink liquor belonging to a European that they do not know, they ask him to drink first that they may see that there is no poison (98). They use no bread, but eat the flour of their various grains. They use the Indian corn when green, roasting it on the coals—or make flour by pounding in mortars.   The

WOMAN OF WESTERN AFRICA POUNDING MEAL.

houses are like beehives, and have pointed roofs : persons of quality have palisades round them.   The domestic utensils are only earthen pots, calabashes, and baskets (c).   They use bows, poisoned arrows and assagais.

The Mahommedan negroes of the West Coast practise circumcision in some place remote from a village (52).

The above customs of the Western African are taken from the older writers on the subject.   After coming into contact with Europeans the natives are apt to change their more primitive manners.   They are fond of discarding round huts in favour of square.   The above illustration shows a basket very different from the East African ones, all of which are carried on the head.

NORTHERN CENTRAL AFRICA.

The BONGO believe that evil and not good comes from spirits. Old people procure roots in the forest glades at night to destroy others. The Nubians, besides having superstitions of their own, confirm them in all this. Old women are compared to hyenas, and believed to enter their bodies by night. The dead are put in a crouching form—as prescribed in the law of Islam *(Schweinfurth)*. Among the NYAM-NYAM no bodies are rejected as unfit for food except those that died of a cutaneous disease. The eldest son of a chief succeeds his father. Chieftains rarely lead their armies (98). A man that wishes a wife goes to a chief or sub-chief, who endeavours to procure one (48). The women eat alone in their own huts. The game "mungala" is played sometimes on a board, sometimes with holes in the ground (51, 5).

The BALONDA (Livingstone) ratify friendship by partaking of each other's blood. They believe in a kind of supreme deity. When they take a poison ordeal they hold up their hands, as if to appeal to a great judge above. [It will be observed that the last clause is an inference.] They have idols, and a cross-road is considered sacred (40).

The WANYAMWESI have also a ceremony of making "blood-brothers".

The WAGANDA have a stringent code of etiquette. A man that makes any mistake in saluting the king is executed at once. The account given by Speke of the chief of Uganda shows what a terrible curse a strong government may become (104). A powerful chief kills scores of people in cold blood, till the thing becomes an established custom, and ceases to be wondered at. Stanley's details are equally instructive. When a warlike expedition is thought of, the sorcerer flays a child, and lays its body on the path as the soldiers pass forth to battle.

The GANI go quite naked, but instead of sitting on the ground as most natives do, they carry a small stool. In this district mothers wash their children and then lick them dry with their tongues as cats do. Towels are no part of native appliances.

Among the OBBO, when a man dies, his relatives take off his hair and wear it in his memory.

The DJOUR country resembles the Yao in being infested by the *tsetse-fly*, which kills cattle ; consequently the people, though with a taste for agriculture, have nothing except goats.

In many tribes the women wear no clothing till marriage. The birth of twins is often considered unlucky ; among the Ishogo the mother of twins is forbidden to speak to any but relatives for six years.

The APINGI offered Du Chaillu a "tender and fat" slave for his "evening meal".

Among the FANS (Ba-Fan) the executed wizards (*cf.* 107) are eaten, and cannibalism (according to Reade) is made no secret.

Among ABYSSINIANS (like the Gallas, Samali, &c.) we find customs like the following :—

Children are circumcised the eighth day. The baptismal name is concealed, to prevent an evil spirit from taking possession of the party. They have civil marriages which are readily dissolved. On a death the relatives of the deceased shave their heads. There is much "wailing," for which professionals attend, and a funeral banquet.

Lobo, the Abyssinian missionary, was cupped by a native by three cups of horn about half-a-foot long (I.).

The GALLAS have a god called Wak. Their priests divine by the fat of goats and intestines. It is honourable to kill an alien, to kill a countryman is criminal. On death the relatives feast on the cattle. Wood that has been burning a little is put on the grave. If the wood grow the man is happy in the world beyond *(Krapf)*.

The ARABS are found everywhere in Northern Africa, and their customs are better known : still I shall note a few for the sake of comparison.

Boys are named at the ceremony of circumcision. This is about their seventh year among the Turks. Some make it the 13th after the analogy of Ishmael (compare 52). Whatever is touched by a corpse is defiled (34). They pay visits to the graves of the dead ; pilgrimages are a great feature in their religion. There are a few superstitions connected with the use of salt, *e.g.*, when an infant is named, some may be put into its mouth. An assemblage of families all from a common stock forms a tribe—the government is paternal (62).

RACES OF ANTIQUITY.

It would be interesting to determine to which of the ancient nations known to history these Bantu tribes are most related. For light on this question we must look at the great nations of antiquity that had most to do with Africa.

The first race that we find in African history is the ANCIENT EGYPTIANS, whose country, Mizraim, is named after one of the sons of Ham. Whether they pressed farther south at an early date it is difficult to determine. It would have been strange if they had not: they had enterprise enough to build the pyramids. As dynasty succeeded dynasty, many that were driven before invaders in those barbarous times may have discovered that the world was wide. It is agreed, however, that in the 18th dynasty, about 1400 B.C., Sesostris found tribes in Nubia, Abyssinia, Senaar, &c., and subdued them. It is instructive to note that about 718 B.C. Egypt had a dynasty of Ethiopian kings; and that about 600 B.C. Necho, an Egyptian king, sent a Phenician fleet down the Red Sea, which appeared in the Mediterranean three years after—having sailed round Africa.

The next of the ancient races that may be mentioned in connection with Africa is the PHENICIANS or CANAANITES. Before Homer's time they had the commerce of the Mediterranean. By the time of Solomon they were making voyages down the Red Sea to a place called Ophir, regarding which there have been many theories. In connection with one of these, we quote the following from Baines. Speaking of the long-sought ruins in the land of Ophir, he says:—"They are extensive, and one collection covers a considerable portion of a gentle rise, while another, apparently a fort, stands upon a bold granite hill. The walls are still thirty feet in height,

and are built of granite hewn into small blocks about
the size of our bricks, and put together without mortar.
The most remarkable of these walls is situated on the
very edge of a precipitous cliff, and is in perfect pre-
servation to the height of thirty feet. The walls are
about ten feet thick at the base, and seven or eight at
the top. In many places there remain beams of stone,
eight or ten feet in length, projecting from the walls, in
which they must be inserted to a depth of several feet,
for they can scarcely be stirred." This explorer finds
Ophir in Southern Africa.

The JEWS had contact with most of the nations of
antiquity, and it is said that the kings of Abyssinia
were descended from Solomon, through the Queen of
Sheba, who on her return was accompanied by many
Jews. It is also maintained that numbers of Jews
found refuge in Abyssinia at various periods. The
Abyssinians, as their name implies, are a mixed race.

Herodotus mentions a party of young men that travelled through the desert and went on till they came
to a black people who lived by a large river which
flowed westwards.

On comparing the customs of the modern tribes of
Africa with those of the Ancient Egyptians, the Phenicians, or the Jews, we find many points of difference.
Still there are points of similarity also. In describing
African manners we have already noted many agreements with old Jewish customs. The customs of the
Canaanites need not detain us long. Even in the time
of the Patriarchs this race could make seals and graven
images, had silver money, and could dye purple. It

may be mentioned, however, that they believed themselves to have sprung from slime ; while the worship of
Ashtaroth involved the pollution of the young of both
sexes, and Moloch demanded sacrifices of children.
Divination was also practised.

It is interesting to note the following particulars
regarding Ancient Egypt :—

The civilisation of Egypt did not come down the Nile
—the black people from the land of Cush being represented on Egyptian monuments as Pharoah's servants.
The Egyptians are akin in customs to the Asiatics.
Some say the Egyptians and Indians are of the same
origin (*cf.* Prichard).

Weapons, Tools, &c.—The old Egyptians had bows,
shields, javelins, and slings. [The latter we have not
seen among Eastern Central African tribes, but their
hoes and wooden pillows resemble the Egyptian.] The
old Egyptians pounded in stone mortars with metal
pestles, and knew something of glass-blowing 3500
years ago—a trade which our African pupils considered
" too wonderful ". Young children were carried at
their mother's breast, rarely at her back as in Central
Africa.

Offerings, &c.—The people inquired whether the
deceased deserved the rites of burial. Weapons, &c.,
were buried with him (39). When mourning, they
abstained from " the bath, wine, delicacies of the table,
or rich clothing " (49). (The priests in their purifica-
tions excluded *salt* from their meals, . . . shaved
the head and the whole body every third day.) They
called on the deceased according to the degree of rela-

tionship, as " O my father ". A dirge was chanted to the sound of a tambourine. Mummies were kept in their houses in order that relations might have their deceased with them. (So the Romans gave funeral oblations to their dead, flowers, libations, and victims.) The offerings to the dead were similar to the ordinary oblations in honour of the gods. Offerings were made to Osiris in name of the deceased after the burial.

The first fruits of the lentils was placed on the altars of the Egyptian gods (20). The offering of first fruits was an offering of obligation. Offerings of wine (24), oil, bread (21), salt, were offerings of devotion. Ears of new corn were parched at the fire. There is some testimony to the effect that human beings were sacrificed.

Mysteries.—Circumcision was practised from the earliest times, and when it was administered instruction was given in the mysteries. One part of the initiation was to see the figure of the god (53).

Oracles were consulted on all important occasions (14). Dreams were regarded with religious reverence (15), and thus the gods told the proper remedies for disease (Diodorus). But it was known that most diseases proceed from " indigestion and excess of eating ". Bodies were examined to find the causes of death (Pliny).

Women suspected of infidelity drank a cup of bitter water to prove innocence or guilt (107). The king was the chief of the church and of the state (7).

On studying tribal customs we find that much similarity arises from the very constitution of human nature. Circumstances also exert a great influence. Races are so modified when they obtain cows, horses, or even the rudiments of a calendar, that we are at once puzzled by the difference between them and the rest of their clan. Besides, we must ever remember the enormous influence of the individual. A whole tribe like the Ovambo derived the habit of squirting water in the face to prevent witchcraft from one king. If a stray man settled in Negroland with two or three wives 3000 years ago, the descendents of this person would now count by millions on millions! What are now large African tribes evidently descended from an ancestor that lived not so many centuries ago. The whole tribe naturally follows and develops certain characteristics of this ancestor, and as it keeps aloof from other tribes, it soon has distinct peculiarities in speech and customs. Even in England almost each county has certain peculiarities, a fact which will illustrate to what a great extent such developments may grow among tribes that have no written literature, and no means of keeping up communication with their neighbours. Often have I wondered, as I gazed on these African mountains and valleys, what tales they could tell, if they only found a tongue. Much, I believe, may be yet learned by the study of native legends and mythologies, which frequently condescend on names; but after all, there are many secrets which will remain undisclosed until those mountains and valleys give up their dead.

CHAPTER XVII.

AFRICAN PHILOLOGY.

"There is a notion that African languages are rude and imperfect. They are no such thing."—Bishop Steere.

What makes one language more perfect than another? What is a philosophical language? We judge a language by the way in which it fulfils its purpose : its great purpose being to express thought. Every language is a means of expressing thought by words. In one tongue we express certain thoughts easily and conveniently, which in another we have to express in a cumbrous manner. Thus instead of saying "inapplicabilities," we might have to say "the-plural-condition-of-not-being-able-to-fold-one-thing-into-another". To express thought words must be used in a particular way: the words themselves are the vocabulary, the particular way in which they are used is the grammar. In estimating a language, we must consider (A) its vocabulary, (B) its grammar.

A. THE VOCABULARY.

1. *The Number of Words.*—(*a*) A language may have too many words. In English, multitudes of words

have been taken from other tongues.   Thus we have the numeral *one,* and also *unit* (Latin) and *monad* (Greek). Unless such words are necessary, there is a loss of simplicity, which is felt by a foreigner trying to learn the language ; and which we could make apparent to ourselves by introducing from three other languages three additional words for *one,* with all their derivatives.   So long as such new words indicate different shades of meaning, their presence shows fertility in thought ; but where they do not each indicate a separate and necessary meaning, they encumber the language.   As writing is the chief means of giving permanency to unnecessary words, we find that an unwritten language like Yao is not thus burdened, and seldom uses two or three words where one might do.   There are, however, cases of apparent excess.   We have a word for *his elder brother,* and quite a distinct word for *his younger brother.*   Many such cases, however, arise really from deficiency—there is no word in the language for *brother.*   Again, we have words for *my younger brother, your younger brother,* &c., but no word for *younger brother.*

(b) A language may have too few words. I have never seen Africans of the same tribe trying to talk with each other and breaking down for want of vocables. They have always language enough to express their ideas.   But they have often to use circumlocutions. Instead of saying a *pen* they speak of a (thing) with which to write or mark.   It would be unfair to expect the Yao to have a name for *ice,* any more than the English have a name for anything they don't know of,

but every language should have easy methods of forming new words where they are wanted.

While sufficient for ordinary purposes, the words of a language may be too few for exact translation. The English vocabulary enables us to speak of: (1) Objects (and actions) in the material world. (2) Relations between these objects; such relations are numerous. (3) Things and relations in the mental world, which are named through analogies in the material world, for material things are more readily named than mental. (4) Besides there are the names of Science. In names of the 1st kind, Yao is as full as English. In names of the 2nd, 3rd, and 4th kinds, where a greater abstraction is implied, it falls short. An African, while able to perceive all such relations, &c., does not find it necessary to name many of them. Even though he named all that he observed, his names would be lost, for in the absence of writing, few words acquire fixity except those in general use. Take the word *grey*; present a grey object to a Yao, and he calls it black or white, but as a matter of fact, he knows perfectly that it is different from either of these colours. In English we speak of a man as being good, upright, straightforward, true, honest, honourable, just, strict, religious, pious, holy, pleasant, courteous, &c.; but in Yao there are not names for so many shades of character, and one or two words must do service for the whole list. We shall not wonder at this if we consider how many of the above epithets have been taken into the English language from other tongues. A modern mission to our Saxon ancestors would have found their vocabulary as poor as we find the African.

2. *The Nature of the Words.*—Where one language
has an easy word, another may express the same idea
(a) by a word dreadful to pronounce—" a vocable sufficient to splinter the teeth of a crocodile"; or *(b)* by a
cumbrous combination of words.

(a) The Yao words are easy to pronounce, the rule
being that every consonant is followed by a vowel. But
they are longer than English words. If a Yao had to
say *transubstantiations*, he would say *tiransubisitantia-
tion(i)si*. Again, where we say " You believed him,"
he prefers to say " You-him-believed," in one word.

(b) A language may have a cumbrous combination of
words. When the Romans had to work with their
numerical notation of IX. and XI., we can excuse them
for not making much of simple multiplication and division. So when the Yao express 99 by *makumi msanu
ni makumi mcheche kwisa msanu ni mcheche,** we may
expect that their numerical system will not care to go
any farther !

B. GRAMMAR.

What parts of speech are first used ? Interjections
like *ah !* and imitations of sounds like " crow " come
very soon. Now, when children utter the word " crow "
what is its nature ? Is it a noun meaning the sound, or
is it a verb in reference to the production of the sound,
or is it too indefinite to be classed ? When it does

---

* Tens five and tens four, to this comes five then four. The inflexion of certain adjectives, and the negative inflexion of the verb,
are also felt cumbrous by a European.

become definite, it is certainly more like a noun or a verb than anything else. The only other part of speech that might come into competition is the adjective ; but if we look at what the adjective does in Grammar, we see that it already implies the noun.

The noun and the verb are the parts of speech that are most readily obtained,—that lie nearest to hand in nature. But the nouns and verbs that we meet with generally go far beyond the individual. Such a word as house, though denoting a single object, could not have been formed without abstraction. This position is illustrated in any text-book on Logic under the Logical notion. The word " house," while denoting a special object, implies that this object has certain characteristics. Yet the degree of abstraction is greater for other parts of speech. To take an illustration. We know that " John built houses," and that " John did not enter these houses". Now, we might state these two ideas without anything farther ; but most languages bring in another idea, thus, " John built houses *but* he never entered them". The new idea marked by *but* arises from contrasting the other two ideas, and could not exist till both of them existed. So we cannot speak of a good house till we know of a house, neither can we speak of " building well," or " building for a friend " till we first know about " building ".

Thus, the more concrete words are the nouns and verbs ; adjectives and pronouns are less so, while adverbs, prepositions, and conjunctions are very abstract, and are often so few in many languages as to be classed together as particles. The concrete words describe the easier thoughts, the primary modifications of thought, the abstract words describe secondary or more abstract modifications of thought. Hence, as we might anticipate, we find the Yao language well supplied with nouns, verbs, and even pronouns, but as we go beyond these to adjectives, the supply is less, and still less as we pass on to adverbs, prepositions, and conjunctions. The scarcity of prepositions and conjunctions often discourages the European who studies the language. It is a great shock to discover that the English words *to* and *from* are represented by one and the same native word !

We shall now show how the Yao language deals (1) with the principal parts of speech, (2) with the subordinate.

1. The chief thing to note regarding the *principal parts of speech* is their inflexion. The fewer the inflexions, the greater is the simplicity.

(a) Inflexion for Concord.—We have

In English.	In Latin.
good hill	bon*us* mons
good tree	bon*a* arbor
good field	bon*um* arvum

The change in the adjective (like good-us, a, um) is cumbrous, and is seldom necessary. A boy trying Latin at school mistakes in saying *bonus arbor*, but he has little chance of being misunderstood. Yao gives ten concords of this kind with their plurals. This is a severe infliction, although we can generally tell by inspection what concord is required.

(b). Inflection for Government.—English nouns have one inflexion for case, Latin nouns have six. The Yao

noun has no inflexion of the same kind, but it modifies the verb so as to indicate its relation to the noun. These modifications correspond in number (ten) with the concords.

The advantage of many inflexions is that related words are marked so clearly that they may be separated from each other or have their order changed. The Yao could speak of ten nouns and say *that* is hard, *that* is soft, &c., without ambiguity, where our word *that* (which never changes) is powerless. Again, in English we cannot say " the sire the son addressed ". In Latin, *sire* and *son* are so marked that the meaning is unmistakeable in any order. But such advantage is small. So great explicitness as inflected languages mark at every step, is seldom necessary. The Yao, then, as compared with English, takes too much trouble with the principal parts of speech. Its process of fitting out nouns and verbs (which affects also adjectives and particles), is too minute and cumbrous.

2. Coming now to the more abstract and *subordinate parts of speech,* we find that while the English language has many of these, the Yao language has not ; and to make up for the want it throws more work on the principal parts of speech. In English we say, "to build a house for him"; the Yao modifies the verb " build " till it means " build-for," and dismisses the preposition. In most of these cases the English language has an advantage like that which arises from the principle of division of labour in other matters.

We shall now sum up these results, and add a few more in the following table :—

	ENGLISH.	LATIN.	HEBREW.	YAO.
SYLLABLES	May end with consonant	May end with consonant	Preference for open syllables except where accented	Natives find difficulty in pronouncing syllables ending with a consonant: theirs all end with a vowel
PLACE OF ACCENT	Not uniform	...	...	Great uniformity (nearly always on the penult in Chinyasa).
VOWEL SOUNDS	Numerous	...	...	Few.
INFLEXIONS FOR NUMBER IN NOUNS	At end (of words)	At end	At end	At beginning.
DUAL NUMBER	Traces of (*both*)	Traces of (*ambo*). Common in Greek	Used	No trace: *e.g.*, a word like *both* is translated by *all* (all the two).
CASE INFLEXION (Nouns or Prons.)	Only in pronouns	Highly developed	Traces found	Entirely absent.
CONCORD INFLEX.	Only in pronouns	Much used	Used	Exceedingly numerous.
CHARACTER OF THE CONCORD	Pronouns are masc., fem., or neut.; but the distinction disappears in the plural	Masc., fem., and neuter	Masc. and fem.	No trace of masculine or feminine inflexion even in pronouns: but distinctions like (1) personal or personified, (2) impersonal; the latter being subdivided into names of objects in nature, collective, abstract, ampliative, diminutive, &c.
RULES FOR APPLYING THIS CONCORD	According to sex	Faintly indicated by the termination of the noun	Faintly indicated by the termination of the noun	Almost infallibly indicated by the beginning of the noun.
NUMBER INFLEXION IN VERB	At end; rare	At end, almost superseded by the inflexion for person	At end and at beginning	At beginning.

			Used	Used.
CONCORD INFLEXION IN VERB	None	None (exc. when a verb is made up of participle and auxiliary)	Used.	
INFLEXION FOR PERSON	Rare; at end	General; at end	Gen.; at beginning and end	General; at beginning.
INFLEXION OF VERB TO INDICATE ITS OBJCT.	None	None	Pronomenal suffixes	General, and used to distinguish definite and indefinite objects.
INFLEXION FOR MOODS AND TENSES	At end. When words are put at the beginning they retain their independent character, and are called auxiliaries	At end	At beginning and end	At beginning (and end).
MODIFICATIONS OF ACTION GENERALLY	Few	Many	Not so many for moods & tenses, but modifications of action are expressed often by modifications of verb instead of adv.	Numerous. Instead of an adverb *not*, there is a complicated negative inflexion.
USE OF ADVERBS, PREPOSITIONS, & OTHER PARTICLES	Large	Fewer prepositions than in English owing to case inflexions	... ...	More work is thrown on the principal parts of speech, and particles are not much used.
COMPOUND W'RDS	Numerous	Numerous	... ...	Hardly any except in names; but derivative nouns can be formed very readily.

We select Latin and Hebrew, because the one is of the Aryan family of languages and the other of the Semitic.

What is a family—and when are languages said to belong to the same family?

Languages, like everything else, are classed with reference to similarity. The similarity may be in grammar, or in vocabulary, the former kind of agreement being the more decisive. Let us take an example of agreement in vocabulary. In the Aryan group of languages the word for five is *pantshan* in Sanscrit, *pente* in Greek, *quinque* in Latin, *pump* in Welsh, *funf* in German, and *fif* in Anglo-Saxon. Agreements of this kind go to prove that the languages belong to one great family. Next we reach the conclusion that the races that used them had a common ancestry who dwelt in an old "Aryan home". But can we prove that the Semitic languages have any kinship to the Aryan? Some try to do so by looking for coincidences in certain words, as in the numerals. For instance, the Hebrew for five is *chimasha*. Has this any relation to *pantshan?* In looking at the Yao language we often find certain coincidences. If the Yao had ever derived a word for five from *pantshan*, they would have put a vowel at the end, and further, they would have treated the beginning of the word as being less important (just as the Greeks treat the end of the words as of less importance). Now, it is singular that the Yao word for five is *msano*, the Swahili *tano*, the Chinyasa *sanu*, and the Nyamwesi *nhanu!*

Resemblances of this kind, if numerous and not accidental, would point us towards a time when all "the earth was of one language and one speech".

As we have already hinted, the Bantu family of languages, to which the Yao belongs, fills nearly the whole of Southern Africa. Besides the Bantu people there are the Hottentots. As early as 1850 we find Dr. W. H. J. Bleek writing, "The Hottentot language is to me at this moment of greater interest than any other. The facts have now so increased upon me and offer such strong analogies, that there is no further doubt in my own mind, that not only the Coptic but also the Semitic and all other languages of Africa (as Berber, the Galla dialect, &c., &c.), in which the distinction of the masculine and feminine gender pervades the whole grammar are of common origin". Although the Yao is a genderless language, much of its folk lore resembles the Hottentot. Dr. Bleek has published 42 Hottentot tales. I have heard amongst the Yao, tales corresponding to 16 or 18 of these.

Chapter XVIII.

AFRICAN PHILOLOGY.—*(Continued)*.

Before stating the peculiarities of the Yao language, I shall illustrate the subject by reference to the speech of children. This form of illustration applies to unwritten languages generally; and although not much alluded to in books on Philology, it is, I venture to think, exceedingly important, not only for the theory of language, but for the guidance of persons that are confronted with unwritten tongues. While children are learning to speak, their slowness comes not entirely from the intellect, but from want of command of the vocal organs. On encountering a word that they cannot pronounce, they frame a word of their own which they employ instead. In imitating the word *table*, a child may say *dodo*, a sound which at first sight seems to have no relation to the word "table". Yet the child employs it uniformly, and often for more than a year. Such imperfect imitations are not by accident: they follow laws similar to those principles that operate in changing the same original sound into the *quinque* of Latin, the *pump* of Welsh, and the *five* of English.

Form of Words.—The syllable easiest for a child is

a single consonant followed by a vowel. For *basket* a child says *tase*; for *purse*, he says *tuse*. Where two consonants come together, as the *sk* and *rs* of these words, the child throws out one of them. He also drops the final *t* in *basket*, and obtains a syllable ending with a vowel; and where no vowel exists he supplies one, as in *tuse* for *purse* (purs).

Beginning of Syllables.—Some maintain that we cannot begin a syllable without a consonant, or at least an aspirate like what the Greeks wrote. Children seem to be exceptions as they leave out a difficult consonant and begin with a vowel—*that* becomes *at* as well as *tat* but even in *at* there exists the kind of aspirate contended for. In the Yao language syllables almost always begin with a consonant. Here arises an important principle of spelling. I should not like to decide whether we ought to write *Ya-o* or *Ya-wo*. The natives themselves had no writing till we taught them, and on words like *Yao*, my best pupils were divided. Some pronounced and spelt *Yao*, others *Yawo*. I believe that the sound at first was *Yawo*, and etymology in many cases bears out my conclusion. But in course of time the original *Yawo* may be rendered *Yao*, as an original h*onest* has become *onest*.

End of Syllables.—It is not so easy to end a syllable with a consonant. The child's earlier syllables end with vowels as *papa*. The difficulty of pulling up the voice at once is seen in the utterance of certain words like rock, especially by Scotchmen who often unconsciously pronounce as if the word were *rocka*. All Yao syllables end with a vowel.

Parts of Speech.—The language of childhood shows that man observes things before he observes the relations between them. Nouns and verbs come before the other parts of speech, but when first employed they are more like interjections. The imperative of the verb, which is as near to an interjection as may be, forms a large element in infantile speech : thus adjectives when first used are in effect imperatives or interjections. The expression *Doto dad* (doctor bad) is synonymous with *Doto, go-way* (doctor, go away). Whether nouns or verbs come first is hardly worth discussing, because it is misleading to apply the distinction of parts of speech at a stage where speech has no parts. But it may be noted that what we call nouns are used by the child like verbs : thus, *No tair* (chair) means " Do not put me on the chair ".

The Meaning of Nouns.—Nouns at first denote individuals like *papa, mamma*. But the child by and by sums up in these words a great deal of meaning, and if he were placed in a world where he saw no white woman but his mother, the next female that appeared he would call mamma. So if the only animal he is acquainted with be a dog, he at first calls goats, sheep, or rabbits all dogs.

Inflexion of Nouns.—A child sees no need of inflexions, and forms his first sentences accordingly. He says *more man* for *more men, see more camel* for *see more camels*. After he feels the need of a plural, his first impulse is to express it by old materials, and then *see more camel* is used where the meaning undoubtedly is *see the camels* or *see camels*. The possessive case is similarly dispensed with : for *John's book* we get *John boop.* This has a strong relevancy in the explanation of African tongues, where *Kumlomba brother* is used for *Kumlomba's brother.*

Adjectives are at first used exactly like nouns. We tell a child *it is hot in there,* and he says *hot in 'ere,* and immediately adds *fire in 'ere,* thus showing that he considers *hot* as a substitute for the corresponding noun. Moreover adjectives, on their first appearance, are often used to make compound nouns in which the adjective meaning is lost. The child says, *Dem dood-doy* for *James is a good boy. Dood-doy* is really one word, and is rather a noun than an adjective. This explains why it is that in African tongues simple adjectives are very few. In the Yao language, adjectives being so unimportant, have no inflexion for comparison. *Articles* are entirely dispensed with by children. *Look at the man, look at a man,* are both rendered *ook man.*

Pronouns are not easily understood at first. A child hears the words, *Come, and I will bathe you* : by and by he asks for his *bathe yow, bathe-you* being understood as a single word, which he construes as a noun. It is long before he says *I did it;* he says *James did it* instead. Also for *my boot* he says *Dem toot* (James' boot). Indeed, the interrogative pronoun *who* seems to be understood before the personal pronouns.

Relative pronouns come very much later. Hence in African tongues they are poorly represented. They resemble conjunctions, and are introduced into the vocabulary of childhood, we believe, even later than they.

Verbs.—Children are fond of viewing a complex phenomenon as an action. When we tell a child to look at the men tying on a sail, we call forth the expression *tat tying on* for *that is a tying on*. The subject and object are thus ignored in comparison with the action itself. So in African tongues the verb is of overwhelming importance. Besides the imperative, one part of the verb frequently used in childhood is the participle : as *James eating food* for *James is eating his food*. The *eating* is used as a noun or an infinitive. The infinitive is largely used in Yao to express action in general, and the indicative mood is formed from it.

Adverbs are by children often used as imperatives, as *quick !* (Adverbs of place as well as demonstrative adjectives are soon used in company with vocal gestures.) Negation is early expressed by putting *no* before verbs or nouns, as, *Doto no go*, for *the doctor did not go*, *no home*, for *we will not go home*.

Often adverbs make but one idea with the adjective or verb that they are attached to, as *go-away*. The same thing is seen in the case of prepositions. *Put on your coat* is rendered *tut on toat* and even *ton toat, pu* falling out and *ton* being used for a verb. So, *put off your coat* is *toff toat*. This principle illustrates what has been called applied verbs and causative verbs. A neuter verb like *put* is made transitive by placing another word like *on* after it, and this other word is liable to become part of the verb, as if *put on* was the transitive form of *put*. The principle is of the greatest use in explaining African derivative verbs. Again, children often omit prepositions. *Look man*, is used for *look at a man*; *man 'os* for *a man on a horse.*

As regards *conjunctions*, simple people like children are often content to express one idea or sentence at a time. When they have to join two ideas or sentences they put them side by side without any connecting word. *James and papa* becomes in the infantile language *James, papa.*

In the same way, connecting words like the logical copula, are at first omitted, as *Dem dad boy*, for *James is a bad boy.* The tendency to omit the copula, throws light on the earlier use of adjectives. When the child says *bad-boy*, the expression is to be taken as a single word, and we may call it a noun. But often the child sooner understands, *boy bad*, the equivalent to him, of the *boy is bad*; which thought is ultimately developed as it is written, though at first the child views it as being the equivalent of *boy, go away.*

Unwritten languages are marked by a peculiar *graphicness*, arising partly from the omission of connecting words, and partly from other causes. The expression, "if you be sufficiently warm, you will be sufficiently braw (well-dressed)," is very weak, when compared with the proverbial "warm enough, braw enough". A savage, or a child, would feel it very tame to say, "if you do not cover your well, some one will walk into it". He would say, "cover your well, a man will go into it, plump!" Instead of an intangible, "one cannot say what one would think, if one fell into a well," the more natural language of childhood is, "I cannot say what I would think, &c.," or, "you cannot tell what you would think, &c." Instead of "he stabbed him very deeply," we have, "he put the knife into him that length !"

The above remarks on the imitation of sounds and speech by infants, besides illustrating an unwritten language, will enable a reader, to whom the subject really is new, to understand how languages that are of the same family, may yet differ immensely. It is to be remembered that different individuals imitate differently. While some find it easier to throw out consonants, others put them in, as some men find it easy to say *Amelia-r-an* for *Amelia Ann*. Again, children often modify their vowels to compensate for some consonant they cannot pronounce. When a child says *tate*, for *blanket*, the *a* is emphasised through an effort to embrace the *n*. Some African races say Nyansa, others Nyasa, with the *a* so modified that we might write, Nyaasa, or Nyassa.

Like children beginning to speak, certain races have few consonants, and are obliged to throw much work upon them. Thus one tribe had to call Captain Cook, the first Englishman that they met, Taptain Toot, making the *t* do duty for the *c* (*k*).

When we think of the various ways in which a language may be modified, we are much struck by studying a work like Koelle's *Polyglotta Africana*, which points to striking affinities, traceable among African tongues. Moreover, such works are liable to be at first obscured through misleading data. Perplexity is caused by words from languages that had not been perfectly studied at the time. Thus where there are two words for "woman," the philologist may hear only one, which instead of being the proper instrument for tracing affinities, may be derived from another word within the special dialect. Again in one language an old word for "woman," may have been superseded, although some derivatives from it yet remain. As more languages are gradually reduced, a rich harvest awaits the philologist in Africa.

These illustrations from the speech of children, include nearly all that will be expected from one giving a general account of an African language. We are aware of the danger of converting illustrations into principles without stating their limitations : as did the man who wanted to prove that all speech was but a development of the utterances of the lower animals. After making observations on two of his children, he found his theory much confirmed ; but when he tried the third child, its first utterance was, "Don't tease, go away". This wonderful sentence brought his theory into discredit ; but it is clear that I may claim this child in confirmation of what I have adduced. Its first utterance is made up of imperatives, and this on our principles, is just what it ought to be !

It remains only to give a short account of points not yet touched on.

Sounds. Vowels and consonants are much modified for euphony. The consonant changes may be exemplified in connection with the letter *n, e.g.*, ku-n-lola becomes kundola ; and in ku-n-sosa the *n* is entirely dropped, but the preceding vowel is lengthened, and the word might be written kuusosa. In this way,

n-l becomes nd, n, l, or nil
n-f   ,,   f
n-m   ,,   m
n-n   ,,   n
n-s   ,,   s
n-u   ,,   u
n-ng   ,,   ng'
n-j   ,,   ny
n-k   ,,   ng
n-t   ,,   nd
n-w   ,,   mbw, &c., &c.

In African spelling, some advocate the disbanding of *j* and *ch* in favour of *tsh* and *dzh*, but the changes of *ch* and *j* after the letter *n* afford an argument against writing these letters *tsh* and *dzh* in the Yao language. Thus, for kunchondelela (kuntshondelela) we hear kunjondelela (kundzhondelela), and not kundshondelela. But such questions turn greatly on expediency.

Words.—An English word like *loved*, is found to consist of two elements, a simpler word *love*, and the ending *d*. If the simpler word *love* be not traced farther back it is called a root. The other element *d* indicates the modification of the root. In order to give an account of such a word we have to explain (1) the root, (2) the modification of it. The modification of it by the addition of *d* is well explained when we have found that *d* is for *did*.

But how do roots arise ? A great many are imitations of sounds in nature, others may be utterances which were at first accidentally associated with certain objects.

Yao words we may explain in the following manner. In the case of kulemba (to write, mark), we may suppose that the root *lemb* or rather *lembe* expresses the

sound made by some scratching instrument. Hence we
have *lemba* the shortest form of the verb. From this
verbal root we may form ten nouns which express different meanings and fall into ten classes. Strangely
enough these classes correspond to a great extent with
the classifications of the noun stated in some English
grammars (see Bain's Grammar). They may be exemplified as follows :—

1 { Mlemba, a writer / Ju-akulemba, one that writes } (personal)

2 Ulembe, writing, marking (abstract)

3 Ndembile (nembo), a writing

4 Chilembo, a great mark (ampliative)

5 Lilembo, a mark } names of natural objects
6 Lulembo, a mark

7 Kalembo, a little mark (diminutive)

8 Kulemba, writing (verbal noun or infinitive)

9 Pakulembila, a place-for-writing-at, desk

10 Mukulembila, a-place-for-writing in, office

These ten classes of nouns may be formed in connection with every verb. The 2nd class, besides embracing
abstract nouns includes the names of all trees that begin
with *m;* while the third class embraces the names of
birds and animals, especially such as appear in flocks;
as deer, sheep ; and the words in this class have now no
plural though there is some evidence that they had a
plural formerly.

Sentences.—A noun in a sentence demands the concord of adjectives, pronouns, and verbs. This is the
only important concord in the language. The absence
of gender is a great peculiarity. A native may make a
long speech about a person while his audience do not
know whether it is a man or a woman that is spoken

of. Again, when a native speaks of persons it may be impossible to tell whether he means one person, or several. Originally, the singular of the third person was distinct from the plural, but by the use of a plural of excellence one man is habitually spoken of as *they*. This is a refinement of politeness.* In the same way the English language employs *you* instead of *thou :* these natives go farther on the same lines, throwing away not only number, but person also. In England, where the question is asked " where are you going " the reply will be " I am going to *your* house ". The African for the same meaning would reply " I am going to *his* house ". Traces of the same refinement exist in England: thus, instead of " What do you want " we may hear " What does *his* Reverence want ? "

The following will show the method of tense formation. The present indicative, I love, may be analysed into I-a-loving or I-to-love (person, preposition, and verb). The perfect tense, indicating completed action, is made up of the root meaning love, and an affix which seems to be akin to a demonstrative pronoun, and signifies that the action is *there* or *at a distance* now. One future tense is formed from a participle with a negative, so that I shall love = I-a-loving but-*not-yet*.

These are the three leading tenses, but the fertility of tense forms is amazing—thus we have a tense for " Why should I neglect to love ? " Yao has a great

* A certain kind of politeness comes natural to the African. Seldom will he say anything to irritate a neighbour, knowing as he does, that in a country where there is little law, a neighbour may kill him without any scruple, and get absolution by paying over a few siaves.

wealth of participles, which seem to be wanting entirely in Chinyasa.

Derived verbs are numerous. From a word leka, *to leave,* we have lechela (for lekela) *leave for;* lechesya and lekasya (whose terminations remind one of the Greek idso) with *causative* meanings; lekana (= leka na ; na = with) *leave each other,* or *together;* lekanya, *separate* with causative lekanisya; as also lekwa and lecheka with passive and neuter meanings.

In the study of these languages we are often reminded that what are now to us familiar words, were really formed with much difficulty, and we are not so ready to laugh at the Etymologist who derived the Latin word *nihil* for *nothing* from a *bean,* as if it originally meant " not a single pea " !   In some African dialects there is great difficulty in getting a word to translate "nothing". Yet, after all, the English language has not much to boast of here ; some of these dialects can also furnish a derivative word like no-thing.

Chapter XIX.

ESTIMATE OF NATIVE CHARACTER.

" The savage is essentially cruel, not having the least regard for the sufferings of others, and inflicting the most frightful tortures with calm enjoyment. As for morality, as we understand the word, the true savage has no conception of it, and the scenes which nightly take place in savage lands, are of such a nature that travellers pass them over in discreet silence. Honesty in its right sense is equally unknown, and so is truthfulness, a successful theft, and an undetected falsehood, being evidences of skill and ingenuity, and by no means a disgrace."—T. G. Wood's *Nat. Hist. of Man.*

In speaking of Native Character we begin with the Physical side. The *features*, despite thick lips and flat noses, are by no means unpleasant. The forehead is well formed. At first all black faces seemed alike, but this was because the blackness was then strange to us, and not because the faces wanted variety : after returning from a long stay among negroes, we felt the same difficulty in distinguishing white faces.

Their *figures* are tall and graceful. Some of the men are six feet high, while few can be called little. The women, owing to their out-door work, are strikingly tall and strong. After becoming accustomed to their " want of dress," one feels that natives are seen to most advantage in their own costume. They don't look well in garments of the ordinary coat-and-trousers description,—coloured shirts, or even white shirts with red borders suit better.

Their *powers of endurance* are very great. Men and women will carry sixty pounds on the head, and walk at a brisk pace for two days' journey of forty miles. As they march thus under a burning sun, their whole body is covered with beads of perspiration, yet they do not succumb. In estimating the value of certain Roman Generals, Livy was careful to note, that they had the power of enduring hunger for a long time. The Yao would have merited his praise, for they possess this power in an extraordinary degree. They will march for days without any "ostensible" means of keeping themselves alive. On occasions when we misjudged distances, and were obliged to pass about 20 hours (mostly of great exertion) without food, our anxiety about our companions, was met by the polite assurance that "they had eaten". They even contrived to turn the sympathy the other way by saying, "We are used to hunger, but the white man will faint". The white man might endure hunger nearly as long, but the native has this advantage—when food comes he has an enormous capacity for quantity, he is a "dreadful eater," while the white man can scarcely taste a morsel. The natives can also endure the burning thirst of this land. On a long day's march, they pass all the streams in the morning without drinking : it is not till three or four o'clock in the afternoon that they become thirsty. But the white man may drink by the end of the first hour, and then he becomes "demoralised" for the day. As he continues the hot march his thirst increases but he cannot quench it. He arrives at a clear rippling brook, hastily puts a stone under his knees—a drinking jug is a mockery now, he must get at the stream itself—still he is never quite satisfied. He craves the drinking for its own sake. After imbibing a great quantity of water, he is grieved that he cannot go on drinking more, and no sooner has he left one stream than he begins to long for another. The unpleasant craving continues till the sun begins to sink in the west. He may avoid the torture by abstaining from drinking at first, only to exercise this self-denial, it is almost imperative to shut the eyes when passing a stream! Some natives suffer in the same way, but they are chiefly boys.

When much exhausted the natives light a pipe, each takes one or two whiffs and passes it on to his neighbour. In a few minutes all are inspired with fresh energy. In work that they do not like, they very soon complain of fatigue, but in other cases, even when asked to rest, they redouble their energies, while they make the whole welkin ring with some wild song. They are never so tired that the sight of game does not rouse them to every energy necessary for pursuit.

The natives are vegetarians not of choice, but of necessity. Few can procure much flesh, and they avoid milk and eggs on superstitious grounds. They are, therefore, in the opinion of some, deficient in muscle. They certainly do not excel in doing work that requires a dead strain, but this is due to want of practice—they are not used to such work. At their

own homes they never require to raise heavy stones or
weights, and their naked legs and arms are out of
keeping with the task. Constant exposure of their
bodies to the elements, renders them very hardy. This
feature in the African has almost become proverbial.
"From constant usage, the soles of his feet are de-
fended by a thickened skin as insensible as the sole of
any boot. He will walk with uncommon unconcern over
sharp stones and thorns, which would lame a European
at the first step."

Mr. Wood remarks that, "Their state of health
enables them to survive injuries which would be almost
instantly fatal to an ordinary civilised European," and
mentions a wonderful case of two young girls that were
removed from a heap of corpses. "One had received
19 stabs with the assegai, and the other 21. They
survived their dreadful wounds, reaching womanhood,
though both crippled for life." "The dreaded 'stick'
of the Orientals, would lose its terrors to a Kaffir, who
would endure the bastinado with comparative impunity."
The same writer speaks of a Hottentot wagon-driver
who fell under the wheels of his wagon. One of the
fore-wheels passed over his neck, and as the wagon was
loaded with some two tons of firewood, it might be
supposed he was killed on the spot. He was not only
alive, but had the presence of mind to roll out of the
way of the hind wheel. In answer to anxious inquiries,
he said he was not much hurt, except by some small
stones which had been forced into his skin, and which
he asked a gentleman to remove. In Africa we often
saw instances of endurance, which would make us

exclaim with Buffon, that civilised man does not know his own powers.

Judged by a European standard, these natives would not be commended for *cleanliness*. Their habit of smearing the body with oil or grease, is very repugnant. When a boy was cooking our dinner, he delighted to put his fingers into the fat and smear his whole body. "Kafirs," says Mr. Wood, "are charming savages, but it is always as well to keep to the windward of them, at all events, until the nostrils have become accustomed to their odour." Judged by an African standard, this habit would be highly approved; for a European when obliged to dress like a native, feels the necessity for his grease!

As they lie about on the ground their bodies and scanty dresses become very dirty. In some districts they bathe a great deal. Our pupils at Zomba availed themselves of the beautiful stream daily. Bathing in the morning is avoided; the streams are then cold, especially on the hills. But when a traveller rests by a brook at mid-day his native companions generally bathe.

Passing now to the MORAL side of their character I shall first point to their great want of *truthfulness*. "Telling lies" is much practised and is seldom considered a fault. The way in which it comes before the European is like this. He enters the country with half-a-dozen bath-towels expecting them to last for a long time. In a few weeks the majority of them have disappeared. He then begins to open his eyes, and in a short time he sees his "boy" making off with the last of them. I have been much amused at the earnestness

with which the new-comer will exclaim : "I actually
saw him take it and found it in his hands, and yet he
denied"! In such cases the denial of the native is
made all the stronger. What is wanting in probability
must be supplied by boldness. The negro often thinks
that he is flattered by being accused of falsehood. So,
when natives wish to pay a high compliment to a
European who has told them an interesting story, they
look into his face and say "O father, you are a great
liar !"

Avarice is strong in these people, and prompts to
much cheating. A native comes to the Mission store
to sell eggs. When asked if they are fresh, as a matter
of course he says they are. The storekeeper after trying
them in water declines to buy, and the native calmly
retires. He has been outwitted on this occasion and
that is all, he hopes to play a better game next. He
carries his eggs home, and carefully lays them past. A
few weeks after, learning that this storekeeper is absent,
he forthwith takes his eggs, hastens to the new storekeeper, declares that they are fresh, and succeeds in
selling ! In making a bargain the native has but one
principle, he tries to get as much as he can. As avarice
and selfishness are often too strong for the civilised
man, we must not expect too much from the savage.
Still, the natives have many motives against a wretched
greed. The teaching at their Mysteries condemns the
wretch who " concentres all on self ". Again, the members of a community have their meals in common, and
when a stranger arrives at a village he is treated with
the greatest hospitality. One night I came upon a

village at the side of a wood, just as its two male inhabitants were beginning their evening meal. I was
accompanied by twelve boys, two of whom were close
by me, and at once received an invitation to supper. I
expected that the men would be much puzzled when
they found out the real number of their guests. But
no. As soon as the other ten boys came out of the
wood, they invited them likewise, gladly giving up their
own meal to my party. Knowing that the hungry men
would have to wait till more food could be cooked, I
could not but admire their strict adherence to native
custom under such difficulty   It would have demoralised
them to offer payment, but I quietly sought an opportunity of meeting their daughters and presenting them
with a quantity of beads. Still, it may be doubted
whether the natives on the whole are more generous
than Europeans. Their insecurity makes them lazy,
their laziness makes them poor, they have little to give,
and expect a large return for a small present. In our
first contact with the Portuguese after emerging from
the atmosphere of the native kings, we were received
with great hospitality, and, having been so long used to
the natives, I became concerned about repaying the
kindness, when one of our party said, " Why, you are
among Christians now, don't think you are dealing with
some old chief who gives for the purpose of getting ".

Any *novelty* has a great attraction, though the emotion
of fear sometimes overpowers that of wonder. A white
man, sitting quietly after his day's march with a crowd
of people round him, proceeds to light his candle. In
a few moments there is a terrible stampede. Shrieks

of terror drown the laughter of the traveller's native retinue. What can it mean ? Why, he has struck a match ! As soon, however, as the first scare is over, the crowd increases and comes nearer. When satisfied that there is no danger, the old men ask to see more of the wonderful little fire-stick ; and by and by, all admire it so much that if the traveller were to listen to their entreaties, he would sit lighting matches all night. When the Missionaries first came into the country, the revolver produced a profound impression ; it was looked upon as a supernatural weapon, the idea being that its possessor could fire without ever requiring to reload. Certain powerful chiefs near Nyassa, on being shown some revolver practice, at once put their hands to their throats and said to the Missionaries, "You are the kings of this country ". Such an impression as this, gives the Missionary a breathing time till the natives become acquainted with him. If they thought him quite defenceless many would kill him at once, especially if he had any goods. But apart from revolvers, the very appearance of a white man at first inspires the native with fear. Nor is this strange, for if a black man had shown himself in any quiet English hamlet before its inhabitants knew that negroes existed, there would have been a terrible scare. So, when a white man appears in an African village, natives that are unfamiliar with such specimens of humanity take to their heels ! But gradually their fears subside, and they come to look at the man. They examine his long hair, his hat, his umbrella, his boots and his stockings, and when he goes away they follow him, and he can see that they will soon become his friends. The children are particularly drawn to the stranger : while those who rank highest as sorcerers are most influenced by superstitious fear.

The emotions of *tenderness* and *sympathy* are strong among some, while others are as callous as can be conceived. But few of them would say with Hobbes, that "pity is a weakness, and that the best men have least of it," for on one occasion, where a mourner produced a copious supply of tears by taking snuff, the others administered a grave rebuke, telling him that, "his was no true sorrow ". Usually their grief for their friends is intense. In this respect (as throughout the whole emotional side of their nature), they resemble children. They are easily impressed, but they do not keep grief longer than grief keeps them.

The *humorous* side of a subject has great attractions for the natives. In cases where there is any disposition to quarrel, one joke is worth ten arguments. They are always polite enough to laugh at the Englishman's jokes, especially if he speak with a half serious air. In any discussion, it is the humorous side that they most appreciate. In the course of a conversation with Kapeni and his people, about the custom of killing slaves to accompany the dead, after trying the arguments that most readily suggest themselves, I pointed out that the slaves were big powerful men, while the deceased was very weak, and that if a quarrel took place beyond the grave, the deceased would have no chance against them. They laughed immoderately at this, and when reporting the discussion to their friends, they dwelt chiefly on the idea that slaves

would be as good as their master " on the other side
of the grave," and might avenge their death. In
conversation with each other they have a great capacity
for presenting the laughable side of events. It often
happens that a stranger regards the natives as beings
to be patronised and amused by; so much does he
consider himself superior to them. Now as might
almost be expected, they view the new-comer in the
very same light! Most of them humour him and
allow him to treat them as children, but all the same,
they amuse themselves at his expense after he is gone,
and, indeed, while he is present, if they know that he
cannot understand their speech. They are careful not
to laugh if there be any danger of giving offence. Once
at the close of an open air meeting, an Englishman
happened to get up on the trunk of a large tree, which
one often sees used for a seat in the native villages.
The log revolved, and the man fell heavily on the
ground. Yet the whole meeting looked as grave as if
the accident had been part of the programme.

Their *anger* though sometimes violent, soon exhausts
itself: but where the passion cannot be readily grati-
fied, it may settle into a lasting enmity. Many people,
especially headmen, will not visit a village two miles
distant on any account; rather than pass through it,
they will fetch a wide circuit, and that although their
children and dependents visit the place quite freely.
The negroes are very cruel, and sometimes take a
positive delight in inflicting the greatest tortures they
can devise. They reserve much of this for enemies from
whom they would expect the same treatment themselves.

Of their INTELLECTUAL powers I venture to speak very highly. I knew a number of boys that came to school at the ages of from twelve to fifteen, without knowing a single letter, and in six weeks, they could, after a little consideration, read any word in their language. This they accomplished without any unnatural cramming. There were many school children whose progress I watched with great interest, and who, I am certain, if they had enjoyed the usual training, could have taken no mean place among the Cambridge Wranglers.

The natives possess great powers of *argument*. Though some are swayed by feeling and admit irrelevant matter, others stick well to their subject, and soon pull up a debater that changes his ground. In public speeches they use a style more elaborate than in ordinary conversation. Many English speeches are so different from ordinary talk, that to one who only knows English conversationally, they seem to be in another language. So native speeches may be greatly polished, and lose much of the bluntness of conversation. Public speaking is much practised, as an important meeting may last for days. Many of the speakers have a tone of quietness and self-possession that any orator might envy; others believe in loud words and bold gestures. An excited native orator presents an appearance never to be forgotten. I have one before my mind just now. He stands near an ant-hill, and at the close of each stirring sentence, he makes a wild rush to the top. " Are we all to be killed," he cries, " by Chekakamila ? " Having said this, he runs

up the hillock.   Coming back he confronts his audience
and resumes at the pitch of his voice, "Is he to come
and catch our wives and children ?   We'll go and kill
him !   We'll go and eat him ! "   The orator again runs
up the ant-hill.   He continues in the same strain till
his hearers also begin to rush about and brandish their
weapons in frantic excitement.

Natives have the bump of *locality*.   I once lost my
way when about nine miles distant from any dwelling.
I was accompanied by a little boy, who followed
wherever I led.   After wandering for some time, I sat
down in despair, unable to tell the direction I wanted.
I asked the boy whether he knew the way, and to my
great surprise he said he did.   Advancing to a small
knoll, the little fellow caught a glimpse of a distant
mountain.   He looked at it carefully for a few moments,
and then marched off with confidence.   For more than
an hour I followed in great anxiety, fearing that he
might be in the wrong direction.   But whenever we
escaped from the denser parts of the jungle, he stopped
to gaze intently at some hill.   This gave me confidence,
and when at last I found myself on a native path, I
could not sufficiently admire my youthful guide.

We often hear the expression "I don't believe in a
nigger ".   It is common to assert that negroes have no
redeeming quality.   But much of this severe criticism
springs from prejudice.   The African is physically
superior to most of the Indians that we see along the
Mozambique coast, and I am materialist enough to
hazard the opinion that this superiority will "mean
something " in the long run.   As it is, these Africans

are not mere animals composed of greed and selfishness. They often shew great bravery and devotedness. I can point to one man who saved my life on three separate occasions at the risk of his own. Every one that tries to understand these negroes, will acknowledge that the better natives have in their breasts all the qualities that constitute the hero, and only want favourable circumstances for their development. But this is a great want. No doubt there are in Africa, natural differences both among individuals and among tribes. Mr. Rowley says, "Compare an ordinary Yao with an ordinary Anyasa, and the former is at once seen to be physically superior". "A phrenologist would say, that firmness and self-esteem predominated, but that caution which prevails to a deformity among the Anyasa was barely evidenced." The difference between the Yao of the hills, and the Anyasa of the plains is so very great, that I could generally tell a man's tribe by his appearance. But admitting natural differences to the fullest extent, we cannot ignore the effect produced on the natives by their circumstances and customs. The institution of slavery is demoralising in the extreme. The master is a cruel tyrant, the slave is a thief, a liar, and a miserable coward. The government of the country has also a deplorable influence. Where it is weak, it gives the people no protection, where it is strong, it preys upon them. There is nothing to keep the headman of a village from robbing his people, and many a bitter complaint have I heard on the subject. Speke has some instructive observations on the African. "He works his wife, sells his children, enslaves all he can lay hands on, and, unless when fighting for the property of others, contents himself with drinking, singing, and dancing. They store up nothing beyond the necessities of next season, lest their chiefs or neighbours should covet and take it from them." He adds, " If some government could be formed for them, like ours in India, they would be saved, but without it, I fear there is little chance. For at present the African can neither help himself, nor be helped by others, because his country is in such a constant state of turmoil." Owing to the unsettled state of their land, they are victims of fear. The men never go unarmed, the women and children never venture far from home without a guard. A great proportion of their villages are built far up the mountains, for security against their neighbours. Hobbes says that men are naturally distrustful of their fellows— witness the barring of doors at night. Such distrust is greater here, and well it may. It is not that they fear for their property; that is too small to deserve anxiety! They fear for dear life—though they lie down quietly at night, they may awake to receive a mortal wound, and see their wives and children carried into slavery. One in this country finds a meaning in prayers for protection, that he does not realise in a civilised land. These circumstances of the native develop also a peculiar kind of patience and·servility. He looks on injustice and hard treatment as something to be expected at every step.

Superstition also has a dismal influence. Throughout his whole life the native is haunted by the dread of being bewitched. As he grows older the shadows become darker—he has now escaped " the evil eye " so long, that he is judged guilty of witchcraft himself, and the few last days of his life are made unspeakably bitter. What a dreadful cry comes from the old men or women that are convicted by the witch-detective ! Forsaken by friends, disowned by relatives, and detested by the whole community, they appeal with confidence to the poison. Oh ! how must the iron fetters of superstition crush the very soul, when the victim finds recovery hopeless, and knows that in a few hours his dishonoured body will be cast forth to the vultures, and that his name will go down to posterity covered with infamy.

The *musical tastes* of the natives may here be alluded to. Many villages have in the forum a large piano with wooden keys, while men often carry a smaller in-

MUSICAL INSTRUMENT (WITH IRON KEYS).

strument with iron keys. The native musical scale is not the same as ours, and although there is a certain method about the instruments, it is rare to find two of them tuned exactly the same way.

Other traits of native character will appear when we describe our life among them.

As a Missionary with the Bible in his hand looks on the natives, he seriously ponders how the truth can, humanly speaking, be most readily commended to them. His first aim must be to reach their intellects. They stand before him as a people that are entirely unbelievers, and who cannot be blamed for being so. How shall they believe without a preacher? It is well when they state plainly that they disbelieve and point out their reasons, but alas! they often assent to everything from mere politeness. Still, they are well able to appreciate the narrative parts of the Scriptures. Persons fond of doctrine in its purest form think that the tales of Joseph and his brethren, of Saul and David, are so much packing in the sacred volume, but on coming into contact with the strong unsophisticated intellect of the savage, one becomes alive to the sublimity and power of this part of Scripture. These natives readily understand the Old Testament; familiar as they are with a state of civilisation, where a "younger brother" may be sold like Joseph, where a chief (like Saul) hunts a rival among mountains and caves, and where a headman thinks nothing of dividing a child to settle a dispute. A person in Britain thinks it almost incredible that a king could break promises like Pharoah; but to the subjects of an African chief, the narrative of this is the merest commonplace, while they feel that such falsehood in the prince would rather call forth the applause of his people so long as it seemed to be in their interest. Our pupils had often to write about these Scripture subjects

in their own words. When they wrote on English
affairs their remarks were extremely ludicrous; but by
reading their Bible themes I have benefited as much as
by studying a commentary. Again, they can understand and appreciate *parables*. They are all familiar
with this species of literature, since many of their own
tales have double meanings. The natives of course hold
no theory of the universe that excludes *miracles*. In
their own tales they have the miraculous and look for
some teaching in connection with it, a habit which they
may be taught to carry with them in using the Scripture
records. In my first effort at translating Jonah, my
little tutor thought there was some mistake and changed
my proposed version. He felt it would be more natural
for Jonah to " swallow the fish ". But it was a " great
fish !" Still the same answer came. " No, a very
great fish like a crocodile." The dark countenance
turned fully round upon me, and the sharp eyes regarded
me with a strange quiet stare. He approved of my
original rendering, amd wondered what I would venture
on next. Perhaps he thought I was " far gone " or
perhaps I had come near something he had heard before.
They have themselves a story of a man that was caught
by a crocodile and effected his escape while laid past till
the crocodile should be hungry. Their literature also
contains some stories regarding the division of the
waters of a river or lake, while one tale would pass for
an account of Jethro's interview with Moses.

The Africans have a liking for ontological speculation.
Being ill one day, I asked one of our best students to
speak to the people, when, to my utter disappointment,

he dashed into an explanation of "three persons in one
God"; but what surprised me most of all was that the
people listened to him with the greatest attention. I
felt that there was here the working of a mode of
thought that the Western mind has seldom sympathised
with. The discussion seemed to have such a practical
interest to them that I could not but think of the butchers
of Alexandria, who, during the early Church controversy, when asked the price of mutton, would make
some remark about Trinity in Unity. Little did the
lecturer know what an amount of thought had been
bestowed on this subject, and yet he showed he had
been thinking himself, for every statement he made
had evidently passed through the crucible of his own
mind.

Our older pupils formed the habit of asking me about
everything in the Bible that they did not understand,
and I have watched them with breathless interest as they
read passages bearing on "Free-Will". But they were
never "pulled up" by this subject, although I fancied
that one boy came very near the difficulty. They
would doubtless hold that God could foresee, much as
a wise man can. It was a subject where to them
"ignorance was bliss," and I could not be so cruel as to
suggest the difficulties that encompass this antinomy
(as Kant calls it). Still, it might not have been such a
puzzle to these young lads, as they had not lived in a
country where will is evoked in a struggle with the elements. Again, where the vast majority are entirely at
the disposal of guardians or slave-masters, a species of
resigned fatalism is apt to be developed. Once when

translating the sermon on the mount, " Be not anxious for to-morrow ; sufficient for the day is the evil thereof," I was admonished, " Don't tell them that ; their sin lies the opposite way. They never think of to-morrow at all!" Such is the fact, these creatures of God have little or no anxiety. Like the bird of the air and the beast of the forest, they "believe and live".

END OF VOL. I.

APPENDIX.

NATIVE TALES LITERALLY TRANSLATED.

APPENDIX.

———————→∗←———————

1. PEOPLE.

PEOPLE came from *kapilimtiya* [an unsteady (soft)
stone]¹. There came forth two, a man and a woman,
and they married and had children. Then there was
seen another man who was sick, being a leper, who had
come from *kapilimtiya*. The sick man sent the woman
to draw water, then he opened a bag and took out
maize and millet. On this earth there was no grass,²
and he said, "You two may sleep in a cave". The

---

¹ The Africans have a widespread tradition that man sprung in this
way from the earth. The world is viewed as a house with three
stories. The higher story, the region of the sky, is now occupied by
Mulungu, and the sun, moon, &c. We inhabit at present the second
story, but we came originally from "the first flat". But all races
did not come at the same time. According to the Kafirs, the white
man staid till he cast off the skin of imperfection—much as a snake
casts its skin. When a man dies, "he is summoned by those that
are beneath". This might be explained by saying that he joins the
dead who are buried beneath, but Bishop Callaway thinks that such
expressions intimate an old faith, now no longer understood, in a
Hades or Tartarus.

² *i.e.*, to make a house, grass being a main constituent of a native
hut.

sick man died, and the other man put an offering on the ground [3] saying, "You have left us here, now give us grass". So grass grew and trees; and his children grew and had children; hence the tribe of the Yao.

2. THE SUN.

It came to pass that two men went to the hunting-field and arrived at a cave. One said, "Here is heat!" The other said, "Is this fire?" He said, "I don't know, come and help me to search". They began to search in the cave. One peered and saw the sun [4] in the cave. Then he said, "Look! look!" his companion said, "Come, let us run away". The other said, "I will look," and he went into the cave and put away a stone, then the sun burned him and he died. His companion said, " Please, please, don't burn me " (by this time the grass was on fire). The stone being thus removed, the sun went on high.

3. THE MOON.

Out here there lived Machelenga, and he said, " I want a firefly to make a lamp of". A great man said, " Come, I'll shew you a good fire ". And he said, " It is a good fire this"—it was just the moon. Then he took the moon and put it in a pot. And he said, " My children, don't take off the cover of this, it contains my

[3] They postulate that some one died before man could find any being to pray to. This is in accordance with their theology.

[4] Of course they think the sun is not bigger than a plate.

fire. I go to the garden." [5] So he went to the garden.
The children then went to fetch the fire, then there was
light with a brightness! And he said, " My fire has
come out, they have brought it out of the pot ": and
he said to them, " My children, where is the fire ? "
And they said, " We—no ".[6] And he said, " Don't
meddle with the place where I have put my fire".
And they said, " We understand ". Another day he
said, " Good-bye,[7] let me go down to the garden," and
he staid for the night at the garden.[8] One of the
children then took the moon, which burned him, and
flew away to settle right on the top of the hill.[9] The
father awoke and looked out and said, " Outside there is
light," and he ran and said, " But now, see ! is not my
fire gone ? Seek ladders, take it thence." So they
climbed the mountain ; though they tried thus to go to
fetch it they failed. The child fell down a precipice.
The father next tried to climb, then the moon flew,
going up to the clouds, and he said, " Now it is gone,

[5] Or "field" where he raised his food.

[6] A good specimen of native truth. The narrator assumes that the
children will lie, and that the father will take it as a matter of course.

[7] The native good-bye is managed thus : The person that goes away
from his friend says "Stay," while his friend replies "Go". In their
intercourse this is not always a mere form. If a party with goods
have rested at a village whose chief is powerful, and covets their
goods, they are much relieved when he says "Go !"

[8] There are little huts in the fields where people stay to drive away
such animals as would destroy the crops.

[9] In this simple nursery tale Perspective is ignored, but this will
be excused by one who has observed how strikingly the moon rising
over a hill resembles a distant grass-fire.

it is settled in the clouds. Now my enemies will see
quite well, because you have taken out my fire."

His wife said, "Your moon has killed my child for
me; I do not want to see the moon". She went to
another country, she looked on high and the moon was
still there, and she was weary and said, "Dig a pit for
me," and they dug a pit. Then the woman went in
and the man covered it over. The woman died in the
pit.

Yonder moon was the fire of Machelenga.[10]

4. STARS.

It came to pass that the children of Mkwilima [10] said,
"We will go to play," and they arrived at the sands,
and found many stones, and they threw them at each
other. Their father said, "My children, do not strike
each other, stones will pain you". Then a stone was
thrown, and one child was struck on the head and fell;
and the stone ran away and leapt forth and became
fixed on high. People looked, and behold! the stone
was visible, and Mkwilima said, "My children, there I
told you, behold the stone that killed your companion,
behold! now it is on high". When the rain fell particles of it kept floating filling the heavens everywhere.[11]

[11] Here the sky is likened to a great lake, and the stars are the
"golden sands" of "Afric's sunny fountains".

[10] His name implies that he was clever. The 3rd story reminds
one of the Indian widow who refuses to survive her husband.

5. [12] CLOUDS.

Mwangalika sent his son, and said, " In this country there is sun now. Please, please go and burn with fire." Then the fire smoked, and Mwangalika said, " Now I want the smoke to be clouds, that my children may stay in the shade ; " then it went on high.

6. [12] WIND.

A great man had a daughter, and she said, " Father, in this country I am hot, I sweat ".

Then her father said, " Come here, my child, I have pity, I will blow with my breath," so he blew, and thence came wind.

7. RAIN OR LIGHTNING.

The lightning (rain, ula)[13] flashed and killed a man, then it ran on high, and they said, " Please, please, rain but you have killed people ". The rain said, " Now I am sorry, I have done wrong, but I want to send water that you may *drink at the mourning*, and the people said, " Yes, let us consent ". The water of the rain then descended.

[12] V. and VI. seem pointless, except that the etymology and the form of the native words are made to support the simple theories.

[13] Rain, lightning and thunder seem to be almost inseparably associated in the minds of the native. If a peal of thunder is heard, when we ask what it is, the reply is " rain ".

8. THE BOW OF THE LIGHTNING.

The bow of the lightning came from on high and struck a hill, then came Mtanga, and said, "My bow for killing meat". The chief at that land said, "Let us see you killing". He picked up an arrow, threw on high and killed four stars, and said, "I have killed this meat, let me give you to eat". He said, "Give me that I may look at it". He received it and looked, and there was just a flash-flashing. He said, "The meat of my shooting you cannot eat. That comes from on high. But watch what I shall do in the eating of it." He boiled water, and filled a great pot, and picked up the stars and put them in the pot and stirred them, and then they actually found cooked flesh. He said, "Taste it now": when he ate it he found it sweet like honey.

He said, "Lend me, friend, the bow that I may shoot"; but he was killed by his shooting. Mtanga (12) then said, "My bow is dreadful". When Mtanga went away, it was not seen where he went, and he put up his bow on high.

9. MOUNTAINS AND RIVERS.

Mtanga came to the Yao country, and he said, "This country is bad because it is without a hill". The inhabitants said, "What will you do?" and he said, "I will press out mountains". They said, "How will you press them out?" He said, "I will press them out at night". They said, "Come, let us sleep in the houses". At night then passed Mtanga, and came to make a moun-

tain spring forth.   Then he took away his leg when he
had pressed out one mountain, and went and pressed
out another.

In the morning when people arose, they found that
mountains were standing forth (in one place a mountain
sprung up, in another place a mountain sprung up).
He said, "When you thought of me, you supposed I
told a lie.   I am from 'God,'[14] Chitowe sent me.   This
country I have now made right."

He then said, "I will now press forth water, let us
dig a river," then he brought down rain, and the water
flowed in the river.

In the beginning[15] this country was all a plain, and
Mtanga put it right: there was no water and he pressed
it forth.

10. COOKING POTS AND MORTARS.

Long ago 'God' said, "My children, I gave you
food".   He gave them also a piece of iron[16] ore.   Then
he said, "Draw water, boil it on the fire".   Then he
said, "This is a cooking pot".   The iron ore was lost,
and 'God' sent Namawelenga, and he said, "Now I

[14] Chitowe is generally represented as inferior in power to Mtanga.
This passage would lead us, therefore, to understand that Chitowe
called in Mtanga because he could not put the country right himself.
The Yao as they contrast their hilly district with the flat burning
plains around may well thank Mtanga.

[15] Native philosophers accept the existence of the world as an
ultimate fact.

[16] Does this point to the use of 'the pot-stone'?   The native
values his present methods as an advance on something more primitive.

want to dig clay," and they manufactured cooking-pots.

People used to roast (their corn), and there came a woman and she brought a short piece of wood. She said, " I am hungry, I want porridge ". They refused at the village, saying, " At our home, no ; there is no porridge ". She said, " There is maize ". They said, " We have much maize ". Then she brought out her small reed and said, " Give me maize " ; and she put it in her (piece of) wood and set to pounding. When she pounded she said, " Well, this is called a mortar, now pound and eat ".

11. HOES, KNIVES AND AXES.

People hoed with wood [17] and there came a certain man who said, " I have pity, let me give you things-to-hoe-with ". They said, " Give us ". He said, " Bring fire," and they brought fire, and he took iron ore and put on the fire. They collected much fire, and pieces of ore were melted, and they took a stone and beat it, and it was smelted to make a hoe.

Knives and axes came together. People said, " We sleep outside," and there came a man and gave them ; he said, " With this axe cut trees, take the knife, dig down, use it as a pick, and put in your posts ".[18]

[17] Compare the hoeing of the Hottentots.

[18] *i.e.*, to form the sides of the native hut.

12. BASKETS.

He said, "Where do you put your food?" They said, "We put it on the ground," and he said, "But seek for the *mneche*,"(a soft tree),and they sought for it and prepared it (there were no bamboos then). He said, "Take now your maize, put it in the baskets". When they found bamboos then they plaited them: then were made things for holding their goods.

13. CLOTHING.

There were some that did not wear clothes, and a certain man came and stript off bark, and the males wore it. Then he produced a hammer from his bag, and said, "Cut down a *mjombo* tree,"and he stript it. Then he set to hammering, and beat out the juice, and put the bark in the sun to dry. Then he took it and said, "Try to put it on," and the females clothed themselves. Bark-cloth then abounded in this land.

14. DEATH.

This country was one where people did not die, and there came a woman that could not walk. People lived without sleep, and the woman said "sleep," and two persons slept, then she caught one by the nostrils, and the other continued to breathe, and she said, "Arise," the one arose and the other died. She said, "I am sorry, I have done wrong, I caught one by the nostrils, he can not breathe, now mourn" (for him).

Then the people mourned, and continued three days.
Afterwards they said, "Carry him away, dig a grave
and bury him," and they buried him.

People then discovered sleep; death and sleep are one
word; they are of one family.

The woman that could not walk wrought mischief.

MORTALITY,[19] THE CHAMELEON (NALWII) AND THE

SALAMANDER (MLALU).

The chameleon was sent to the graves to say, "When
people die they may return" (to their homes). He
went off and was passing along the road. Afterwards
the salamander was called to go to the graves, and say,
"When people die they must not return". The salamander ran and arrived quickly (while the chameleon
was still on the way), and said, "When people die they
must not return". Next morning the chameleon appeared. He said, "When people die, they may return".
Those at the grave said, "No, the salamander came and
he told us the truth". Then he (the chameleon) went
back to report at the village (from which he was sent),
and said, "The salamander was first. He gave the
order, 'When people die they must not return'." Those
at the village said, "How silly! You were stupid, O
chameleon, you should have made haste."

[19] This tale exists among both the Kafirs and the Hottentots, and
is one of the most noteworthy.

16. OFFERINGS.

A person hoed his field (lit. food), and there came a blind man and said, "You do not eat your corn, what prevents you?" He said, "The corn is without an offering".[20] The blind man said, "I can give the offering". Then he put his arm in his bag, and took out of it flour, and the man that hoed said, "Do it yourself, give an offering that you may see with your eyes". The blind man said, "Please, please, I want to see, help me, O mother!" Then his blindness went away and he saw. Then the man that hoed the garden said, "Now you are able to see". Then the farmer plucked five maize cobs, and said, "Please, please, a blind man told me about the offering, I now want that my maize may be abundant". So the Yao when their child dies say, "Please, please, I give this offering for you which a blind man gave us"; the sick then have health. In this way the Yao continue (to exist).

17. BOWS AND GUNS.

There was a man with three children, one was mad, and he bit, and his father caught him and put him in a slave-stick. Then he said, "Father, I want you to cut wood for me," and he cut the wood. And he said, "Father, now I want a nail" (the iron pin of the slave-stick), and he brought a nail and gave him. In the same way he brought strips of bark, and he (the son)

[20] The offering of 'first fruits' had not been presented.

19

bent the wood with the cords. His father loosed him
and he ran to the bush and returned at night and
pierced his mother with the nail. She said, " My husband, my son whom you loosed has pierced me—pierced
me with a bow" (something bent). These people then
sought bows, and carried pieces of iron, and sought that
madman; but he died in the bush. The people remained with the bow.

Here there were no guns, then came the people of
Misiri [21] and gave to a man (who lived) long ago. The
gun came with the people of Misiri.

18. CANNIBALISM.

There was a certain man, Malyawandu,[22] and an appe-
tite for meat came (to him), and his wife cooked
porridge with vegetables for a relish. He said, " No, I
don't want to eat vegetables ". So she killed a fowl for
him, but he refused and said, " Look for a knife for
me," and he cut himself on the leg and roasted for himself on the fire. And she said, " My husband eating
this meat alone ! " [23] He said, " Delicious meat ". The
man then died of that wound. And the woman said,
" I will look at the flesh of my husband, I will eat it ".

Her children said, " Mother eating father ! " and she
said, " Come ! taste ". One child received it and ate,

---

[21] Described as staying in the north. The word also means crafts-
man. Most of these names are mere adaptations for the story.

[22] i.e., Man-eater.

[23] A breach of etiquette. (67.)

and said, "Give me more". It told its friends that human flesh was delicious. Then they began to kill each other.

At present they say, "We must not eat people". Those that eat people are cannibals (§ 106, 107).

19. MEDICINE.

A certain man was sick; he said, "I shall dig up moles". Then he found a root which was in a hole, he struck it with the hoe, and took it away from the tree and placed it so.[24] Then he killed two moles, and another mole ran away. Then the sick man sat down there to look, and it returned and carried the root and chewed it and spat on the other moles that were dead and they got life. The sick man then said, "Is this medicine? Those dead moles have risen again." The mole said, "This is medicine, do you take it when you are sick, chew it that you may have health". Then he went away to the village and chewed it and had health. Then others said, "Give your friends that they may have health". Then medicine abounded in this land.

20. FLEAS.

People died and went to the graves and became 'Itowe,' and 'God' came and said, "You Itowe come all here," and they came all round. Then he gave them little bags, and said, "You go abroad with these and

---

[24] The narrative shews how.

give people". They all received them. Some had a bag of fleas, and others of seeds, &c., &c. When they came abroad here then people refused the bag of fleas, but wanted the bag of seeds. So they gave the seeds and returned, but on the way they opened the other bags and threw the fleas away.

21. FISHES.

There was a woman, and she took bark-cloth and tore off a long strip and put on as a loin-cloth, and said, "Now let us go to the stream and bathe". (In the waters there were no fishes.) The woman had untied her loin-cloth, and she said, "Give me my loin-cloth to wash". As she was washing it the water took the loin-cloth from her, and she said, "My companions, my loin-cloth is lost". Her companions said, "Sit down, let us go to seek it, that you may wear your clothes". The woman then sat at the water naked; then she saw it coming, it having become a fish. And she said, "I have seen wonderful things; I saw my loin-cloth like an animal". Then they took it, and saw that it was a fish, and they took a knife and opened it at the breast. Then they found inside the eggs of fish (nat. idiom), and threw them into the water, and they brought forth many fishes.

22. BIRDS.

There was a man that had two children, and they said, "We want a bow". Their father made them a bow. And he said, "Don't go throwing at each other". One stood like this,[24] and took a grass wand, threw it at his companion, and struck him in the eyes, and he died. His father then ran, " My son, you have killed your brother"; and he took the grass, and it said, "Your son threw me; I have killed a man. Now I don't want to stay here below," and it flew and lighted on a tree, and became a bird. And this is the origin of birds.

23. ELEPHANTS.

The elephants lived along with men, and the children took them out to eat grass in the plain. Then an elephant killed one child, and another ran saying, "Father, father, an elephant has killed my companion". His father said, " Well, I want to go and kill it". And he carried his bow and arrows and went to shoot it, and he shot it, and it died. The others then ran away, saying, "We have done wrong; now our master is killing us". So they ran away to the bush, and people kept encountering them and shooting them, saying, " You killed a person at the village". Hence there was enmity against them.

24. LIONS.

The lion was a cat dwelling with people. Then it sprung to catch a fowl. The next day it sprang to scratch the baby. Then its master said, " I will kill you," so it ran away to the bush. Whereupon it was at enmity with people.

25. THE SERPENT.

There was a man that hoed a garden and planted cassava, and took bark-cloth and twisted, and took thorns and put through this bark-cloth, and said, "Bark-cloth, I place you in my garden; bite those that come to steal". So he went to hang the bark-cloth[25] in his garden. Then came a thief and took hold of a cassava plant, and the thorns pierced him, and that lad said, "War". It said, "My master left me in the garden, saying, 'If people steal cassava, bite them'." The person died. Then came the man and said, "Bark-cloth, you have bitten a lad; you have a bad heart". Then it went away in the bush, and when it saw people it bit them. Hence came the serpent.

26. BABOONS.[26]

A woman bare three children, but the children stole from the owner of the country, and he killed two. Then the woman ran away, and the other child went away. Her friends said, "Cut your hair".[27] She said, "No, the chief killed my children". And she said on seeing the maize of others, "That maize is ours". On her running away hair grew on all her body. That fur

[25] They have a custom of putting charms round their crops this way (see K.).

[26] All the African races seem to have similar stories about the origin of monkeys.

[27] She would be expected to make herself bald in mourning for her two sons.

of the baboons was the hair of the head, those legs were arms.

27. OTHER ACCOUNTS.

Some tell one way, others another way—telling and telling.

Heavenly Bodies.—'God' made the stars and the moon and the sun likewise. All things in this world were made by 'God'. The sun gave way to fierceness, and said, "Let me shine and destroy people". God refused, and took rain and cooled down the sun.

Wind.—'God' placed a spinning-top on the summit of a mountain, hence the wind.

Rain.—People who died became 'God,' and they said, "Come, let us give our children rain". Others refused, and said, "Come, let us make pots and fill them with water". And they said, "Come, let us break another pot; let us give our children rain".[28]

Animals.—At first the lion was a man; a man died and became a lion. So of the elephant.

28. ANOTHER ACCOUNT OF MAN.

At first there were not people but 'God' and beasts. There was a Chameleon, and he wove his fish-trap; when he had woven it, he went to snare in the river. The day after he went to take it out, and he found

---

[28] Compare the ancient expression, "Who can stay the bottles of heaven."—Job xxxvii. 38.

fishes therein. He took his fishes to the village to eat them. Again in the morning he went early and found that otters had entered the trap and eaten the fishes, and he said : " To-day I have bad luck. I just found that the otters had eaten my fishes. I do not know whether to-morrow I shall find they have eaten them again." Then he departed to the village, empty, without fishes, and he went to sleep. When it was dawn, he went early again, and found man, male and female, entered into the trap.

He said, "To-day have entered things that are unknown. I wonder whether I should take them." Mlungu ('God') was staying down here, before he went away to heaven. And he said, "Father, behold what I have brought to-day ". And He ('God') said, "Place them there, they will grow ". Man then grew, both male and female. But his father said, " Gather the people together, and call your master ". 'God' was called, and he came and said, " Now, Chameleon, where have you brought these from ? " He said, " But they entered my trap ". Then Mlungu said, " Wait till I call my people," and he went calling all the beasts of the earth and all the birds. They assembled. When they came, their Master said, " We have called you for those curious beings that the Chameleon went to bring in his trap ". All the beasts said, " We have heard ". (They had not a word to say.)

" Now let us go to our home." So the beasts all went to their homes. And Mlungu said, " Now good-bye, let me go home ".

The day after they actually saw these people (the

new creatures) making fire [29] (by friction). When they made fire, they set it a blazing, and found a buffalo and killed and roasted it on the fire, and it was cooked. And they kept eating all the beasts in this way. Again Mlungu came, saying, " Chameleon, I told you that you introduced puzzling beings on the earth here. See now my people are finished. Now how shall I act?" They actually saw the bush at their verandah burning with fire. Now the Chameleon ran away, and Mlungu ran away. The Chameleon ran for a tree. Mlungu was on the ground, and he said, "I cannot climb a tree". Then Mlungu set off and went to call the spider. The spider went on high and returned again, and said, " I have gone on high nicely," and he said, "you now, Mlungu, go on high". Mlungu then went with the spider on high. And he said, "When they die, let them come on high here ".

(On this, the lightning when it came down destroyed a tree because the Chameleon ran to a tree.)

And behold, men on dying go on high in order to be slaves of ' God,' the reason being that they ate his people here below.[30]

29. NTEMBE, THE BROTHER OF THE "SPIRIT".

Ntembe came to the mysteries ; and people said, " A great one has come, let us go to see him ". They found

[29] Man is the only animal that can make fire. It is common to set fire to the bush with the view of catching game.

[30] Mulungu is here said to have lived once on the earth, and to have left it because of men. The Chameleon is introduced here as well as in tale No. xv.

him sitting on a stone and he said, " Have these people come "—(he spoke through his nose so). They said, " Yes, we thought we should go and see the great Ntembe the owner of this land ". He said, " You are welcome, I have come myself, I have come to teach the mysteries ". Then came a serpent and he twisted it round his head, and when people passed they were bitten and died. And people complained saying, " The serpent will destroy us all ". ' God ' came saying, " You have a bad heart, you are killing (my) children ". He said, " Take them away and dwell with them, I Ntembe am here ". ' God ' then took the children and went on high with them, and they were happy. Ntembe then became a mountain.[31]

30. THE THREE WOMEN.

There were three Women with their children, and they went to the water. When they reached it, one of them was cheated by her companions who said, " Throw your child into the water, we have thrown our children into the water ". But they had hidden their children under a tree. So their companion threw her child into the water, and a crocodile swallowed it (but did not kill it). Then her companions began to laugh at her and said, " You have thrown your child into the water! We were only cheating you." Then she wept and said, " Why did you cheat me ? " Her companions went to

---

[31] Such metamorphoses are ve y common in native tales.

the village to tell her mother, and said, " Your daughter has thrown her child into the water ". When her mother heard them she said, " Can it be true ! " Her companions said, " Yes ". So her mother wept in great sorrow.

But her daughter climbed a tree and said, " I want to go on high," and the tree grew much and reached upwards. She met many leopards and they asked the girl and said, " Where are you going " ? The girl said, " I want my child ; my companions cheated me and said, ' Throw your child into the water. We threw ours into the water.' " The leopards said, " Indeed ! " and they showed her the way, saying, " You will come to the Nsenzi who will show you the way again ". So the girl went on and met the Nsenzi and they asked, " Girl, where are you going " ? The girl replied, " I want my child, my companions cheated me saying, ' Throw your child in the water ' ". Then the Nsenzi showed her the way and said, " Go, there you will meet the Mazomba " (large fishes ?). The Mazomba said, " What do you want, my girl ". The girl said, " I want (to know) the way ". The Mazomba said, " Where to " ? The girl said, " The way to Mlungu (God) ". The Mazomba said, " Well, be strong in your heart ". The girl said, " Yes, Masters, I understand ".

Then she came to the village of Mulungu and Mulungu asked the girl, " What do you want " ? The girl said, " Master ! I want my child. My comrades cheated me saying, ' Throw your child into the water,' I threw it in, and a crocodile swallowed it ".

Then Mulungu called the crocodile and the crocodile

came. Mulungu [32] said, " Give up the child," and it delivered it up. The girl received the child and went down [33] to her mother. When her mother saw that her daughter brought the child she was much delighted and gave her much cloth and a good house.

When her companions saw that she had fetched her child they asked her, " How did you fetch your child ? " Their companion said, " I went to Mulungu ". When her companions heard that she fetched it from Mulungu, then they threw their children in the water, and also climbed the tree, which grew quickly, quickly.

Then they met the Leopards. The Leopards asked, " Where are you going " ? But the girls were obstinate and said, " We don't want you to question us. No." The Leopards left them, and they went on and met with the Nsenzi who said, "Well, where are you going"? But the girls began to abuse them. They went on and came to the Mazomba. The Mazomba said, " Well, where are you going " ? The girls said, " We don't want you to ask us ".

Then they came to Mulungu. Mulungu said, "What do you want " ? The girls said, " We have thrown our children into the water " But Mulungu said, " What was the reason of that " ? The girls hid (the matter) and said, " Nothing ". But Mulungu said, " It is false. You cheated your companion, saying, ' Throw your child into the water,' and now you tell me a lie."

[32] The narrator pronounces sometimes Mlungu, sometimes Mulungu.

[33] Here as in xxviii. and xxix. ' God ' is on high. He is reached after a journey through a trilogy of Beasts, Birds, and Fishes. Compare with this, one native view that the sky is a great lake.

Then Mulungu took a bottle of lightning, and said, "Your children are in here". The girls took the bottle, and the bottle made a report like a gun. The girls both (lit. all) died.